Smart Organizations in the Public Sector

How does a smart organization model enable self-governments to lead local and regional development in a sustainable and resilient manner? What are key aspects of smart organizations impacting the success of self-governments in attracting and retaining residents, entrepreneurs, and investors? Smart organizations became a relevant construct in economic and management sciences. They supply many practical applications for self-governments and public sector organizations that are looking for effective ways to leverage their resources and capabilities in the local and regional development process. This research monograph indicates how factors of smart organizations in local administration lead to sustainable and resilient development processes. In parallel, the monograph is a practical guide for local government managers looking for the best, international practices in collecting, researching, and interpreting data for making decisions that influence the competitiveness and market position of locations they govern.

Hanna Godlewska-Majkowska is a full professor in economics. She is Director of the Institute of Enterprise and a professor in the Entrepreneurship and Business Environment Unit in the Institute of Enterprise in Collegium of Business Administration at SGH Warsaw School of Economics, Poland.

Tomasz Pilewicz is an assistant professor in the Entrepreneurship and Business Environment Unit in the Institute of Enterprise in the Collegium of Business Administration at SGH Warsaw School of Economics, Poland.

Patrycjusz Zarębski is an assistant professor in the Department of Economics at Koszalin University of Technology, Poland.

Citizenship and Sustainability in Organizations
Series Editors: David F Murphy and Alison Marshall

Exploring how organizations and citizens respond to and influence current and future global transformations, this book series publishes excellent, innovative and critical scholarship in the fields of citizenship, social responsibility, sustainability, innovation, and place leadership in diverse organizational contexts. These contexts include commercial businesses, social enterprises, public service organizations, international organizations, faith-based organizations (FBOs), non-governmental organizations (NGOs), community groups, hybrids and cross-sector partnerships. The role of the individual as citizen may also be explored in relation to one or more of these contexts, as could formal or informal networks, clusters and organizational ecosystems.

Knowledge Management and Sustainability
A Human-Centered Perspective on Research and Practice
Edited by David Israel Contreras-Medina, Julia Pérez Bravo and Elia Socorro Díaz Nieto

Corporate Citizenship and Family Business
Edited by Claire Seaman

Partnership and Transformation
The Promise of Multi-stakeholder Collaboration in Context
Leda Stott

Business Schools, Leadership and Sustainable Development Goals
The Future of Responsible Management Education
Edited by Lars Moratis and Frans Melissen

Smart Organizations in the Public Sector
Sustainable Local Development in the European Union
Hanna Godlewska-Majkowska, Tomasz Pilewicz and Patrycjusz Zarębski

Smart Organizations in the Public Sector

Sustainable Local Development in the
European Union

**Hanna Godlewska-Majkowska,
Tomasz Pilewicz and
Patrycjusz Zarębski**

NEW YORK AND LONDON

First published 2024
by Routledge
605 Third Avenue, New York, NY 10158

and by Routledge
4 Park Square, Milton Park, Abingdon, Oxon, OX14 4RN

Routledge is an imprint of the Taylor & Francis Group, an informa business

© 2024 Hanna Godlewska-Majkowska, Tomasz Pilewicz and
Patrycjusz Zarębski

ISBN: 978-1-032-20907-4 (hbk)
ISBN: 978-1-032-20910-4 (pbk)
ISBN: 978-1-003-26587-0 (ebk)

DOI: 10.4324/9781003265870

Typeset in Bembo
by codeMantra

Contents

Figures

Tables

About the authors

Hanna Godlewska-Majkowska is a professor and Director of Institute of Enterprise in Collegium of Business Administration at SGH Warsaw School of Economics, Poland. She was vice-rector at SGH Warsaw School of Economics in 2016–2020. Scientific interests, including issues in local and regional development, business location, and investment attractiveness of regions, are related to the function of an expert in local government units.

Author's profile at ResearchGate: https://www.researchgate.net/profile/Hanna-Godlewska-Majkowska

Tomasz Pilewicz, PhD, MBA, is an assistant professor in Entrepreneurship and Business Environment Unit in Collegium of Business Administration at Warsaw School of Economics, Poland. He is interested in research collaboration related to smart organizations and technology entrepreneurship. He is a graduate of PhD studies in Economics, specialization innovativeness of economy, Warsaw School of Economics, Poland and graduate of Professional MBA Entrepreneurship & Innovation, Vienna University of Economics and Business and Technical University of Vienna, Austria.

Author's profile at ResearchGate: https://www.researchgate.net/profile/Tomasz-Pilewicz

Patrycjusz Zarębski, PhD, MBA, is an assistant professor in the Department of Economics at Koszalin University of Technology. He is interested in research collaboration related to regional innovation ecosystem, renewable energy, and regional sustainable development. In his work, he combines science with practice. He was involved in implementation projects and participated in the preparation of analyses, reports, and strategic documents. He cooperated with the Polish Investment and Trade Agency, the Ministry of Development, and the Agency for Restructuring and Modernization of Agriculture. He is a member of the Urban and Architectural Commission of the West Pomeranian Voivodeship.

Author's profile at ResearchGate: https://www.researchgate.net/profile/Patrycjusz-Zarebski

Introduction

The 2020s is a time of unexpected and also profound changes in social life worldwide. The Covid-19 pandemic, along with other global hazards of economic, social energy, and climate-linked origin, translates into ever greater challenges faced by local government units.

Hence, in order to foster social and economic development over various spatial scales, it is necessary to come up with new tools to ensure better-than-ever resilience to disruption caused by occurrences or hazards never seen before, the scale and effects of which have become quite exponential.

There is a chance for progress in resilience to development shock in progress in scientific, technological, and organizational terms, in ICT in particular. Local government units may rationalize management decisions, thus forming local development processes, even in an environment that is difficult to predict and unstable at the same time. This is possible if based on smart organizations.

Smart organizations have become a recognized theoretical category in economic and management sciences. The concept and practice of smart organizations embedded in local government units, in spite of the work already being done, still needs to be put into order and aligned with the contemporary exponential changes in the functioning of local communities.

The cognitive gap in the theoretical sense is due to failure to identify mechanisms which smart organizations use to modify the impact of public institutions on local and regional development. This is particularly striking in the case of administrative regions which are not, at the same time, regions objectively existing in the economic sphere, and do not correspond to statistical units.

The empirical gap, on the other hand, is due to an unprecedented lack of knowledge on the current disruption in social and economic development that fails to be covered in local or regional development strategies. How the resilience of local government units to sudden, previously unknown threats, with simultaneous inertia of their organizational structure, can be promoted has not been probed into much to date, even for the leading smart cities in Europe.

DOI: 10.4324/9781003265870-1

There is also a methodological gap. The ways in which the impact of smart organizations on local or regional development, especially in an unstable environment, can be examined still leave much to be desired. This is because the Covid-19 pandemic, energy crisis, and the acceleration of violent climate anomalies are tendencies that emerged in the early 2020s. For now, there are no tested or verified methods of examining the impact of smart organizations on local development. This is because, on the one hand, the needs of local communities undergo great changes, and on the other hand, we are witnessing a rapid growth in ICT and a rising impact of access and sharing economy.

This monograph aims to show how smart organizations in local administration spawn sustainable and resilient development processes. In addition, we wish to create a practical guide for local government managers seeking the best international practices in accumulating, examining, and interpreting data to make decisions that impact local development.

We seek answers to the following questions:

1 How does the model of smart organizations encourage local government in pursuing the policy of local and regional development in a way that is sustainable and resilient to internal disruption?
2 What are the major characteristics of smart organizations that impact local government's effectiveness in attracting and retaining inhabitants, entrepreneurs, and investors?

The co-authors of the study seek answers to the above questions in order to verify research hypotheses derived from systematic revision of literature:

H1 The greater the access to human resources and to infrastructural resources, the greater potential for local government to evolve into a smart organization,
H2 The greater the potential for local government to evolve into a smart organization, the higher intensity of decision processes and the more their effects are palpable at the local government level,
H3 The more mature a smart organization, the more positive effects it has for local development at local government level.

Thus, the concept of "local" needs to be clarified. It is not a straightforward concept, as it depends on the perspective from which spatial units are viewed. In the EU, the term "local" refers to local administrative units (LAUs) reflected in the EU statistics as a municipality, commune, or county (LAU1 vs. LAU2), whereas the regional level mostly corresponds to NUTS2.

In turn, in the global context, the regional level may be identified with a group of countries, and the local level may come down to the scale of single countries. Thus, as digital economy media are towns and cities of varying size, the local level will be construed as local government units which cover not only over a commune, municipality, or county (LAU), but also a subregion (NUTS3) and often NUTS2 when a real-life nodal region goes beyond the scale of a LAU. This is due to interest in exploring, as far as practicable, real-life population clusters and anthropological areas which stand out in economic reality.

This monograph consists of three parts, each divided into chapters. For technical reasons, the current version put forward as the result of statutory research conducted at the Collegium of Business Administration of SGH Warsaw School of Economics comes in Polish and English. In turn, the version to be published by Routledge will be in English only.

In Part I, *"Characteristics and typologies of smart organizations in the public sector"*, the focus is on consideration of the essence, classification, and characteristics of smart organizations formed within local government units. The units have been earmarked for analysis in spite of a broader sense of the term "public sector". This is because, in this case, these are public sector institutions that are responsible for local/regional social, economic, and natural development, including the spatial factor.

In Part I, we seek to address the following detailed research issues which were taken up in the summary and conclusions of the work.

1 How are smart organizations defined, operationalized and classified, special prominence being given to smart organizations in the public sector?
2 How do smart organizations fit into the scientific discourse and how can they be used for further improvement and advancement of public sector organizations?
3 How are smart organizations measured in scientific and academic terms, as well as in industry and business practice?
4 What factors and mechanisms enable the proliferation of a smart organization in local government units?

Part I is made up of three chapters. In chapter one "Characteristics and typology of smart organizations in the public sector", readers will learn what types of smart organizations are formed in local government units locally and regionally. This part examines ways to define, operationalize, and classify smart organizations. The issue of primary importance was the context of emerging smart organizations in management and quality sciences, as well as the predecessors of smart organizations such as intelligent, ambidextrous, or learning organizations. Performance of intelligent organizations and their more dynamic and advanced form was demarcated, which clearly stands out in literature as an organization category in its own right, i.e., smart organizations. Smart organizations are embedded in the context of local government and EU local government units. A literature-derived author's model of a smart organization emerging and functioning on the level of a local government unit was put forward.

In Chapter 2, attention was drawn to ways to measure intelligent and smart organizations. A total of 32 methods of measurement were presented in the academic and business practice domain. Measurement approaches proposed in the domain of scientific discourse and smart city-related, professional services were particularly highlighted. A few dozen measurement methods are reviewed, along with their limitations. The chapter concludes with a proposal of the author's approach to the measurement of smart local government organizations, whereby indicator examples along with relevant sources are cited.

In Chapter 3, factors and tendencies affecting the emergence of smart organizations, as well as the related ways of working and workflows in the local government context, were investigated. Attention turns to tendencies related to a knowledge-based economy, Industry 4.0, digitalization of how the public sector works, the COVID-19 pandemic as a transformational and developmental impulse, and investment funds available from 2021 to 2027 in the European Union to promote the evolution of local government units into smart organizations.

Part II, "*Smart organization in a local government – institutional context*", is focused on issues bearing on innovation institutions and systems and their role in how smart organizations develop and function.

Chapter 1 is an introduction to categories related to the new institutional economics and the concept of an institution in the context of economic choices and the functioning of social and economic systems. The position and importance of institutional theory versus the present scientific discourse, as well as their relationship with other research domains, are shown. The importance of an economic, social, legal, and technological environment in the functioning of local government and in the generation of competitive advantages is presented. What follows in the final part of the chapter is a description of the evolution of EU policies and strategies, that is, of the inextricably bound elements of an institutional environment oriented toward territorial and local government development.

Chapter 2 ventures to address the size of the impact of institutional environment on the processes of creating and exchanging knowledge in the context of European countries' technological transformation and digitalization. The role of knowledge and innovations in the functioning of smart organizations is presented. It was assumed that sustainable development based on innovations boosts the competitiveness of local government units and enables building of regions' competitive advantage in the global economy. The chapter provides a comprehensive look at smart organizations from the perspective of innovation systems' institutional environment. Knowledge and innovations derive from institutional structures present in organizations such as institutions of higher education, research centers, innovative enterprises, and local government units. The chapter elaborates on the institutional importance of human, relational, innovative, scientific-and-research, and IT technological capital which collectively promote the development of digitalization processes and digital skills. A typology of EU regions was shown as a reference point for the creation of smart development policy.

Chapter 3 touches upon issues associated with the response of smart organizations to shocks and changes. An attempt was made to examine how institutional potential may foster smart organizations in times of uncertainty, pandemic, and war-related and economic crises. An ability to implement innovations and new solutions is a prerequisite for the resilience of the local economy and the skills to foster sustainable development. Research has shown that not all local government units fully tap into the regional potential for the development and functioning of smart organizations. The chapter investigated why it is important for smart organizations to be anchored in their local and regional innovation systems embedded in strong institutional structures. The institutions collectively help to learn how to respond to the changing environment and how to use the strategic knowledge flows oriented toward shocks and hazards. The public sector's institutional environment provides numerous types of potential to implement smart solutions. Owing to their multidimensional character, it is difficult to pinpoint the most important of these, as they perform specific functions and are mutually related through synergy.

Part III, "Results *achieved by smart organizations in local government units during the COVID-19 pandemic"*, aims to show how smart organizations in local government may give rise to sustainable and resilient development processes. In addition, the authors wish to propose a practical guide for local government managers seeking the best international practices in accumulating, examining, and interpreting data to make decisions that impact local development.

In this part, the following issues were examined:

1 How does the smart organization model enable local government units to pursue local and regional development in a way that is sustainable and resilient?
2 What are the major characteristics of smart organizations that impact local government's effectiveness in attracting and retaining inhabitants, entrepreneurs, and investors?

The considerations fall into three chapters. The first one ventures to properly organize the major tendencies that determine what sustainable local development is and how it is analyzed, in particular the forms in which it manifests itself. Theories that may be the source of knowledge about how smart organizations impact sustainable local development were also reviewed. The chapter concludes with an indication of how good practices in identifying the impact of smart organizations on local development may be applied.

Chapter 2 is an attempt to determine whether smart local government organizations may give rise to sustainable development, be it amidst strong regional development destabilizing factors. To this end, research of 2021 and 2022 was cited. It was undertaken by the authors and their colleagues at SGH Warsaw School of Economics, and it regarded innovative new solutions for the functioning of Polish local government units during the pandemic.

As the research identified a local government unit as the principal initiator of innovative and development-fostering solutions, further analysis focused on good practices undertaken by local authorities of selected European smart cities. Solutions were sought as regards promoting local development using ICT methods, based on auditing websites of outstanding European smart cities.

Chapter 3 offers a more profound analysis based on the experience of European cities which are the leaders in the development of the smart city concept. It aims to define the development measures undertaken by local government units, based on tools and solutions typical for smart organizations. For the purposes of this chapter, representatives of nine European and five Polish cities were interviewed.

In this chapter, possible mechanisms supporting the implementation of smart organizations in local government units as a tool to foster local development were identified. Relevant good practices were shown, too.

An appended list of the uses of smart organizations as instruments fostering local development, broken down into legal, economic, social, technological, ecological, and legal factors, comes as an important supplement of the chapter. This list was drawn up based on an audit of websites, as well as interviews with representatives of selected smart cities in the EU and UK.

In order to investigate the ways to define, operationalize, classify, and measure smart organizations in local government units, a systematic literature review (SLR) was applied which included stages typical for the method: (1) review design, (2) literature search, (3) literature screening, (4) deep reading and content analysis, and (5) reporting results. The review design included queries with phrases such as *intelligent organization* and *smart organization*, along with phrases such *as definition, characteristics, examples, methods, tool, results, development, local development, regional development,* and *sustainable development*. The literature search was based on peer-reviewed scientific writing released in the form of scientific articles, in English, from January 2022 to June 2022 in Web of Science (WoS), SCOPUS, and Director of Open Access Journals (DOAJ). Once duplicates had been removed, a total of 656 scientific articles were screened (i.e., their titles and abstracts were analyzed) in the identified three databases mentioned above. The contents of 95 publications were earmarked for deep reading and content coding. Content coding included major categories of the scientific knowledge sought, and in particular specific examples of definitions, methods, and tools used by organizations labeled as smart, and their functioning mechanisms, both for internal and external interactions, ways of working and cooperation, as well as the influence smart organizations have on the internal and external environment. The SLR was complemented with a traditional review of literature, including scientific monographs, expert studies, and reports by professional organizations, all of which are relevant to smart organizations.

For the purposes of potential analysis of smart organizations existing in varying European regional ecosystems, **theoretical frameworks** of the regional innovation systems concept were used along with statistical methods to operationalize and evaluate the territorial potential. In line with the concept, institutional capital along with economic and social (linking) types of capital are the major constructive elements in the regions that make it possible to delineate and account for the mechanism of sustainable development. A total of ten indicators were employed to evaluate the determinants, each of which represented one of the five types of capital: human, social, innovative, scientific and research, and relation based. In the study, data for the years 2018–2020 for 240 regions in 22 EU Member States, Norway, Serbia, Switzerland, and the UK, at varying NUTS levels, were used. Data availability for NUTS levels varied, hence the indicators gathered pertain to 47 NUTS regions and 193 NUTS-2 regions. In the EU member states of Cyprus, Estonia, Latvia, Luxembourg, and Malta, NUTS 1 and NUTS 2 correspond to the country's territory. Therefore, in their case, the country level was applied. Given the purpose of the study, that is, defining the potential of regions and spatial regimes, the same weights of model indicators were used. The following steps made up the process of preparing region typology for smart development: defining the types of capital, selection of empirical features, standardization of variables, calculation of zero–sum unitarization for the types of capital, clustering the units of the population being studied based on capital groups, and the evaluation of indicator sustainability (k-means classification). For easier interpretation, the indicators were grouped into four clusters that are the model's components. The K-means algorithm is a clustering technique that is widely used in numerous studies for input classification. In the last chapter, a smart city ranking (Report Smart City Index, 2021) produced by the International Institute of Management Development (IMD) was used in mapping smart cities in the EU.

The study is, to a degree, limited. Potential for the growth of smart organizations is complex, and measuring them requires various indicators which account for numerous occurrences. Measurement is difficult in that it involves translating theoretical assumptions into measurable empirical indicators. The problem intrinsic in research on institutions lies in their non-tangible character, and thus it is more customary to observe the effects of how they function, and what policies and rules of conduct are in place. The research focused on the types of potential created by the policy of innovation and the human and social capital growth aiming to develop digital skills and create social networks based on new IT technologies. Indicators were selected both for a broad range of potential of IT technologies and innovations, as well as human potential and the ability to implement new technologies in social structures. Hence, they show incomplete institutional potential that may affect the development of smart organizations. In further research, it would be worth expanding the observation range, for instance to include local laws, the quality of government, and informal rules.

As it is not possible to draw in-depth conclusions regarding the influence of smart organizations in local offices on local development, this monograph also includes methods allowing an analysis of case studies in the context of website audit and interviews with the officers of local government units, and managers of departments for economic development or special units promoting smart city development.

Websites of cities outstanding in terms of potential for smart organizations growth (cf. chapter two), as well as of those ranked the highest on the Smart Cities list, were audited. They include Amsterdam, Berlin, Birmingham, Bordeaux, Brussels, Copenhagen, Dublin, Duesseldorf, Glasgow, Gothenburg, Hamburg, Hannover, Helsinki, Cologne, Leeds, London, Madrid, Manchester, Munich, Rotterdam, Saragossa, Stockholm, and Vienna. In addition, a survey was carried out in these cities, however, there was a low rate of returns. Surveys were received from such cities as Vienna, Brussels, Leeds, and London.

In addition, 15 in-depth interviews were carried out with representatives of the smart cities to identify the measures they undertake to foster local development, as well as the difficulties in implementing the smart city concept using smart solutions.

A total of 50 European cities were selected that made up the Smart City ranking. Moreover, representatives of six Polish cities known for using solutions typical of the smart city and at the same time showing similarities in terms of development path or economic base to the previously mentioned European cities were invited to the interview. All in all, representatives of cities such as the following agreed to be interviewed: Warsaw, Gdańsk, Katowice, Łódź, and Wrocław, and European cities: Barcelona, Duesseldorf, Gothenburg, Hannover, Leeds, Lisbon, Rotterdam, Verona, and Vienna. The research lasted from August to October 2022.

Owing to triangulation of methods, it is possible to reduce the limitations attributable to a relatively small research sample, and also lack of access to all the chosen cities. Regrettably, quite a numerous groups of cities commonly considered smart were at a loss to share knowledge either in the form of a survey or consent to be interviewed. This is understandable as, during the research, there were serious global and regional disruptions that impacted the functioning of cities and other regions (not only in the EU and UK), as well as of other regions of the world.

Nevertheless, based on the case study collection, it is possible to identify the mechanism whereby smart organizations impact local development, and thus to formulate relevant good practices. Hence, we would very much like to thank the representatives of cities who supported our activities for sharing knowledge, and for their willingness to continue our study.

The authors express their gratitude to the authorities of the Collegium of Business Administration at SGH for their support in the process of producing and publishing this work. It was made possible owing to the analyses carried out for the purposes of this book as part of statutory research at the Collegium, *"Smart business -smart regions -smart society: towards a new paradigm"*, headed by Prof. Dr hab. Hanna Godlewska-Majkowska (KNOP/S22:1.1).

The authors are immensely grateful to anonymous reviewers representing the international scientific community who, at the stage of contracting the monograph with the publishing house, came up with a number of comments, both substantive and essential from the perspective of managerial practice.

Authors also express gratitude to Mrs Professor Wieslawa Lizinska from the University of Warmia and Mazury in Olsztyn, Poland for thorough review of the manuscript prepared by the authors for the publishing house and for critical remarks provided before the final manuscript submission.

Warsaw – Koszalin, Poland, December 2022

Part 1

Characteristics, typologies, measurement, and enablers of smart organizations in public sector

1 Characteristics and typologies of smart organizations in the public sector

I.1 Smart organization construct in sciences – introductory remarks

Intelligence has usually been attributed to living organisms and considered in relation to the ability to learn, understand, and formulate judgments based on reasoning.[1]

Intelligence has been characterized as the ability of organisms to convert collected information and stimuli into knowledge and capabilities enabling a response to stimuli demonstrated by observable behaviors.

These aspects of intelligence, typical to living organisms including humans, are the reference point and managerial metaphor for intelligence looked for among organizations, understood as social phenomena of people working together toward the achievement of shared goals. In management sciences discourse, organizations are examined in relation to the basic constructs operating in all sectors of the economy, including the private, public, and non-governmental sectors.

In life sciences, the application of intelligence in response to a change in the environment of an organism is examined in relation to the attribute of being smart, and it is indicated as a practical aspect of using intelligence, or in other words – being smart. Therefore, smartness refers to reacting to a given situation in the best possible way, using intelligence gathered by the organism. Smartness expresses easiness and quickness in responding to a challenge or problem and the related decision-making process. In this monograph, we distinguish between intelligence and smartness and refer to smartness as purposeful application of intelligence.

Application of accumulated intelligence requires from a living organism an ability to learn, including learning from mistakes and failures and being able to apply the lessons learnt in decision-making, oriented toward achieving expected outcomes. The aspect related to the capability of making informed decisions further distinguishes intelligence and smartness. The latter is an ability to make informed decisions.

The terms intelligence and smartness are used in everyday context interchangeably, however, there are additional criteria enabling a clear distinction to be made between them.

DOI: 10.4324/9781003265870-3

Intelligence and being intelligent in the measurement context are referred to as gradable (low, medium, high intelligence) and measurable variable (e.g. through intelligence tests). Smartness on the other hand is a dynamic, continuously evolving quality that is hard to measure in the same way as intelligence.

In recent decades, the performance of machines in activities requiring human-level intelligence has been a domain of research dedicated to augmented and artificial intelligence. Therefore, the total intelligence of a smart organization must refer to both human intelligence and artificial intelligence resources an organization uses.

Discourse on intelligent and smart organizations is relatively new, as scholarly research dedicated to them has intensified in the last three decades, with a vast majority of the research papers dedicated to organizational intelligence, and a minority of papers dedicated to organizational smartness. Systematic literature review analysis of smart organizations indicates a continuum of smart organizations evolving from earlier types of organizational paradigms such us intelligent organizations, ambidextrous organizations, and learning organizations.

From the science disciplines perspective, intelligent and smart organizations are researched in the context of human resources and capabilities management, knowledge management, and organizational strategy domains.

Intelligent and smart organizations are part of the broader management sciences discourse on how organizations specialize and improve their structures and interactions to dynamically respond to changes in their environment, deliver on the goals set, and adapt to shocks.

Models of organizational intelligence and smart organizations researched over the past decades evolve from the types oriented toward data and knowledge collection and processing in general to become purpose-oriented types, where collection and processing of data are done to achieve defined goals, such as increased competitive advantages, strengthened market position of organizations, organizational agility, and responsiveness to changes in the competitive environment.

Table I.1 Intelligence and smartness distinguishing criteria – general context. Own work. Smart organization definitions journey

	Intelligence	*Smartness*
1	Ability to learn	Practical application of intelligence to respond to a problem or challenge
2	Ability to formulate statements and judgments based on a learning process	Ability to make educated and informed decisions based on a learning process
3	Gradable and measurable (e.g. low, medium, high intelligence)	Dynamic and evolving in nature, not easily gradable and measurable

Table I.2 Various aspects of intelligent organizations outlined in research dedicated to them. Own work

No.	Key characteristics of intelligent organizations	Author(s)
1	Converts intellectual resources into a chain of service outputs and integrates them into a form most useful for the customers. Leverages skills and the intellect of its key professionals and adds value based on knowledge-based activities.	Quinn (1992)
2	Absorbs information, data, and knowledge, analyses them, and invests in teaching its participants to solve problems. An intelligent organization is an interactive, dynamic, and evolving construct.	Armstrong (2000)
3	Is capable of responding and formulating changes in its environment in advance and owns intellectual assets which are hard to imitate.	Wachowiak (2004)
4	Leverages a whole community of participants of the organization, and their knowledge, know-how and experience, not only of top management.	Maryta in Nonaka and Takeuchi (2000)
5	Utilizes the knowledge of all employees toward creation of innovation, is oriented toward teamwork in delivery of work through projects and openness to leveraging data.	Ziębicki (2000)
6	Combines self-learning practices, organizational reflection, business transformation, and transcendence beyond its current state. Reacts to the challenges in its environment and can find a new environment for its development and contribution to growth of environment found.	Schwaninger (2001)
7	Is sensitive to trends in its environment, able to respond to trends identified in a fast manner through capability to absorb knowledge and capability of knowledge development, continuous improvement of employees, and processes within the organization. Achieves competitive advantage through continuous development and organizational learning.	Łobejko (2009)
8	Dynamically exchanges knowledge between participants in the organization enabling integration of various activities.	Brzeziński (2014)
9	Leverages intellectual potential of each employee to enable a response to market opportunities and challenges based on collective intelligence.	Nawrocki (2015)
10	Effectively solves problems and leverages decision-making impacting on competitiveness and market position.	López-Robles Otegi-Olaso, Porto Gomez and Cobo (2019)

Intelligent and smart organizations have been the subject of numerous studies, and their characteristics can be investigated in terms of literal focus on intelligent organizations and on smart organizations separately. Analysis of groups of definitions enables a key definition and distinguishing aspects of both types of organizations to be identified and enumerated.

The presented definitions of an intelligent organization emphasize the following aspects related to their modus operandi:

- Absorbing and leveraging data
- Promoting internal knowledge sharing
- Practicing organizational reflection and decision-making
- Applying internal learning, self-learning, and teaching processes
- Leveraging intellectual resources, capabilities, and experiences of each person.

This set of characteristics distinguishes an intelligent organization from a smart one, which can be perceived as the next stage of intelligent organization evolution with a set of advanced characteristics.

Definitions of a smart organization differ from definitions of intelligent organizations developed earlier and extend characteristics of an intelligent organization by:

- Additionally focusing on a clearly identified and articulated organizational purpose beyond organizational existence or survival (e.g. serving defined customers, responding to the relevant market needs).
- Depending on relevant organizational stakeholders' feedback (e.g. customers), agile and entrepreneurial organizational culture, and abilities required to serve organizational stakeholders effectively.
- Exploiting existing organizational knowledge to leverage the ability to fulfill the organizational purpose and exploring new knowledge not existing in the organization to serve relevant organizational stakeholders, also by applying intra- and inter-organizational learning.
- Being dynamically adaptable, practicing an internetworking approach, using collaborative networks reflected by transitory structure, often exceeding defined organizational boundaries.
- Leveraging support of a technology-based solution and other tools for purposeful utilization of information and data for its operations.

Compared to an intelligent organization, a smart organization seemed to be more advanced in orientation on purpose, stakeholders it serves, and feedback loops it uses to enhance learning. It also uses technology in data analysis and operations, which is an aspect we can attribute to this specific organization type.

Table I.3 Various aspects of smart organizations outlined in research attributed to them. Own work

No.	Key characteristics of smart organizations	Author(s)
1	Smart organization as knowledge-driven, interworked, dynamically adaptable to new organizational forms and practices, learning as well as agile in their ability.	Filos and Banahan (2001)
	Customer-focused, committed to intra- and inter-organizational collaboration organized to master change and uncertainty, leveraging the impact of people (entrepreneurial culture) and knowledge (intellectual capital).	
	Smart organization understood as an emerging organizational paradigm collecting models, ideas, and concepts which are relevant and of growing importance in the new economic framework shaped by information society technologies.	
2	Defines activities based on knowledge and exploits the knowledge to respond to concrete market opportunities within the reach of the organization.	Filos (2006)
3	Smart organization as rapidly developing, marked by transitory layout and agile structure able to integrate seamless with specific, ever-changing processes.	Iapichino, De Rosa and Liberace (2018)
	Highly dependent on the customers' feedback. Appointments and tasks organized according to specific processes and goals entailing specific skills and seniorities, with workload designed and distributed to respond to dynamic patterns of consumers' needs and expectations and to workers' skills and availability.	
4	Smart organization defined within a broader concept of sensing, smart and sustainable organizations (S^3), where sensing refers to continuous monitoring of organizational context and operations, smartness refers to decision-making creating collaborative networks that enhance reactive and proactive organizational capabilities, and sustainability refers to usage of technological and human resources to become sustainable in the environmental, economic, and social aspect.	de Sousa, Yamanari and Guerrini (2020)
5	Smart organization understood as a state where an organization develops and uses knowledge as an integrated resource that combines the expertise provided by human resources with the support offered by technology-based platforms. A smart organization effectively utilizes tools harnessing information age and management practices within an organization.	Adamik and Sikora-Fernandez (2021)

I.1.1 Smart organization in the public sector

Investigated definitions of intelligent and smart organizations were very often embedded in the context of private enterprises. This monograph focuses on the public sector context exemplified by organizations oriented toward satisfying public needs. The public sector consists of entities owned by and reporting to the state, local government authorities, or autonomous entities, where the majority of ownership and equity can be attributed to public entities. The public sector and public sector organizations at the country level are often defined by legal regulations underlying their purpose, obligatory tasks, and budgeting.

By its nature, the public sector is primarily oriented toward the satisfaction of needs and legal entitlements of stakeholders its serves, less the

Table I.4 Various aspects of smart organizations in public sector in research dedicated. Own work

No.	Key characteristics of a smart organization in the public sector	Author(s)
1	Defined as organizational units implementing their fundamental tasks determined by legislative acts, providing employees with education and skill improvement opportunities, searching for effective and innovative sources of finance, implementing changes to respond to market megatrends, encouraging new economic entities and residents to settle in its territory by leveraging its brand and local government fiscal and financial incentives, leveraging education and skills of its citizens, especially in the digital skills domain, exchanging experiences and best practices with other public organizations, and creating value through nurturing and managing relations with their partners and stakeholders.	Wereda (2010)
2	Organizations able to generate and manage knowledge, including using it to carry out public tasks, creative and innovative in problem-solving, and capable of forecasting social needs and flexible in responding to social needs.	Sikora-Fernandez (2013)
3	Organizations able to anticipate needs and discover their new combinations, which utilizes existing and searches for new development resources for an efficient set of innovation abilities.	Sasinowski (2015)
4	Organizations leveraging knowledge for decision-making, applying continued learning and continued process improvement to effectively pursue its mission.	Olejniczak and Śliwkowski (2014)
5	Defined as a unit that effectively manages information, knowledge, communication, and relations with partners, leverages technology to deliver upon public tasks, and dynamizes local development processes to achieve and maintain competitive advantages.	Godlewska-Majkowska and Komor (2019)

economic profits. This monograph focuses on public sector organizations responsible for governance over given local administrative-territorial units and responsible for providing defined public goods and services.

Therefore, a smart organization in the public sector must be oriented toward better satisfaction of needs of stakeholders it serves and other characteristics related to the nature of the public sector.

The basic reference point for public sector organization analysis is Local Administrative Units (LAUs) exemplified by various local characteristics in European Union (EU) countries, elaborated further in this chapter.

The public sector consists of entities owned by and reporting to the state, local government authorities, or autonomous entities, where the majority of ownership and equity can be attributed to public entities.

In recent years, the public sector has become a subject of debate on public sector management reforms which make a distinction between a few prominent reform-oriented propositions, such as *new public governance, neo-weberian state*, the concept of *networks and joining-up*, and the concept of *governance* (Pollit & Bouckaert, 2011). Public sector reform propositions point out the importance of multi-level and multi-layer management aspects required for the efficiency of public policy realizations, including local development policies. *New public governance* emphasizes the relevance and importance of practices typical in a private sector economy for a public sector economy. *Neo-weberian state* relates to a *new public management* school that emphasizes formal rules, hierarchic organization structure, and operations that are lean in nature. *Networks and joining-up* are understood through the context of self-organization, flexibility, and inclusivity of various entities belonging to the networks, often created and orchestrated by public sector entities. Propositions focused on *governance* refer to effective decision-making by a broad range of stakeholders included in the decision-making process.

Operations based on acts of law and utilization of resources and knowledge, generated to perform tasks, and oriented toward satisfaction of public needs, distinguish between a smart organization in the public sector and a smart organization in general. The purpose of smart organizations in the public sector based on local administration units relates to the advancement and acceleration of local development processes and increase of governed territory competitiveness supporting further attraction of development resources to the territories such as new economics entities, such as enterprises, and residents.

López-Robles, Otegi-Olaso, Gómez, and Cobo (López-Robles et al., 2019) with a team of researchers synthesized over 30 years of smart organization research and stated that the universal characteristics of intelligence in an organizational context relate to decision-making processes based on collection, analysis, interpretation, sharing, and gathering of relevant data and information that can be used to solve problems and challenges in a prompt manner.

According to scholars, leveraging intelligence in organizations enhances organizational performance.

The common denominator of the smart organization definitions and conceptualizations presented is practicing collecting, analyzing, interpreting, and sharing relevant data and information to solve problems and challenges in a prompt manner, to generate competitive advantages, and achieve a strengthened market position.

López-Robles says that collection, analysis, interpretation, and dissemination of high-value information transmitted at the right time to decision-makers and specialized information service units are a key prerequisite of increased efficiency in decision-making. This context of smart organizations will be explored in the smart organization explanatory and measurement model proposed below.

I.1.2 Smart organization in the public sector in smart cities discourse

The proliferation of the smart cities and smart municipalities concept in the last decade in the EU raises a question whether and to what extent a smart organization in public sector overlaps with smart city concept. Smart cities are defined through the specific capability of utilization of information and communication technologies to increase the quality of living of their inhabitants. Smart cities are discussed in an urban planning and governance context with predominance of technology solutions enabling collection, processing, and leveraging of data from municipal networks and media installations such as parking spaces, traffic lights, water supply systems, sewers, or public monitoring systems to advance and improve urban planning, urban management, and governance (Jiang, Luo & Chen, 2018).

The initial focus of smart city initiatives investigated by the OECD pointed to the usage of digital information and communication technologies to improve the efficiency of urban services planning and delivery. Later, the debate started to include the effects of smart city initiatives on people, the environment, and the local development model (OECD, 2020). The smart city definition in the EU proposed by the European Commission emphasizes enabling higher efficiency of traditional networks and services using digital and telecommunication technologies for the benefit of inhabitants and businesses (European Commission, 2014).

As the smart city concept is continuously evolving and a subject of debate, a smart organization in the public sector defined in this monograph can contribute to this concept. Especially in the context of the organizational purpose of a smart organization, over the technology, orientation toward educated and informed decision-making, dynamization of local development processes, increase of local competitiveness, and attractiveness for its development stakeholders. A smart organization in

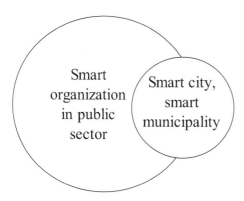

Figure I.1 A smart organization in the public sector and smart cities and municipalities. A graphical representation of areas of definition. Own work.

the public sector is proposed as a broader and more general approach for administration units that are different in nature to a city or a municipality, including smaller and bigger units of functional type and regional scale, exceeding boundaries of a geographically delimited city or municipality.

I.2 Smart organization construct in sciences – context of management and economic sciences schools and paradigms

I.2.1 *Smart organizations in the context of the 20th–21st management and organization schools*

In the twentieth century, there was an abundance of various organizational theoretical perspectives, which gradually contributed to professionalization of managerial practice and also the emergence of the smart organization concept.

The first part of the twentieth century was characterized by the development and advancement of the first scientific management schools, such as division of labor, which, in essence, had been focused on the separation of tasks in an organization to enable specialization for its participants, and thus increase efficiency of the work process (Taylor, 1997). Another management and organization perspective, which was formalized at that time, is a functional hierarchical organization, which utilized organizational design with a function-related and organizational hierarchy structure oriented toward efficient resources flow within the organization, including information, and fostered managerial control over the work results (Thompson, 1961).

In the latter half of the twentieth century, new perspectives in theory of organization were introduced, such as Theory X, outlining the role of managerial supervision, external rewards, and penalties as key determinants of work efficiency, and its opposite, called Theory Y, focusing on the relation of job satisfaction with employee engagement and impact of this engagement on work results (McGregor, 2006).

Other perspective introduced at that time, which dominated the management science discourse, was management by objectives (MBO), outlining the role of a proper process of setting the objectives, followed by planning resources and tasks to achieve them (Drucker, 2006).

MBO developed in parallel with the school of formal strategic planning related to setting organizational goals and broader formation of organizational structures and resources in a way enabling them to be pursued effectively (Porter, 2004, 2009). MBO and strategic planning contributed to emergence of the so-called market-based view (MBV), an approach in management stressing the importance of following external market trends and occurrences, and formulating organizational goals in a way that capitalizes on these external trends, also through purchase and acquisition of external resources, not existing in the organization at the moment of formulation of objectives.

Capability management and so-called resource-based view (RBV), contrary to MBV, was an approach that emphasized the necessity of understanding an organization's own internal and external capabilities to build competitive value propositions and market responses (Barney, 1992; Penrose, 2013).

In parallel to the organizational perspectives discussed in the latter half of the twentieth century which had an impact on strategy formulation (MBO, MBV, RBV), an important topic related to an organization's performance and operations management emerged. Around the mid-twentieth century, companies started to analyze whether their manufacturing processes and activities contributed to value or were waste from the end-customer perspective. The lean manufacturing school popularized by Taiichi Ohno and the example of Toyota proliferated the usage of lean management methods and tools in manufacturing, and, later on, in services (Liker & Convis, 2012).

Another school related to an organization's performance oriented toward organizational process improvement through work efficiency and quality measurement was total quality management (TQM) (Deming Cahill, Orsini & Deming, 2012). This, together with lean management, dominated for decades in both management and organization sciences theory and practice.

The end of the twentieth century brought new aspects to the work efficiency and enterprise competitive advantages discourse in the form of knowledge management. Increased amounts of data and information impacting decisions and operations of economic entities drew the attention of scholars to collection, analysis, and sharing aspects of information

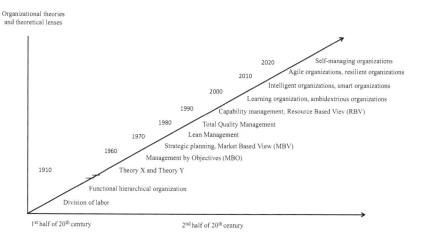

Organizational theories
and theoretical lenses

2020 Self-managing organizations
Agile organizations, resilient organizations
2010
Intelligent organizations, smart organizations
2000
Learning organization, ambidextrious organizations
1990
Capability management, Resource Based View (RBV)
1980 Total Quality Management
1970 Lean Management
Strategic planning, Market Based View (MBV)
1960
Management by Objectives (MBO)
1910 Theory X and Theory Y

Functional hierarchical organization

Division of labor

1st half of 20th century   2nd half of 20th century

Figure I.2 Organizational theories and theoretical perspectives in twentieth and twenty-first-century discourse. Own work.

within organizations and the relationship between such practices and the emergence of competitive advantage.

The domain of knowledge management is intrinsically linked to learning the organization construct, elaborated upon in detail later in this chapter, as per its character of the direct predecessor of ambidextrous, intelligent, and smart organization types.

The most recent perspectives influencing development of management science and practice in the first half of the twenty-first century relate to agile and self-managing organizations (Laloux, 2014), and shock-resistant and resilient organization structures with previously secured resource buffers enabling them to resist and respond to shocks (Hobfoll, Halbesleben, Neveu & Westman, 2018).

I.2.2 Smart organization construct in sciences – emergence and evolution

The emergence of the smart organization concept in management sciences is related to the transformation of economy in the latter half of the twentieth century, induced by the increase of data in the world, and its potential to be used in economy for creation, manufacturing, and delivery of goods and services.

In 2022, the amount of data created, captured, copied, and consumed in the world was estimated to be 97 zettabytes (a zettabyte has 21 zeros) and is estimated to double in three years and reach 181 zettabytes in

2025 (Statista, 2022). Data and the ability to use it in the right way at the right time started to become perceived as competitive advantage of an enterprise. Meanwhile, knowledge management as a domain in both the academic and real economy context gained importance.

An early predecessor of a smart organization is a learning organization characterized through the ability to create, acquire, and transfer knowledge within its boundaries and an ability to modify organizational behaviors in a way reflecting knowledge and insights (Garvin, 1993).

A specific type of learning organization advancing and mastering organizational learning ability is an ambidextrous organization, defined through simultaneous capability of two types of learning: exploitative learning, making it possible to improve and advance capabilities and resources existing in the organization, and exploratory learning oriented toward monitoring the organizational environment and identification and acquisition of relevant new insights and knowledge (He & Wong, 2004).

An intelligent organization, characterized earlier in this chapter, builds on those two concepts and exceeds them with quality of organizational reflection on existing and not yet existing knowledge required for an educated and informed decision-making process. According to M. Yolles, organizational processes related to self-awareness of an organization in the context of new knowledge to be acquired to be competitive are key factors distinguishing an intelligent organization from ambidextrous and learning ones (Yolles, 2006).

B. Kaczmarek (2013) argues that an intelligent organization is an advanced type of learning organization that uses system thinking, extensive teamwork, collection and analysis of data, and experiences.

A smart organization advances the intelligent organization type in focusing on a clearly defined purpose and stakeholders it serves, feedback loops used to enhance learning, and technology solutions used for data analysis and operations.

At the beginning of the twentieth century, new organization types and ways of working oriented toward dynamic reaction to change in the volatile environment of the organization intensified. An agile concept of an organization emerged first in the information and communication technology services and was later popularized in the broader services sector. An agile organization is a concept that is also in flux and is influenced by earlier organization types elaborated upon in this chapter.

Agile organizations focus on rapid adaption to requirements and expectations of their stakeholders, namely, external customers and end users of their products and services. Agile organizations are indicated as excellent in information management, and knowledge sharing (Smite, Moe, Levinta & Floryan, 2019). Agile organizations rapidly apply flexibility in product and service design, and delivery thanks to excellent capabilities, resource management, and decision-making processes. This type of organization has been closely investigated in recent years due to its resilience to external development shocks such as the global pandemic in 2020–2022.

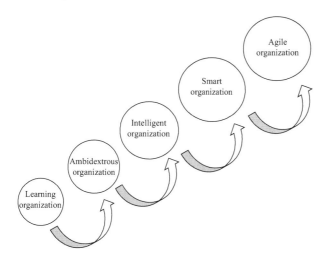

Figure I.3 Evolution of organization types in a knowledge-driven economy. Own work.

Agile organizations are also investigated from the perspective of self-management capability (Kuusinen et al., 2017) of its smaller units, such as classic strategic business units (SBUs) of which those organizations very often consist. Knowledge exploitation and exploration capability, together with informed and educated decision-making processes, enables smaller units of bigger organizations to be self-reliant and respond to changes faster than in other types of organization structures.

The presented perspective provides a broader context for foundations of the agile type of organization and partially contributes to the explanatory context of failures (Chavarría-Barrientos et al., 2015) of agile ways of working in organizations which have not recognized and practiced mechanisms typical for learning, ambidextrous, intelligent, and smart organizations.

I.3 Smart organizations in the public sector – the context of Local Administrative Units and self-governments in the European Union

I.3.1 *Local Administrative Units in the European Union*

The territorial context of this monograph is the EU – an international organization with common economic, social, and security policies fostering cooperation and development of countries in Europe and territories they cooperate with, which in 2022 consisted of 27 countries.[2]

In the EU, for the purpose of normalization of policy-making related to locations and regions, a specific system of territory demarcation was introduced. Basic territorial units usually governed by a respected public sector local governance body are called LAUs.

LAUs in the EU are used to manage physical territories for the purpose of providing statistics at a local level. Level 2 LAUs are the lowest level of administrative division of a country, below the state, macroregion, mesoregion, submesoregion, and microregion. Not all EU member states classify their locally governed areas in the same way, and LAUs may refer to a range of different administrative units mentioned earlier.

Prior to LAUs, other statistical nomenclature was used for territories in the EU – *Nomenclatures des Unites Territoriales Statistiques* (NUTS). Former NUTS V units are currently reflected by the current level 2 LAU.

At the specific country level, LAUs have their own naming system, such as *sogne* in Denmark, *Gemeinden* in Germany, *comuni* in Italy, *gminy* in Poland, or *freguesias* in Portugal. Normalization of taxonomy of LAUs fosters not only policy-making but also research and comparative studies.

LAUs in the EU, in economic geography terminology, refer to a local, microregional scale of spatial unit taxonomy, whereas regions and the regional scale refer to larger territorial areas. In colloquial speech, local and regional terms are used interchangeably, whereas in the EU a spatial taxonomy region consists of local spatial units. In some examples, the term region is used as the proprietary name of the location (e.g., Brussels-Capital Region in Belgium).

The number of LAUs in EU countries varies and depends on local administrative law and regulations.

In this monograph, a local government organization managing LAU level 2 territorial units in reference to the EU are used to explore and validate its fit with the smart organization concept.

From the perspective of how local government units work in relation to the territorial units they manage, a taxonomy of smart organizations can be introduced. In all EU countries, local self-governments are adopted structures stating that local authorities adjust internal administrative

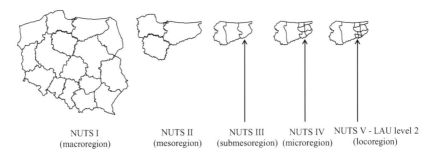

NUTS I
(macroregion)

NUTS II
(mesoregion)

NUTS III
(submesoregion)

NUTS IV
(microregion)

NUTS V - LAU level 2
(locoregion)

Figure I.4 Example of level 2 Local Administrative Unit in territorial statistics nomenclature of the European Union. Own work.

Table I.5 Number of level 2 Local Administrative Units in European Union member states and their total population in 2021. Own work based on Eurostat, https://ec.europa.eu/eurostat/web/nuts/local-administrative-units, accessed on 8.6.2022 Local government in the European Union and its obligations

No.	European Union member state	Number of LAU level 2	Total population
1	Belgium	581	11 566 041
2	Bulgaria	265	6 916 548
3	Czech Republic	6 258	10 701 777
4	Denmark	99	5 840 045
5	Germany	11 002	83 155 031
6	Estonia	79	1 326 425
7	Ireland	166	4 761 865
8	Greece	6 137	10 816 286
9	Spain	8 131	n.a.
10	France	34 966	12 289 638
11	Croatia	556	4 284 889
12	Italy	7 903	59 257 566
13	Cyprus	615	n.a.
14	Latvia	119	1 892 623
15	Lithuania	60	2 795 680
16	Luxembourg	102	634 730
17	Hungary	3 155	9 730 772
18	Malta	68	516 100
19	Netherlands	355	17 407 585
20	Austria	2 095	8 932 664
21	Poland	2 477	38 265 013
22	Portugal	3 092	10 562 178
23	Romania	3 181	22 089 211
24	Slovenia	212	2 108 977
25	Slovakia	2 927	5 459 781
26	Finland	310	5 525 292
27	Sweden	290	10 379 295
	TOTAL	95 201	347 216 012

structures to respond to local needs and to assure effective management of the defined territory. Therefore, local government units are institutionally closest to living and working communities. Local government refers to government under the control and direction of the inhabitants of a given territorial, administrative unit. Local government units at level 2 LAUs means local communities which elect official representatives of self-government and thus empower them to act on their behalf. In the EU, the basic reference point for the concept and foundations for local self-government is the European Charter of Local Self-Government (Council of Europe, 2013).

Local government units focused and limiting their activities to a given LAU in isolation from the neighboring areas represent a simple and autonomous type of smart organization in the public sector. Local government units managing LAU territory in cooperation with other local government

Table I.6 Types of smart organizations in public sector in reference to a level 2 LAU. Own work

No.	Smart organization in the public sector	Reference point for level 2LAU
1	Simple and autonomous smart organization	Self-government of level 2 LAU managed in isolation from neighboring LAUs
2	Complex and functional smart organization	Local government units of level 2 LAUs in given territory interested in integrated management

units (directly and indirectly neighboring ones) represent a complex and functional type of smart organization in the public sector, oriented toward integrated planning and development of their own areas.

The rationale for proposed taxonomy assumes that local government units' activities in physical space can be either focused and autonomous ones, or of a broader, integrative nature, as contemporary ways of working also enable virtual cooperation of local government units located in distant areas using information and telecommunication technologies (ICT).

This perspective sheds additional light on taxonomy of smart organizations in the public sector in terms of effective boundaries of such organizations ranging beyond the LAU itself and LAUs it directly neighbors.

Smart organizations in the public sector might emerge and function beyond taxonomic classifications. In this monograph, the basic reference point for a smart organization in the public sector LAU2 (locoregion) is referred to. Smart organizations in the public sector might however operate as network organizations at microregional, submsesoregional, mesoregional, and macroregional levels. The method of operation of organizations to which a smart organization relates may exceed the taxonomic, geographical boundaries of locations.

Organizations follow lifecycle logic related to the stages of their organizational maturity over time. An organizational lifecycle is congruent with the product and services lifecycle widely used in the marketing domain (Kotler, 2011). An organizational lifecycle will also apply to smart organizations in the public sector with typical stages of entrance, growth, maturity, and decline. The lifecycle logic of smart organizations in the public sector provides an additional dimension to their basic typology and perspective of analysis. Smart organizations in the public sector can be simple and autonomous, complex, and functional, and at the same time at a different level of their development lifecycle.

Formal Governance over the spatial, physical territory of an LAU is conducted by the local government unit responsible for the enforcement of acts of law related to providing public services in the local territory. The local government unit usually consists of legislative and executive bodies,

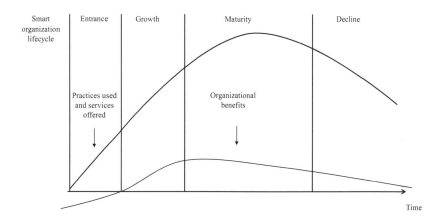

Figure I.5 Smart organization lifecycle. Own work.

with the leader of the executive body usually elected in local elections, represented by municipal, town, or city mayors, depending on the LAU size and their location across EU member states.

From a managerial perspective, employees of a local self-government organization are public sector managers, often referred in academic discourse as *local government managers*.

A broader definition of a public sector manager defines them as managers at different organizational levels, whose basic responsibilities include effective management of an organization and delivery of high-quality public services (Kożuch, 2004).

A narrower definition of public sector managers proposed by the European Group of Public Administration defines them as persons that are professionally responsible for the execution of a program, product, or service, directly or indirectly report to a public institution, and are autonomous in the decision-making process in financial, organizational, and human resources aspects (Barlow, Farnham, Horton, & Rodley, 1996).

Literature on the capabilities of public sector managers emphasizes the role of network-based models of public organization service delivery. Such models are enabled through public sector managers networking with multiple, diverse groups of local development stakeholders in order to enhance responsiveness to needs of communities they serve.

Engagements of public sector managers oriented toward the cultivation of collaborative relationships with a diverse range of stakeholders can take place during delivery of public services, meetings, and training (Andrews & Beynon, 2017). Scholars emphasize the growing role of technology and digital platforms in interactions between public sector managers and local development stakeholders (Kowalik, 2021).

A local government organization usually operates in a physical location, serving as an office, enabling interactions within the organization between its employees, and serving the local community through appointments, consultations, and other types of interaction.

Activities of local government units oriented toward the implementation of their obligatory tasks are mostly financed by public funding from local tax and regional and central government provisions.

Multiple local government units exceed the agenda of tasks they are required to implement by including facultative tasks, financed by additional sources, oriented toward meeting additional needs of local stakeholders.

Managerial and decision-making processes in local government units evolve, and over the last century of research into public government professionals, a trend related to professionalization of this practice has been observed.

A local government unit uses and applies methods, techniques, and tools typical for the private business sector in its practice. Strategic planning, development, and deployment of documents of strategic nature are not obsolete for them. Public statistics and other publicly available data are used in the planning of local government tasks and related budgets.

In the EU, the European Statistics Office – Eurostat – is considered a reliable source of standardized data, often from national statistical offices of countries belonging to the EU (Eurostat, 2022). Eurostat's data are considered a comparable, reliable, and objective source of statistical data available free of charge in the public domain.

Typical local government challenges are related to the fulfillment of obligations provided for in acts of law related to providing local public services, meeting needs of the community served, and continued increase of local attractiveness of the LAU for development resources such as entrepreneurs, investors, existing and new inhabitants, and tourists.

In this monograph, a local government organization, together with its purpose and internal ways of working, is used to explore and validate its fit with the smart organization concept.

In the next chapter of Part I, a review of smart organization measurement approaches is introduced and followed by a proprietary smart organization operationalization and measurement model for public sector institutions' advancement.

I.4 Proposed model of a smart organization in the public sector

I.4.1 Key premises of the model proposed

The explanatory model we proposed for smart organizations in the public sector is based on a set of premises. For the construction of the logic of the model, we assumed that there are inputs and outputs, and a transformation process related to them.

The basic premise of the model is that thanks to an informed manner of working, resources endowed at local government level can reveal their potential and result in smart-organization-related phenomena including development results at local government level and beyond.

On the input side of the model, we identify human capital resources and infrastructure resources. Human capital resources mean local inhabitants of the local government unit and employees that come to the local government unit to perform work in the workplace. The basic qualities impacting the potential of human capital resources are the demographic (age) and health status of inhabitants and external employees, the level of their professional knowledge, know-how, and capabilities, as well as attitudes toward pre-requirements of smart organizations including learning and knowledge-sharing (outlined in the literature by Wereda, 2010; Sikora-Fernandez, 2013; Olejniczak & Śliwkowski, 2014).

Another type of resource endowment critical for emergence of a smart organization at local level is infrastructure resources, meaning available knowledge management infrastructure in the form of ICT needed for collection, processing and management of data, information, and knowledge. The parallel parts of knowledge infrastructure are methods for data, information, and knowledge processing.

We proposed that infrastructure resources, referring to endowments in the operational domain of local government, relate to both public and private sector entities, as internetworking and spillovers between them are outlined in the literature by Filos and Banahan (2001) and Godlewska-Majkowska and Komor (2019).

Both human capital resources and infrastructure resources are the foundation of a smart organization. They demonstrate its development potential through a set of mechanisms such as flow of data, information and knowledge leading to decisions of short-term, long-term and strategic nature fostered by links between key stakeholders of the smart organization, and its system profile. The system profile of a smart organization refers to its life-cycle stage described in detail above (introduction, growth, maturity, decline stage).

Smart organization potential at local government level refers to inclusiveness of the decision-making process of smart organization stakeholders, response time to decisions made, costs of decisions, including financial and non-financial costs, a set of decisions of complex or selective nature corresponding to local government development strategy, and risks attributed to decisions made in the short- and long term.

The direct results of a smart organization oriented toward inclusive, and time- and cost-effective decisions, aligned with local government strategy, are a cornerstone for the outcomes at both local government level, and beyond − at regional level.

The types of outcomes of smart organizations are investigated in further chapters of this monograph, with particular attention to economic, social, and environmental ones.

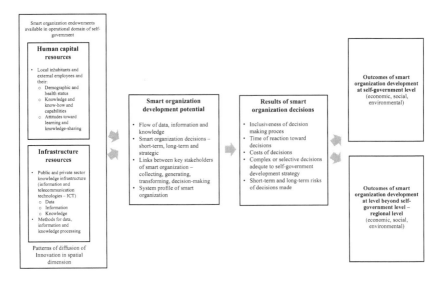

Figure I.6 Smart Organizations in the Public Sector: Sustainable Local Development in the European Union. Own work.

I.4.2 Correspondence rules between components of the model

Theory should relate to the empirical domain and practice, otherwise it could be considered as a set of imagined statements (Czakon, 2022). The proposed model for a smart organization in the public sector derives from the abstract devised above, theoretical constructs which are further operationalized in the form of a theoretical model proposed in this chapter. Theoretical models are constructed for explanatory purposes of observable phenomena and are verified or falsified through research.

From the scientific rigor perspective, what is between the theoretical model and observable phenomena is the rules of correspondence, which refer to relations between dependent and independent variables measured, and take the form of hypotheses.

Hypotheses are statements later verified or falsified through research, and a set of such hypotheses has been formulated in relation to the model for a smart organization in the public sector.

Dependent variables relate to phenomena which the theoretical model aims to explain and are usually located on the right of theoretical models constructed. Independent variables, usually located on the left of theoretical models, are those which are used to explain dependent variables. Theoretical models might also include intermediary variables located between independent variables and dependent variables. If the relationship between independent variables and dependent variable is weaker than between the independent variable and intermediary variable, then the

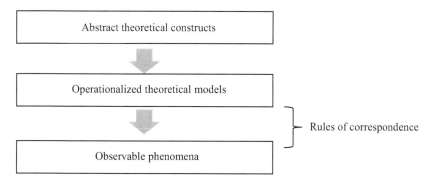

Figure I.7 The place of rules of correspondence in the context of the proposed theoretical model for a smart organization in the public sector. Own work.

model with the intermediary variable has a better explanatory value than that without the intermediary variable one.

In a smart organization in the public sector model, the proposed dependent variables are outcomes of smart organization development at local government level and regional level, which are explained through independent variables in the form of resource endowments in the form of human capital resources and infrastructure resources, which together make up the smart organization development potential. In the model, the proposed intermediary variables are results of smart organization decisions and their components.

A set of hypotheses (H1, H2, H3) related to a smart organization in the public sector is based on an earlier smart organization theory review, including their definitions and measurement aspects:

- H1: The greater the human and infrastructure resources at local government level, the greater the smart organization development potential – hypotheses inspired by findings of Filos and Banahan (2001) and Filos (2006).
- H2: The greater the smart organization development potential, the greater the decision-making intensity, and the higher the number of results of smart organization decisions – hypotheses inspired by findings of Olejniczak and Śliwkowski (2014).
- H3: The more mature a smart organization, the higher the number of local development-related outcomes at local government and regional level – hypotheses inspired by findings of Godlewska-Majkowska and Komor (2019).

The set of hypotheses proposed is verified in Part II and Part III of this monograph using various academic research methods, techniques, and tools.

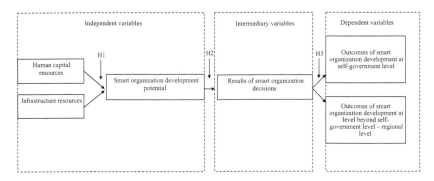

Figure I.8 Independent, intermediary, and dependent types of variables and location of hypotheses for the proposed theoretical model of a smart organization in the public sector. Own work.

Notes

1 Intelligence as defined in the English language Cambridge Dictionary Online – https://dictionary.cambridge.org/dictionary/english/intelligence, accessed on 6.4.2022.
2 The European Union member states in 2022 were Austria, Belgium, Bulgaria, Croatia, Cyprus, the Czech Republic, Denmark, Estonia, Finland, France, Germany, Greece, Hungary, Ireland, Italy, Latvia, Lithuania, Luxembourg, Malta, the Netherlands, Poland, Portugal, Romania, Slovakia, Slovenia, Spain, and Sweden, The European Union. What it is and what it does - https://op.europa.eu/webpub/com/eu-what-it-is/en/, accessed on 7.6.2022.

References

Adamik, A., & Sikora-Fernandez, D. (2021). Smart Organizations as a Source of Competitiveness and Sustainable Development in the Age of Industry 4.0: Integration of Micro and Macro Perspective. *Energies*, 14, p. 1572, https://doi.org/10.3390/en14061572.

Andrews, R., & Beynon, M. J. (2017). Managerial Networking and Stakeholder Support in Public Service Organizations. *Public Organiz Review*, 17, pp. 237–254. https://doi.org/10.1007/s11115-015-0340-0.

Armstrong, M. (2000). *Zarządzanie zasobami ludzkimi, Oficyna Ekonomiczna, Dom Wydawniczy ABC*. Kraków, pp. 438–439.

Barlow, J., Farnham, D., Horton, S., & Ridley, F. F. (1996). Comparing Public Managers. In Farnham, D., Horton, S., Barlow, J., & Hondeghem, A. (Eds.), *New Public Managers in Europe. Public Servants in Transition* (pp. 3–25). London: Macmillan Business Ltd.

Barney, J. (1992). Integrating Organizational Behavior and Strategy Formulation Research: A Resource Based Analysis. In Shrivastava, P., Huff, A., & Dutton, J. (Eds.), *Advances in Strategic Management*, vol. 8 (pp. 39–62). Greenwich, CT: JAI Press.

Brzeziński, M. (2014). O organizacjach przyszłości raz jeszcze. *Kwartalnik Nauk o Przedsiębiorstwie*, 30(1), pp. 44–48.

Chavarría-Barrientos, D., Molina Espinosa, J. M., Batres, R., Ramírez-Cadena, M., & Molina, A. (2015). Reference Model for Smart x Sensing Manufacturing Collaborative Networks – Formalization Using Unified Modeling Language. In Camarinha-Matos, L. M. (Eds.), *PRO-VE 2015, IFIP AICT 463* (pp. 243–254). https://doi.org/10.1007/978-3-319-24141-8_22.

Council of Europe (2013). *European Charter of Local Self-Government*, https://rm.coe.int/european-charter-for-local-self-government-english-version-pdf-a6-59-p/16807198a3.

Czakon, W. (ed.), (2022). *Podstawy metodologii badań w naukach o zarządzaniu.* Wydanie III rozszerzone, Wydawnictwo Nieoczywiste.

Deming Cahill, D., Orsini, J., & Deming, W. (2012). *Essential Deming: Leadership Principles from the: Leadership Principles from the Father of Quality.* The McGraw-Hill Companies, Inc.

Drucker, P. (2006). *The Practice of Management.* Harper Business.

European Commission (2014). *EC Digital Agenda for Europe: Smart Cities*, http://eige.europa.eu/resources/digital_agenda_en.pdf (accessed on 7.6.2022).

Eurostat (2022) – https://ec.europa.eu/eurostat/web/nuts/local-administrative-units, accessed on 8.6.2022.

Filos, E., & Banahan, E. (2001). Towards the Smart Organization: An Emerging Organizational Paradigm and the Contribution of the European RTD Programs. *Journal of Intelligent Manufacturing*, 12, pp. 101–119.

Filos, E. (2006). Smart Organisations in the Digital Age. In Mazgar, I. (Ed.), *Integration of ICT in Smart Organisations* (pp. 1–38). Hershey, PA: Idea Group Publishing.

Garvin, D. (1993). Building the Learning Organization. *Harvard Business Review*, 1(4), pp. 78–91.

Kuusinen, K, Gregory, P., Sharp, H., Barroca, L., Taylor, K., & Wood, L. (2017). Knowledge Sharing in a Large Agile Organisation: A Survey Study. In Baumeister, H. (Eds.), *XP 2017, LNBIP 283*, pp. 135–150. https://doi.org/10.1007/978-3-319-57633-6 9.

Godlewska-Majkowska, H., & Komor, A. (2019). Intelligent Organization in a Local Administrative Unit: From Theoretical Design to Reality. *European Research Studies Journal*, 22(4), pp. 290–307.

He, Z. L., & Wong, P. K. (2004). Exploration vs Exploitation: An Empirical Test of the Ambidexterity Hypothesis. *Organization Science*, 15(4), pp. 481–494.

Hobfoll, S. E., Halbesleben, J., Neveu, J.-P., & Westman, M. (2018). Conservation of Resources in the Organizational Context: The Reality of Resources and Their Consequences. *Annual Review of Organizational Psychology and Organizational Behavior*, 5, pp. 103–128.

Iapichino, A., De Rosa, A., & Liberace, P. (2018). Smart Organizations, New Skills, and Smart Working to Manage Companies' Digital Transformation. In Pupillo, L., Noam, E., & Waverman, L. (Eds.), *Digitized Labor* (pp. 215–227). Cham, Switzerland: Palgrave Macmillan.

Jiang, M., Luo, X., & Chen, C. (2018). The Factors and Growth Mechanism for Smart City: A Survey of Nine cities of The Guangdong-Hong Kong-Macao Greater Bay Area, 4th International Conference on Economics, Social Science, Arts, Education and Management Engineering (ESSAEME).

Kaczmarek, B. (2013). Tworzenie organizacji inteligentnej jako nowej wartości firmy. *Zeszyty Naukowe Uniwersytetu Szczecińskiego* no. 786, *Finanse, Rynki Finansowe, Ubezpieczenia* 64(1), pp. 157–162.

Kotler, P. (2011). *Marketing Management*. Fourteenth Edition. Prentice Hall.

Kowalik, K. (2021). *Social Media as a Distribution of Emotions, Not Participation. Polish Exploratory Study in the EU Smart City Communication Context, Cities 108*, https://doi.org/10.1016/j.cities.2020.102995.

Kożuch, B. (2004). *Zarządzanie publiczne w teorii i praktyce polskich organizacji, Placet.* Warszawa.

Laloux, F. (2014). *Reinventing Organizations: A Guide to Creating Organizations Inspired by the Next Stage in Human Consciousness.* Nelson Parker.

Liker, J. K., & Convis, G. L. (2012). *The Toyota Way to Lean Leadership: Achieving and Sustaining Excellence through Leadership Development.* McGraw-Hill.

López-Robles, J. R., Otegi-Olaso, J. R., Porto Gomez, I., & Cobo, M. J. (2019). 30 Years of Intelligence Models in Management and Business: A Bibliometric Review. *International Journal of Information Management*, 48, pp. 22–38, https://doi.org/10.1016/j.ijinfomgt.2019.01.013.

Łobejko, S. (2009). *Trendy rozwojowe inteligentnych organizacji w globalnej gospodarce, PARP.* Warszawa.

McGregor, D. (2006). *The Human Side of Enterprise.* Annotated Edition. McGraw-Hill Companies.

Nawrocki, T. L. (2015). Identyfikacja organizacji inteligentnych na podstawie analizy porównawczej wielkości i wskaźników finansowych spółek giełdowych. *Zeszyty Naukowe Politechniki Śląskiej. Organizacja i Zarządzanie*, 86, pp. 71–82.

Nonaka, I., & Takeuchi, H. (2000). *Kreowanie wiedzy w organizacji. Jak spółki japońskie dynamizują procesy innowacyjne, Poltext.* Warszawa.

OECD (2020). Smart Cities and Inclusive Growth. Building on the Outcomes of the 1st OECD Roundtable on Smart Cities and Inclusive Growth.

Olejniczak, K., & Śliwowski, P. (Eds.) (2014). *Jak diagnozować mechanizm uczenia się w organizacjach rządowych.* Warszawa: Wydawnictwo Naukowe Scholar.

Penrose, E. (2013). *The Theory of the Growth of the Firm.* Oxford University Press.

Pollit, C., & Bouckaert, G. (2011). *Public Management Reform. A Comparative Analysis – New Public Management, Governance, and the Neo-Weberian State.* Oxford University Press.

Porter, M. (2004). *Competitive Strategy: Techniques for Analyzing Industries and Competitors.* Simon + Schuster Inc.

Porter, M. (2009). *On Competition.* Harvard Business School Publishing.

Quinn, J. B. (1992). The Intelligent Enterprise a New Paradigm. *The Executive*, 6(4), pp. 48–63.

Sasinowski, H. (2015). Zarządzanie publiczne jako element innowacyjności w warunkach gospodarki rynkowej. *Przedsiębiorczość i Zarządzanie*, 16 (12/I), pp. 191–204.

Schwaninger, M. (2001). Intelligent Organizations: An Integrative Framework. *Systems Research and Behavioral Science*, 18(2), pp. 137–158.

Sikora-Fernandez, D. (2013). Inteligentna administracja publiczna jako element smart cities w Polsce. *Prace Naukowe Uniwersytetu Ekonomicznego we Wrocławiu*, 285, pp. 103–111.

Smite, D., Moe, N. B., Levinta, G., & Floryan, M. (2019). Spotify Guilds: How to Succeed with Knowledge Sharing in Large-Scale Agile Organizations, IEEE Software, March/April. https://doi.org/10.1109/MS.2018.2886178.

Sousa, T. B., Yamanari, J. S., & Guerrini, F. M. (2020). An Enterprise Model on Sensing, Smart, and Sustainable (S^3) Enterprises. *Gestão & Produção*, 27(3), p. e5624. https://doi.org/10.1590/0104-530X5624-20.

Statista (2022). *Volume of Data/Information Created, Captured, Copied, and Consumed Worldwide from 2010 to 2025*, https://www.statista.com/statistics/871513/worldwide-data-created/.

Taylor, F. (1997). *The Principles of Scientific Management*. Dover Publications.

Thompson, V. A. (1961). Hierarchy, Specialization, and Organizational Conflict. *Administrative Science Quarterly*, March, 5(4), pp. 85–521.

Wachowiak, P. (2004). Inteligencja organizacji. In Romanowska, M. (Ed.), *Leksykon zarządzania* (p. 171). Warszawa: Difin.

Wereda, W. (2010). Gmina inteligentna–podstawowa charakterystyka i perspektywy rozwoju. In Adamik, A., Matejun, M., & Zakrzewska-Bielawska, A. (Eds.), *Problemy i wyzwania w zarządzaniu organizacjami publicznymi*. Łódź: Wydawnictwo Politechniki Łódzkiej.

Yolles, M. (2006). *Organizations as Complex Systems: An Introduction to Knowledge Cybernetics, Managing the Complex*. Information Age Publishing.

Ziębicki, B. (2000). Współczesne tendencje w zarządzaniu. In Potocki, A. (Ed.), *Zasady tworzenia i funkcjonowania organizacji inteligentnych*. Chrzanów: Wyższa Szkoła Przedsiębiorczości Marketingu w Chrzanowie.

2 Measurement of smart organizations

I.1 Organizational smartness measurement. Academic and professional domain approaches

I.1.1 Academic domain approaches – advantages and limitations

Measurement of smart organizations has been discussed in academic discourse since the late 1990s, thanks to the first smart organization models clearly indicating such organization dimensions, measurement scale, and measurement tools. In the course of the last two decades, the number of smart organization measurement models has proliferated, also thanks to the advancement of the discourse led in the industry domain on how to increase readiness and capabilities of enterprises related to knowledge-based economy and Industry 4.0, understood from the perspective of management of data in manufacturing processes.

Investigation of intelligent and smart organization measurement methodologies in past decades produced two basic approaches related to their nature.

The first set of methodologies identified focuses on the measurement of organizational potential, resource endowment, organizational abilities, and their respective maturity levels. The second set of measurement methodologies focuses on organizational activities and results, considered as a proxy of a certain model of operations.

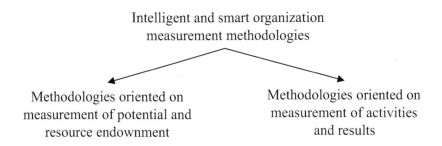

Figure I.9 Domains of intelligent and smart organization methodologies. Own work.

DOI: 10.4324/9781003265870-4

This distinction between the two approaches is clearly visible in reference to methodologies that commenced in the academic domain, whereas professional and business-led domain approaches emphasize measurement of potentials, resulting from organizational resource endowment.

Among intelligent and smart organizations measurement approaches, there are multiple aspects of learning and ambidextrous types of organizations elaborated upon above, which in this context are among the variables proposed to be considered in measurement. The advantage of smart

Table I.7 Academic domain-led intelligent and smart organization measurement methodologies oriented toward the measurement of organizational potential and resource endowment

No.	Key phenomena measured related to intelligent and smart organization types	Author(s)
1	Approach oriented toward measurement of added value of intellectual capital in the enterprise expressed through a ratio called *Value Added Intellectual Capital* – VAIC. VAIC sums up effectiveness of utilization of enterprise capitals including working capital, human capital, and structural capital and their ability to contribute to generation of value of the enterprise.	Pulic (2004)
2	Organizational intelligence research from the perspective of determinants of economy and enterprise agility, including aspects relating to organizational intelligence, such as (1) Human Development Index level, (2) ratio of researchers in the R&D domain per million population, (3) ratio of scientific and technical journal articles per million population, (4) patent applications granted per million population, (5) high technology exports as a percentage of manufactured exports, (6) Internet access in schools, (7) local availability of specialized research and training services, (8) mobile phones per thousands of people, (9) international Internet bandwidth measured in bits per person, (10) Internet users per thousands of people, (11) government online service index level, (12) percentage of GDP spent on information and telecommunication technologies.	Trzcieliński (2016)
3	Smartness level measured in relation to the regional economy and urban environments with intent of the author to apply them to another of smart organizations. Smartness of the regional and urban environment scale measured using a set of variables, including (1) number of broadband internet users, (2) number of patents, (3) number of pending patents, (4) number of registered private enterprises, (5) regional GDP, (6) carbon emission levels, (7) number of scientific and technological personnel, (8) R&D spending, (9) number of scientific institutions.	Jiang, Luo and Chen (2018)

(Continued)

Table I.7 Continued

No.	Key phenomena measured related to intelligent and smart organization types	Author(s)
4	Smart organization framework introduced with specific dimensions and sub-categories applicable for regional and urban environments. Dimensions include (1) smart environment (green buildings, workspace design, sustainable systems), (2) smart mobility (flexible structures, working anywhere, collaborative information technologies), (3) smart governance (open data, participation, transparency), (4) smart economy (ecosystem integration, productivity tools, open innovation), (5) smart living (social cohesion, well-being, meaningful values/CSR), and (6) smart people (diverse skills, lifelong learning, creative environments).	Lima (2020)
5	Approach based on a set of quantified indicators applicable for national economy level and available in the statistical office of the European Union (Eurostat) including (1) enterprises with business processes automatically linked to processes of their suppliers and/or customers, (2) individuals with broadband access to the Internet, (3) enterprises with Big Data analysis, (4) individuals employed in science and technology, (5) enterprises with broadband access to the Internet, (6) employees using computers with access to the Internet, (7) enterprises with integration of internal processes, (8) individuals ordering or purchasing goods or services over the Internet for private use, (9) enterprises using cloud computing services, (10) individuals obtaining information from websites of public authorities, (11) enterprises sending electronic invoices suitable for automatic processing, (12) students of information and communication technologies as the share of students in total, (13) enterprises providing portable devices to the persons employed, (14) adult learning and training in the last four weeks, ICT risk assessments in enterprises, (15) individuals with achievements in reading, maths, or science, (16), enterprises that employ ICT specialists, (16) enterprises with a high and very high level of digital intensity index (17) individuals' use of cloud services.	Adamik & Sikora-Fernandez (2021)

organization measurement approaches is that they strive for quantification of variables measured, and contribution to understanding aspects impacting organizational intelligence or smartness.

Some of the approaches have been validated in the economic practice domain among enterprises. Also, indication of dimensions of smart organizations helps with understanding smart organization operationalization

Table 1.8 Academic domain–led intelligent and smart organization measurement methodologies oriented toward measurement of organizational actions and results

No.	Key phenomena measured in relation to intelligent and smart organization types	Author(s)
1	One of the first intelligence–oriented measurement methodologies in smart organizations discourse. Focused on *principles of smart organization* such as (2) continual learning, (2) value creation culture, (3) creating alternatives, (4) alignment and empowerment, (5) disciplined decision–making, (6) open information flow, (7) outside–in strategic perspective, (8) embracing uncertainty, (9) systems thinking. According to the research method proposed by D. Matheson and J. E. Matheson, nine principles of smart organization were investigated in the form of 45 questions in total, complemented by a survey, interviews, workshops, and summing–up survey. The model proposed by Matheson and Matheson was tested on 1000 enterprises and made it possible to set up baselines for aspects measured. Currently, the model is used and offered through SmartOrg (https://smartorg.com) and enables recognition of strengths of smart organizations measured.	Matheson and Matheson (2001)
2	An approach indicating that the potential of an intelligent enterprise is determined by eight areas: (1) information intelligence – ability to quickly collect and process information to make decisions, (2) social intelligence – care for employees and their wellbeing at work, (3) marketing intelligence – ability to create the market, recognize needs of the customers, and the ability to search for market niches, (4) organizational intelligence – ability to adapt to changed tasks, (5) financial intelligence – skillful financial management, investments sustaining future existence, (6) ecological intelligence – concern for protection of the environment and the reduction of harmful activities, emissions and pollutants, (7) innovation intelligence – constant search for innovative solutions, promotion of innovation and modeling of behaviors of employees, (8) technological intelligence – creation, acquisition and use of appropriate technologies in order to obtain products of the highest quality and develop new fields of production.	Grudzewski and Hajduk (2004)
3	Intelligent organization is characterized through a set of aspects such as (1) economic growth, (2) market position, (3) acquisition and creation of knowledge, (4) organizational learning abilities, (5) investments in information technology infrastructure and knowledge management systems, (6) flexibility in operations, (7) recognition and reaction to relevant market signals, (8) applying long-term vision and strategy to actions.	Łobejko (2009)

(Continued)

Table 1.8 Continued

No.	Key phenomena measured in relation to intelligent and smart organization types	Author(s)
4	Intelligent organization characterized through (1) systems thinking, (2) knowledge management, (3) environment monitoring, and (4) innovation activity.	Gomez Degraves and del Valle Gomez Marquina (2012)
5	Intelligent organization characterized through (1) information flow, (2) creation of technology, (3) creation of an innovation activity environment for employees, (4) sustainable financial management, (5) search of market niches, (6) adaptation of an organization to new tasks, (7) work improvement orientation, (8) caring for motivation and development of employees, (9) caring for the natural environment.	Kaczmarek (2013)
6	Effective management of information, knowledge, communication and relations with partners and making use of innovative technological solutions to execute public tasks and add dynamics to local development processes to achieve and maintain a competitive advantage.	Godlewska and Komor (2019)
7	Intelligent organizations analyzed from a cybernetics perspective and set of systems oriented toward specific aspects, including "system 1" – regulatory capacity of the basic units, autonomous adaptation to their environment, and optimization of ongoing business, "system 2" – coordinates activities via information and communication, "system 3" – establishes optimum among basic units, provides synergies, allocates resources, "system 3*" – integrates and validates information flowing between systems 1, 2 and 3, "system 4" – deals with the future, especially the long term, and with the overall outside environment, diagnoses, and model organization in its environment, system 5 balances present and future as well as internal and external perspectives and moderates interactions between systems 3 and 4.	Schwaninger (2018)

aspects, however, no clear correspondence rules between the inputs and outputs of smart organizations have been identified within the measurement approaches and methodologies studied.

Among the disadvantages and limitations of approaches identified, the various references for organization types and sizes ranging from economic entities to regions and countries need to be identified. No specific approach or methodology for the measurement of a smart organization in the public sector measurement was identified.

There is also no clear distinction between intelligent and smart organization types in the approaches proposed, which demarcation aspects were presented in Chapter 1.

I.1.2 Professional domain approaches – advantages and limitations

The first professional domain and industry-led approaches oriented toward smart organization measurement identified commenced later than the academic ones, and from the beginning they focused on aspects related to information and data management, connectivity, and organizational capabilities enablement in the digital transformation of the global economy. Business-led measurement approaches are oriented toward the assessment of organizational maturity in defined domains and the related organizational potential.

Having reviewed the definition of both an academic and professional domain intelligent and smart organization, in this monograph the definition proposed by H. Godlewska and A. Komor was assumed when a smart organization in the public sector is referred to. The definition proposed by H. Godlewska and A. Komor clearly correspond to the specificity of public sector organizations at the local government level and their goals. According to this definition, a smart organization in the public sector performs public tasks and adds dynamics to local development processes to achieve and maintain a competitive advantage through effective management of information, knowledge, communication and relations with partners, and making use of innovative technological solutions (Godlewska & Komor, 2019).

All approaches oriented toward smart organization measurement in the professional and industry-led domain focused on private sector enterprises with great attention to data, information, and intellectual capital management. Not all approaches focused on the indication of activities enabling continuous improvement of the gaps identified, and often they were limited to indication of intelligence or smartness levels. Because of growing importance of the smart city concept and its theoretical overlap with smart organizations, a set of smart city measurement approaches have been reviewed and proposed by both scholars and professional services domain organizations.

Table I.9 Professional domain and industry-led intelligent and smart organization measurement approaches and measurement methodologies

No.	Key phenomena measured related to learning, ambidextrous, intelligent, and smart organization types	Author(s)
1	*The Connected Enterprise Maturity Model* – an approach proposed by Rockwell Automation, focused on complex assessment of maturity of enterprises in the information and communication technology domain in an organization.	Rockwell Automation (2014)
2	*Industry 4.0 Readineness16* – an approach enabling self-assessment and self-readiness for industry 4.0 by exploration of enterprise domains such as (1) strategy and organization, (2) smart manufacturing site, (3) smart operations, (4) smart products, (5) data-enabled services, (6) employees.	Impuls-Stiftung (2015)
3	*Empowered and Implementation Strategy for Industry 4.0* –an approach of assessment of an enterprise in terms of readiness for industry 4.0 through operational process control, identification of enterprise development gaps, and tools to increase the envisaged maturity level.	Lanza et al. (2016)
4	*Industry 4.0 – Enabling Digital Operations* – an approach supporting self-assessment of an enterprise in the industry 4.0 context through measurement of maturity in several dimensions relating to connectivity and collaboration, capabilities related to data and analytics, and digitization of products and services offered. This approach enables identification of activities in terms of increase of the maturity expected in the given dimension.	PwC (2016)
5	*Manufacturing Operations Management / Capability Maturity Model (MOM/CMM)* – approach developed by the Manufacturing Enterprise Systems Association (MESA) – an international manufacturing community, focused on assessment of maturity and readiness of an enterprise in terms of management of manufacturing operations.	MESA (2016)
6	*Reifegradmodell Industrie 4.0* –an approach based on maturity assessment in the following dimensions (1) data, (2) organizational intelligence, and (3) digital transformation. This approach assumes machines responsible for execution of processes and creation of products, and can become intelligent thanks to information technology tools.	Jodlbauer and Schagerl (2016)

7	*Intelligent Enterprise Index* – an approach based on a set of indicators in the enterprise, including (1) vision of the Internet of Things (IoT). (2) engagement of an enterprise in implementation of the IoT, (3) partnerships oriented toward technology solutions, (4) new technologies implementation plan, (5) change of management plans related to new technologies implementation, (6) ways of new technologies implementation and usage, (7) work safety, security, and norms, (8) extended IoT concept implementation plans, (9) enterprise infrastructure architecture, (10) ways of acquiring and analyzing data. This approach was tested on over 1000 economic entities including enterprises, based on a set of various measurement methods, including an online survey.	ZEBRA Technologies (2016)
8	*The Digital Readiness Assessment Maturity Model* (DREAMY) – an approach oriented toward assessment of digital maturity of an enterprise and its digital readiness in terms of the digital transformation process. The model proposed indicates opportunities for an enterprise related to digital transformation, taking strengths of an enterprise into account. Approach with measurement tool available in the online domain.	De Carolis et al. (2017)
9	*Smart Manufacturing Systems Readiness Level* (SMSRL) – an approach developed by the National Institute of Standards and Technology (NIST) in the USA, concentrated on assessment of readiness of an enterprise to implement smart manufacturing, understood through extensive usage of data in the manufacturing process.	NIST (2018)
10	*Innovative Smart Enterprise* – an approach based on theoretical and practical aspects of enterprise performance, including priorities and goals of an enterprise, their employees, and lean aspects of operations. The approach was tested on almost 200 entities, consisting of an online survey and direct interviews from the methodology point of view.	Crnjac, Mladineo and Veža (2017)
11	DELab approach – an approach focused on assessment of digital maturity of enterprises, deeply anchored in the industry 4.0 context, devised in cooperation between the University of Warsaw, Poland, and the Polish Ministry of Entrepreneurship and Technology in a project on capabilities leading to enablement of the industries of the future.	DELab (2018); Nosalska et al. (2018)

Table I.10 Smart city measurement approaches and measurement methodologies

No.	Key phenomena measured related to the smart city concept	Author(s)
1	The approach taken toward European cities based on a set of 74 statistical indicators clustered in 6 areas, including smart economy, smart people, smart governance, smart mobility, smart environment, and smart living.	Centre of Regional Science, Vienna University of Technology, 2007
2	An original indicator consisting of statistical sub-indicators in the domains of economy, human capital, governance, mobility, environment, and quality of life.	Szczech-Pietkiewicz, 2015
3	The CITYkeys framework developed by the European Commission focuses on data categories of people, the planet, prosperity, governance, and propagation. It contains output indicators (e.g. the number of open data sets) and impact indicators (e.g., reduced energy consumption). The framework contains a set of multiple indicators, as well as details of data availability, sources, reliability, and accessibility. The framework balances quantitative data with qualitative data, gathered through interviews.	CITYkeys framework, 2016
4	The IMD-SUTD Smart City Index (SCI) assesses the perceptions of city residents gathered in research conducted using the survey method on issues related to two pillars – structures and technology applications available to them in their city (1) and existing city infrastructure (2). Each pillar is evaluated over five key areas: health and safety, mobility, activities, opportunities, and governance.	Smart City Index of International Institute for Management Development (IMD) and Singapore University of Technology and Design (SUTD), 2017
5	The smart Sustainable Cities measurement approach of U4SSC focuses on a diverse set of city performance indicators in the economy, society, and environment dimensions oriented toward assessment of smartness and sustainability aspects including usage of ICT, physical infrastructure, social inclusion and equity aspects in access to public services, the quality of life, and environmental and cultural needs of the population.	The United for Smart Sustainable Cities (U4SSC) – United Nations initiative (2017)

6	An original indicator based on 43 public statistics sub-indicators structured using the Preference Ranking Organization Method for Enrichment Evaluations (PRO METHEE) for cities in Poland.	Ogrodnik (2020)
7	An approach based on measurement of indicators in 3 pillars – degree of digitalization and digital innovation implemented at the city level (input and output indicators) including smart city tools (1), indicators of the engagement of various stakeholders in building the smart city (2), and indicators of the core objectives of the smart city (outcome indicators) such as well-being, inclusiveness, sustainability and resilience (3).	OECD Smart City Measurement Framework (2020)
8	A relatively recent approach focusing on an aspect of smart cities related to one of the aspects explored through other approaches, which is digitization. The approach focuses on connectivity (digital infrastructure, quality, affordability), services (e-government services for residents and business, digital finance, transportation, healthcare, education, retail, and hospitality), culture (digital inclusion, government support, innovation ecosystem, public attitude, and engagement), and sustainability (efficient resource management, emissions reduction, pollution, and circular economy).	Digital Cities Index, The Economist Group (2022)

Limitations of smart city measurement methodologies apply to a vast number of indicators. A literature review of smart city indicators identified 1 152 different smart city indicators (Petrova-Antonova & Ilieva, 2018).

In the context of smart organizations elaborated upon in an earlier chapter, the smart city concept can be characterized as having numerous measurement approaches. Some aspects of smart city measurement overlap with a smart organization, however, the former is more quantitative in the data format approach and does not include aspects typical for a smart organization.

Similarly, for business-led intelligent and smart organization approaches, smart city measurement methodologies outline the importance of resources endowment of a location and do not refer to characteristics of a smart organization in the form of decision-making.

Based on an analysis of the reviewed domain measurement approaches of intelligent organizations, smart organizations, and smart cities, both academic and professional, a research gap in the measurement of smart organizations in the public sector has been identified. Identified measurement methodologies do not include aspects related to decision-making, results of smart organization qualities, or risk management. A proposal for addressing this gap is made in the next subchapter.

I.2 Proposed measurement of smart organization maturity in the public sector

I.2.1 Smart organization in public sector measurement variables and data sources

Organizational smartness measurement variables for a smart organization in the public sector relate to human-capital-related variables and infrastructure-related variables. Public statistics reporting enables access to sets of standardized data enabling measurement and comparisons between local government units in the European Union and other taxonomy. In the model proposed for a smart organization in the public sector key reference point for quantitative data is European Statistics Office – Eurostat, considered a reliable source of standardized data with a robust, publicly available online data portal enabling data sourcing – https://ec.europa.eu/eurostat.

Under human capital resources, the key variables measured relate to local inhabitants and external employees and their demographic and health status, knowledge and know-how and capabilities, and attitudes toward learning and knowledge sharing.

Key variables related to human capital resources available in Eurostat are population structure data, including:

- Healthy life expectancy based on self-perceived health.
- Population current activity status.
- Population educational attainment.
- Population occupation.
- Population employment and part-time employment.
- Individual level of computer skills and digital skills.

For attitudes toward learning and knowledge-sharing, the following variables are relevant:

- Population enrolled in early childhood education, primary education, lower-secondary education, upper-secondary education, post-secondary non-tertiary education, students

Key variables related to infrastructure resources available in Eurostat are knowledge management infrastructure data such as:

- Household with availability of computers.
- Households with a connection to the Internet, level of Internet access, and devices with access to the Internet.
- Reasons for not having Internet access at home measured for households.
- Individuals who are computers users, mobile Internet access users.
- ICT technologies usage in enterprises measured by digital intensity, value of e-commerce sales, internet access.

For methods used for data, information, and knowledge processing, the following variables available in Eurostat are relevant:

- ICT usage in enterprises, measured by integration of internal processes, integration with customers, suppliers and supply chain management, cloud computing services, big data analyses.

The majority of data types for human capital resources and infrastructure resources is available for level 2 LAU (former NUTS V), which is adequate for the local government measurement context, and explained earlier in this monograph.

Human capital resources and infrastructure resources together are the foundation for smart organization development potential, of which measurement requires both quantitative and qualitative sets of data (gathered in the form of observations, interviews with relevant stakeholders, etc.). To some extent, links between key stakeholders of a smart organization can be measured by Eurostat's available data such as usage of the Internet by individuals for interactions with public services. Other variables of smart

organization development potential, such as flow of data, smart organization decisions, and smart organization system profile, require quantitative
data sets.

Quantitative data sets and data collection methods are required for an
understanding of smart organization decisions proposed to be characterized by their inclusiveness, duration, costs, complexity, and risks.

Outcomes of smart organization development at local government level
can be measured by a set of data reported for Sustainable Development
Goals (SDGs) for spatial units in Eurostat, which include detailed mea-
surements for all 17 SDGs, including Goal 11 – Sustainable cities and
communities.

Assuming that the more decisions made by a smart organization in the
public sector, the higher the number of local development-related outcomes, the following data sets of Eurostat related to sustainability of local
development would be adequate:

• Severe housing deprivation rates.
• Recycling rates of municipal waste.
• Population connected to at least secondary wastewater treatment.
• Share of buses and trains in passenger transport.
• Population reporting crime, violence, vandalism by poverty status.
• Population that considers that they suffer from noise and poverty
  status.
• Years lost due to PM2.5 exposure.
• Proposed measurement approach limitations.

I.2.2 Proposed measurement method limitations

Depending on the location and size of a local government unit proposed to
be investigated from the perspective of a smart organization in the public
sector, challenges related to measurement might arise. The first type of
challenge and proposed research method limitation is data accuracy from
the measurement timing perspective. Publicly available statistics always
apply to points of time in the past, whereas a smart organization as defined
above is a continuously evolving and dynamic concept. Hence the reflection of smart organization status for a given spatial unit will be limited.

Another measurement-limiting factor relates to the availability of quantitative data proposed to be sourced from Eurostat. Most of the data types
are available for level 2 LAU, which is a spatial unit of interest from the
local government perspective, however, there is often a lack of data for
a particular unit from a particular period (due to it not being reported
in time by relevant lower-level units). Also, combining quantitative and
qualitative data in one approach seems to be challenging, however, some
scholars would argue that mixed data sources are a valuable aspect of the

theoretical model and enable triangulation, increasing the explanatory relevance of the model.

The proposed measurement approach and the set of hypotheses formulated are validated in Part II and Part III of this monograph.

References

Adamik, A., & Sikora-Fernandez, D. (2021). Smart Organizations as a Source of Competitiveness and Sustainable Development in the Age of Industry 4.0: Integration of Micro and Macro Perspective. *Energies*, 14, https://doi.org/10.3390/en14061572.

Centre of Regional Science, Vienna University of Technology (2007). Smart Cities – Ranking of European Medium-sized Cities. Centre of Regional Science. Vienna: Vienna University of Technology.

Crnjac, M., Mladineo, M., & Veža, I. (2017). The Croatian Model of Innovative Smart Enterprise for Different Sizes of Enterprise, 16th International Scientific Conference on Production Engineering – CIM2017, Croatian Association of Production Engineering, https://www.bib.irb.hr/881152/download/881152.81-Crnjac-Mladineo-Veza-CIM2017.pdf (accessed on 10.10.2019).

Czakon, W. (Ed.) (2022). *Podstawy metodologii badań w naukach o zarządzaniu, Wydanie III rozszerzone*. Wydawnictwo Nieoczywiste.

De Carolis, A., Macchi, M., Negri, E., & Terzi, S. (2017). A Maturity Model for Assessing the Digital Readiness of Manufacturing Companies. In Conference: IFIP International Conference on Advances in Production Management Systems.

DELab (2018). *Narzędzie wspierające rozwój firm w kierunku Przemysłu 4.0*, https://dojrzalosc40.delabapps.eu.

Grudzewski, W. M., & Hejduk, I. K. (2004). *Zarządzanie wiedzą w przedsiębiorstwach*. Wydawnictwo Difin S.A.

Impuls-Stiftung (2015). *Industrie 4.0-Readiness. Online-Selbst-Check für Unternehmen*, https://www.industrie40-readiness.de/?sid=62931&lang=de.

Jiang, M., Luo, X., Chen, C., (2018). The Factors and Growth Mechanism for Smart City: a Survey of Nine cities of The Guangdong-Hong Kong-Macao Greater Bay Area, 4th International Conference on Economics, Social Science, Arts, Education and Management Engineering (ESSAEME).

Jodlbauer, H., & Schagerl, M. (2016). Reifegradmodell Industrie 4.0 – Ein Vorgehensmodell zur Identifikation von Industrie 4.0 Potentiale. In Mayr, H. C., & Pinzger M. (Eds.), Informatik 2016 (pp. 1473–1487). Gesellschaft für Informatik, Bonn.

Kaczmarek, B., (2013). Tworzenie organizacji inteligentnej jako nowej wartości firmy, *Zeszyty Naukowe Uniwersytetu Szczecińskiego* no. 786, *Finanse, Rynki Finansowe, Ubezpieczenia* no. 64/1, pp. 157–162.

Lanza, G., Nyhuis, P., Ansari, S., Kuprat, T., & Liebrecht, C. (2016). Befähigungs- und Einführungsstrategien für Industrie 4.0: Vorstellung eines reifegradbasierten Ansatzes zur Implementierung von Industrie 4.0. *ZWF Zeitschrift fuer Wirtschaftlichen Fabrikbetrieb*, 111(1–2), pp. 76–79.

Lima, M. (2020). Smarter Organizations: Insights from a Smart City Hybrid Framework. *International Entrepreneurship and Management Journal*, 16, pp. 1281–1300, https://doi.org/10.1007/s11365-020-00690-x.

Łobejko, S. (2009). *Trendy rozwojowe inteligentnych organizacji w globalnej gospodarce, PARP.* Warszawa.

Matheson, D., & Matheson, J. E. (2001). Smart Organizations Perform Better. *Research Technology Management*, 44(4), pp. 49–54.

MESA (2016). *Manufacturing Operation Management Maturity Assessment Tool*, https://www.nist.gov/services-resources/software/mesa-manufacturing-operation-management-maturity-assessment-tool, and MESA MOM Capability Maturity Model Version 1.0, https://services.mesa.org/ResourceLibrary/ShowResource/a4fcb3cc-bc28-4f87-84cb-3da7432cc3b2.

NIST (2018). *Smart Manufacturing Systems Readiness Level (SMSRL) Tool*, https://www.nist.gov/services.

Nosalska, K., Śledziewska, K., Włoch, R., & Gracel, J. (2018). *Wsparcie dla przemysłu 4.0 w Polsce.* Warszawa: DELab UW, http://www.delab.uw.edu.pl/wp-content/uploads/2019/03/przemysl4.0_Opracowanie_DELabUW.pdf.

OECD Smart City Measurement Framework (2020). *Scoping Note 2nd OECD Roundtable on Smart Cities and Inclusive Growth.*

Ogrodnik K., (2020). Multi-criteria analysis of smart cities in Poland, *Geographia Polonica*, 93(2), pp. 163–181.

Petrova-Antonova, D., & Ilieva, S. (2018). *Smart Cities Evaluation – A Survey of Performance and Sustainability Indicators*, 2018 44th Euromicro Conference on Software Engineering and Advanced Applications (SEAA), pp. 486–493. https://doi.org/10.1109/SEAA.2018.00084.

Pulic, A. (2004). Intellectual Capital – Does It Create or Destroy Value?, *Measuring Business Excellence*, 8(1), pp. 62–68.

PwC (2016). *Industry 4.0 – Enabling Digital Operations*, https://www.pwc.com/gx/en/industries/industries-4.0/landing-page/industry-4.0-building-your-digital-enterprise-april-2016.pdf and *Industry 4.0 – Enabling Digital Operations. Self Assessment*, https://www.scribd.com/document/411453098/Industry-4-0-Self-Assessment.

Rockwell Automation (2014). *The Connected Enterprise Maturity Model*, https://literature.rockwellautomation.com/idc/groups/literature/documents/wp/cie-wp002_-en-p.pdf.

Schwaninger, M. (2018). Governance for Intelligent Organizations: A Cybernetic Contribution. *Kybernetes*, 48(1), pp. 35–57, https://doi.org/10.1108/K-01-2018-0019

Smart City Index, https://www.imd.org/smart-city-observatory/home/ (accessed on 5.9.2022).

Szczech-Pietkiewicz, E. (2015). Smart city – próba definicji i pomiaru. *Prace Naukowe Uniwersytetu Ekonomicznego we Wrocławiu. Research Papers of Wrocław University of Economics*, no. 391.

The Economist Group (2022). *Digital Cities Index*, https://impact.economist.com/projects/digital-cities/ (accessed on 5.9.2022).

The United for Smart Sustainable Cities (U4SSC), Collection Methodology for Key performance Indicators for Smart Sustainable Cities, https://unece.org/DAM/hlm/documents/Publications/U4SSC-CollectionMethodologyforKPIfoSSC-2017.pdf (accessed on 27.7.2022).

Trzcieliński, S. (2016). Research on Intelligence of Medium Sized Enterprises. Proceedings of PICMET '16: Technology Management for Social Innovation, Honolulu, Hawaii, USA, September 4–8, pp. 1993–2001.

ZEBRA Technologies (2016). *The Intelligent Enterprise Index*, https://www.zebra.com/content/dam/zebra_new_ia/en-us/campaigns/brand-campaign/harvard-symposium/how-intelligent-enterprise-survey-index-en-us.pdf.

3 Determinants and mechanisms enabling smart organizations in the public sector

I.1 Anchoring smart organization in the public sector

The framework for analysis of external factors impacting emergence of smart organizations

Aspects related to emergence of smart organizations, which are elaborated upon above, are related to the rapid growth of the amount of data and information in the world and its usage in services and manufacturing processes, the relevance of the amount of data and information for capabilities of organizations to capture, analyze, and utilize it. Knowledge base economy and usage of data in the manufacturing process, the need for learning, and knowledge-based, intelligent, smart organizational design are another aspects contributing to smart organizations emergence (Filos, 2006).

The macro-economic PESTEL framework can be used to structure and investigate in a systematic way factors enabling emergence and anchoring of a smart organization in local government. The PESTEL framework investigates external factors affecting operations of economic entities including their political (P), economic €, sociological or socio-cultural (S), technological (T), environment€ (E), and legal (L) types, hence the acronym PESTEL.

The PESTEL analysis framework is used for investigation and evaluation of an external organizational environment that is dynamic (Gupta, 2013) and through the systematic analysis of factors outlined in the framework, a set of organizational and decision-making-related benefits can be realized (Dwyer & Tanner, 2002). The PESTEL framework is prone to limitations, and for analyses related to a particular organization (micro-level) it is recommended to be used as a complementary framework to the set of other frameworks such as a SWOT analysis, and Porter's Five/Six forces Variations of the PESTEL framework have been investigated from the perspective of their usage in regional development planning (Vasileva, 2018).

From the perspective of the external environment of a smart organization in local government units and the public sector, the following factors draw particular attention:

DOI: 10.4324/9781003265870-5

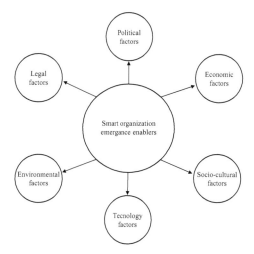

Figure I.10 PESTEL framework applied for investigation of smart organization emergence enablers. Own work.

- Political factors:
  - Legitimacy of local government as a body responsible for local development.
  - Local government local development policy and degree of intervention of local government in stimulation of local development.
  - Rotation of local government employees related to the stability of the political system.
  - Local government ownership of economic entities relevant in local development (e.g. in the water supply domain, waste management domain).
  - Local government cooperation and exchange of knowledge and know-how with central government, partnered local government units (local, international), the private sector, and local business communities.
- Economic factors:
  - Spatial location of a local government unit and its previous development path.
  - The phase of the macroeconomic business cycle (growth, accelerated growth, stagnation decline/recession) and gross domestic product (GDP) attributed to the location and its distribution patterns.
  - Inflation and cost of capital impacting business models and ways of working maximizing efficiency and minimizing costs.

- Public investments including investments in knowledge infrastructure – ICT technologies and knowledge-driven sectors of the economy.
- Private investments including investments in knowledge infrastructure – ICT technologies and knowledge-driven sectors of the economy.
- Funding for research, development, innovation, and digitization of activity of organizations.
- Socio-cultural factors:
  - Demographic and health status of inhabitants and external employees.
  - Attitude toward education and continued, lifelong learning of local government employees, inhabitants, and external employees in the public and private sectors
  - Mobility of inhabitants and external employees.
  - Level of education of inhabitants and external employees including their ICT skills.
  - Knowledge-sharing patterns in the public and private sector (especially related to knowledge-based economy and Industry 4.0 transformation concepts).
- Technological factors:
  - Patterns of adoption of new technologies among the local community, including promotion and education efforts fostered by local government.
  - Intensity of ICT usage at work and communication in the public sector, including the point at which it intersects with realization of obligations toward the local community (e-government).
  - Intensity of ICT usage at work and communication in the private sector.
  - Patterns of diffusion of innovation between local development stakeholders.
- Environmental factors:
  - External threats to demographic and health status of inhabitants and employees (e.g. COVID-19 pandemic).
  - External threats to patterns of diffusion of innovation and external exchange (e.g. COVID-19 pandemic).
  - Orientation of an organization toward sustainable development requirements (minimization of environmental footprint, corporate social responsibility of an organization).
- Legal factors:
  - Legal and policy-making frameworks setting the direction for public and private sector reforms toward a knowledge-driven organization.
  - Legal and policy-making frameworks enabling funding of smart organizations related to development priorities (e.g. in the European Union regulations underlining European Union structural funding for regional development).

I.1.1 Selected determinants and mechanisms enabling smart organization emergence in local government

Several determinants and mechanisms relevant for the emergence and continued development of a smart organization at local government level seem to be instrumental due to their role in nurturing human resources and infrastructure being a base a smart organization is built upon. In this subchapter, particular attention is paid to spatial location, business cycle, gross domestic product, patterns of innovation diffusion, and other elements of a smart organization environment.

I.1.2 Spatial location and path dependence

Spatial location is one of the endogenous local development determinants which is inherited by the location with its resources and location they represent. Local and regional development theories have been investigated for years in the context of dependence of economic outcomes, which could be attributed to the aspects of physical location. An aspect meticulously explored was the context of continuation of the path of the previous development outcomes and their enduring influence on current status and prosperity of a location. The concept of path dependance also relates to consequences of past events and decisions for outlook of a location.

Understanding this aspect requires inclusion of explanatory aspects of economic geography of the location and its historical patterns. Researchers proved, however, that some locations do not develop in an organic and systematic way but can be characterized as having accidental origins and rapidly reinforce their growth by attraction and retention of inhabitants, enterprises, and investors (Krugman, 1991, 1994). Detailed locations and regions have been researched from the perspective of changing development paths and altering their economic trajectories over time related to geographic patterns of economics activity. One of the aspects related to ability to change economic trajectory relates to the role of knowledge and know-how management and institutions (Gertler, 2005).

I.1.3 The business cycle and gross domestic product (GDP) of local government

Economic activity at country level, and regional and specific local levels functions in cycles, relating to recurrence of growth, maturity, and decline stages over time. This economic aspect of the smart organization environment plays an important role as an explanatory factor in formation of different ways of working, management, and decision-making at local government level. The limiting number of resources and development constraints can serve as an accelerator in transformation into a smart organization. Also, GDP reflecting the value of final goods and services attributed to the location determines the wealth local government can accrue through adequate taxes and later distribute in the form of investments and benefits. As a phase of the business cycle, GDP of a location and its physical location are pre-requisites determining whether smart organization emergence would be possible.

Paradoxically, less favorable locations (with scarce access to resources) and in maturity or decline of the business cycle phase may have enough potential to change to the smart organization model due to the push and need to change to respond to environmental development pressures. GDP however and its further distribution is not easily replicable with other types of resource investments (e.g. in capability enhancement and technology) needed for advancement and transformation of a location.

Locations with higher GDP measured in GDP per capita will have a higher potential for switching to the smart organization model at a local government level than those with lower GDP per capita. GDP of locations is calculated by respected public statistical offices, of which data sets enable modeling and forecasting also in the smart organization emergence context.

I.1.4 *Patterns of innovation diffusion*

Diffusion of innovation relates to the aspect of transfer of novel products and processes from one place to another. It could be driven by push processes (outward promotion of new or improved products and processes to the other locations) or by pull processes (inward attraction of new or improved products and processes by the locations). An approach oriented toward pull results from genuine interests, curiosity, and attitude toward adoption and leverage of what is new, better, and effective. Pull and push approaches are used in the management of innovation (Schilling, 2013), but also can be applied to the investigation of how locations switch to the smart organization model at local government level due to the adoption of model-related aspects.

The next determinants of smart organization emergence relate to patterns of innovation diffusion and the ability of an internal mechanisms of the organization to embed and adopt them.

I.1.5 *Knowledge-based economy*

The concept of smart organizations emerged in a context of economy transformation and a shift from a traditional resource-intense, industry-based economy to a knowledge-based and service-oriented one. Intensified research efforts of learning organizations since the 1980s are perceived as an outlining sign of knowledge-based economy formation (Ostrovska et al., 2021).

A knowledge-based economy reflects the importance of intangible resources over tangible ones in creation of a portion of social value and the nation's wealth (Bejinaru, 2018). Over the years, the paradigm shift from industrial economy to a knowledge-based economy has become widely accepted, and nowadays generation and exploitation of knowledge is perceived as a key contributing factor to the creation of wealth (Poppe, 2010).

From an organization research perspective, a knowledge-based economy assumes that knowledge remains an undisputed source of competitive advantage for the most businesses (Gajowiak, 2016). As economic activity is conducted by the private sector and the public sector, the importance of exploiting and exploiting knowledge influenced formation of organizations toward such capability is growing.

Scholars underline the importance of a knowledge-based economy in the adoption of new technologies enabling socio-economic progress and fostering communication and dialogue led between citizens and government at various levels (Szczygielska, 2015).

I.1.6 Industry 4.0 concept

The transformation of an economy into one led by the importance of intangible resources such as knowledge and know-how also affected the way traditional industries operate. An example of how a knowledge-based approach affected transformation of industry is the concept of Industry 4.0, and comparable smart industry and smart manufacturing concepts (Maier, Schmiedbauer & Biederman, 2020). The number 4.0 in the phrase "Industry 4.0" is used to denote the fourth industrial revolution. Earlier industrial revolutions followed the use of steam power mechanization of production (referred to as Industry 1.0), electricity and assembly lines (referred to as Industry 2.0), and computerization and early automation efforts related to production processes (referred to as Industry 3.0).

Industry 4.0 is nowadays discussed world-wide as a reference point for transformation of the industrial sector, and it refers to the set of technologies and technology-related enablers for the advancement of how industries operate and achieve competitive advantages. Industry 4.0 relates to technology solutions deployed for the advancement of various industries such as automation, robotization, digitization, usage of Big Data and the Internet of Things, and integration of these solutions for higher efficiency and productivity of organizations (Lenart-Gensiniec, 2019). Industry 4.0 is researched from the perspective of becoming a technology-enabled business model and emerging philosophy for transformation of traditional industries.

Some countries, such as Germany, significantly contributed through their scholars and researchers to the emergence and advancement of the

Industry 4.0 concept, and perceive it as an opportunity to make the national economy more competitive. Researchers outline the growing ability to self-control, self-configure, self-diagnose, and self-repair of systems in Industry 4.0 and ability to communicate and exchange information between components in Industry 4.0.

Components of Industry 4.0 linked through networks can realize a self-regulating production process and optimize how industries operate nowadays (Lenart-Gensiniec, 2019).

Industry 4.0 laid the foundations for a smart factory, which is a main feature of Industry 4.0, and is characterized by the vision of technology-enabled future manufacturing and a future form of industrial networks. As a type of organization, a smart factory is defined as a cyber-physical system, with implemented flexible and agile production ways of working, high-intensity usage of information management systems, and intelligent machines (Jerman, Pejic Bach & Bertoncelj, 2018). In the Industry 4.0 concept, a smart factory is characterized as an organization that is context aware and assists in execution of tasks of people and machines. The concept of Industry 4.0 provides a broader context for investigation of enablers required for emergence of smart organizations.

I.1.7 E-government

E-government relates to the enablement of public services in an electronic, digital format. Provision of public services in digital format requires regulatory efforts, capability enhancement, and technology advancement.

Digitization of ways of working at the local government level with respect to their external stakeholders (inhabitants, entrepreneurs, investors) can make processes more efficient and increase value added (from the perspective of an external stakeholder). In the European Union, digitization of public services is a priority for systematic research, regulatory transformation efforts, and investments. E-government dedicated reports indicate that in some EU countries e-services made available to citizens at local level are few and unlikely to create a pull effect in promoting digital competencies. The Covid-19 pandemic and restrictions related to direct ways of working, promoting working remotely, are a catalyst for digital transformation of local government units and the way they operate (European Committee of the Regions, 2021).

I.1.8 Covid-19 pandemic

Selected factors outlined in the PESTEL framework for the emergence of a smart organization in local government require additional attention due to not being apparent, including a knowledge-based economy, Industry 4.0, e-government, Covid-19, and European Union (EU) funding for advancement of local government in the European Union in the 2021–2027 EU programming period.

The Covid-19 pandemic in recent years posed a threat for societies and resulted in lockdown, limiting traditional, direct ways of executing transactions, and economic exchange. Scholars outline the role of the pandemic in acceleration of digital transformation of governments in response. In many examples, digital transformation and enablement of communication, and execution of local government obligations primarily using ICT, have become a necessity and further advanced transformation into *e-government* models (Eom & Lee, 2022).

Lockdown and social distancing measures required that public and private sector entities use digital, online solutions for continuity of their activities. According to the OECD, the Covid-19 pandemic caused a crisis that reinforced the importance of ICT, access to the Internet, and governance over digital data (OECD, 2020). Numerous local government units introduced, reintroduced, enabled, and promoted electronic means of communication and performance of tasks with inhabitants and economic entities they served at local level.

The switch to the digital, online domain of activities conducted so far in the physical domain followed with accelerated education and training in skills necessary to use digital tools and benefit from them across all sectors of the economy. Training in the required skills proliferated. From that perspective, Covid-19 is perceived as an external environmental factor catalyzing transformation of local government in aspects directly related to the smart organization model.

According to the European Committee of the Regions, the Covid-19 pandemic raised awareness among individuals and business sectors on the importance of digital connectivity and ICT technologies. Surveys on the impact of the pandemic on the business sector indicated that the acceleration of digitization in business caused by the pandemic can be quantifiable into years of regular development without the shock caused by lockdown and social distancing measures during the pandemic (European Committee of the Regions, 2021). The pandemic resulted in demand for online services and online transactions, through the adoption of distance working models.

In smart organizations of the local government and sustainable development models elaborated upon in further parts of this monograph, the digitization and digital transformation of local governments is one of the key mechanisms for sustainable delivery of obligations and tasks, as they allow for a higher degree of flexibility in cases of shocks to demand. Researchers draw attention to the unevenness of the impact of Covid-19 on digital transformation of local government and provide examples of countries where e-services provided for inhabitants are few and therefore have a limited effect on promoting education of digital competencies. Also, the urban–rural divide in digital services of local government units was not significantly minimized during the pandemic (European Committee of the Regions, 2021).

I.1.9 EU funding 2021–2027

EU funding is a particular type of public funding in the European Union, which can finance or co-finance investment related to priorities of the European Union policies, including digitization. EU funding works in programming frameworks, where the EU funding 2021–2027 programming framework provides funding for digitization on an unprecedented scale. The European Union earmarked EUR 7.5 billion for investments in digital skills and digital technologies through The Digital Europe Program to accelerate economic recovery and transformation of European regions (Digital Europe Program, 2022). Together with digital advancement and investment in digital-related skills and infrastructure, the European Union prioritizes investment in cities and their transformation to become energy efficient and digitally advanced. The *Smart Cities* mission has earmarked EUR 360 million for 100 cities representing 12% of the European population with the goal of providing funding to reach climate neutrality of their emission footprint by 2030. Investments possible from the Smart Cities mission range from clean mobility and energy efficiency to so-called *green urban planning* (European Commission, 2022).

I.2 A smart organization as an operating model of public sector organizations

There is a set of implications of how a smart organization operates in its daily dimension of internal processes and ways of working. An analysis of literature on learning, ambidextrous, intelligent, and smart organizations indicates that a set of practices enables achievement of mastery in information and data collection, analysis and usage for well-informed decision-making and leverage of decision-making processes of local government oriented toward increased competitiveness in the regional investment market.

A review of daily operations attributed to smart organizations and their earlier forms reveals their orientation toward multi-stakeholder and multi-level learning, daily operations focusing on data and information management analysis and management, and a collaborative and network-oriented approach in ways of working.

One of the key mechanisms behind smart organizations is the decision-making process. There is a research gap relating to decision-making processes in intelligent and smart organizations, justifying both theoretical and empirical investigation for the benefit of scaling up the smart organization model in the public sector.

Table I.11 Daily operations and ways of working typical for smart organizations and their earlier development forms

No.	Aspects of daily operations and ways of working in smart organization (and its earlier forms – intelligent organization, ambidextrous organization, learning organization)	Author(s)
1	Learning at team level through exchange of knowledge, experience, and know-how in lower organizational units to increase human resources effectiveness, sharing information about everyday work and related learning	Hovlid et al. (2012); Atiku, Kaisara, Kaupa and Villet (2022)
2	Undertaking systematic activities for increasing efficiency of actions and increasing capacity for change and continuous improvement	Hussein, Mohamad, Noordin and Ishak (2013); Wodecka-Hyjek (2014)
3	Fast learning of public sector managers and individuals, nurturing capabilities of personnel, nurturing a succession system to protect the organizational knowledge base	Schutte and Barkhuizen (2014)
4	Bringing and uniting learning providers to meet and respond to aspirations of inhabitants of a location (externally oriented learning initiatives)	Saraei and Hajforoush (2018)
5	Leveraging knowledge management systems and technologies for improvement of knowledge accumulation and integration, knowledge-sharing (internal and external)	Ostrovska et al. (2021)
6	Promoting and implementing results of learning including new thinking patterns, triggering new collective aspirations based on group learning results, and nurturing collaborative work environments to sustain knowledge and experience exchange and social capital (trust)	Jasińska (2020)
7	Business networking of employees for set-up and strengthening of knowledge and know-how base	Adamik & Sikora-Fernandez (2021)

I.2.1 A decision-making mechanism in a smart organization

Decision-making, together with capabilities related to the decision-making process, has been indicated as one of the key characteristics of intelligent and smart organizations in Chapter I (Olejniczak & Śliwkowski, 2014; López-Robles, Otegi-Olaso, Porto Gomez & Cobo, 2019; de Sousa, Yamanari & Guerrini, 2020). Also approaches and methodologies for intelligent and smart organization types detailed in Chapter II indicated decision-making as one of the key aspects to be investigated and measured in the context of these organization types (Matheson & Matheson, 2001; Grudzewski & Hajduk, 2004).

The topic of decision-making is researched from the perspective of economic sciences (in relation to *transaction cost economics* and both financial and non-financial costs of the decision-making process and decisions themselves), as well as from the perspective of managerial sciences in the context of the scope, depth, and specificity of the decision-making process, the stages, stakeholders involved, and risk managed. Topics related to the decision-making investigated relate to information, data and evidence-driven and evidence-based decision-making, but also decision-making-related resource constraints, governance, transparency, accountability for decisions, and usage (Aqil, Lippevaldz & Hozumi, 2009).

Decision-making as a mechanism requires assumption of a perspective that it is a sequence of steps with various scopes and stakeholders involved, oriented toward reaching the decision. Typical steps in decision-making include the initial stage related to problem or challenge formulation and ensuring that it is well defined and understood. The next stages relate to the generation of problem or challenge response options, their evaluation, and selection of an option, often followed by decision-implementation-related activities.

Scholars have researched the decision-making process from the perspective of the sequence of steps mentioned, and also aspects related to the decision-making environment and enablers (Papamichail & Rajaram, 2007). The decision-making environment relates to information (quantity, quality, accuracy, relevance of information), and technology used for both decision-making-required data collection and decision-making support (management information systems, decision-making support systems). Enablers required for a well-informed decision-making process relate to capabilities of stakeholders involved within the process and include problem-solving, knowledge, experience related to decision-making heuristics, data research and data analysis, data interpretation, learning capability, and also behavioral aspects of attitude toward risk and uncertainties.

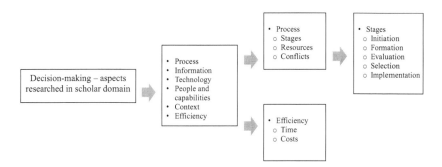

Figure I.11 Decision-making aspects elaborated upon in the academic domain. Own work based on Papamichail and Rajaram (2007).

Scholars investigating learning and ambidextrous organization types indicated that decision-making is one of the key moments and practices for organizational learning and is a form of effective, organization-specific learning practice (Crites, McNamara, Akl, Richardson, 2009).

This specific type of learning related to decision-making, implementing decisions, and comparing their ultimate results with the expected ones at the decision-making stage is called *epistemic learning* and is considered a contributor to the knowledge held in organization members' minds and information and data management systems.

Decision-making was found in the research to be a predictor of organizational learning outlining the importance of the collaborative aspects of decision-making and empowerment of stakeholders involved in the decision-making process (Mishra & Bhaskar, 2010).

From this perspective, decision-making capability, technology, and stakeholders involved are one of the key mechanisms required for emergence and continued development of a smart organization in the public sector. The aspect of decision-making in smart organizations is investigated through empirical research in the next chapters of our monograph.

References

Adamik, A., & Sikora-Fernandez, D. (2021). Smart Organizations as a Source of Competitiveness and Sustainable Development in the Age of Industry 4.0: Integration of Micro and Macro Perspective. *Energies*, 14(6), p. 1572. https://doi.org/10.3390/en14061572.

Aqil, A., Lippeveld, T., & Hozumi, D. (2009). PRISM Framework: A Paradigm Shift for Designing, Strengthening and Evaluating Routine Health Information Systems. *Health Policy and Planning*, 24, pp. 217–228. https://doi.org/10.1093/heapol/czp010.

Atiku, S. O., Kaisara, G., Kaupa, S., & Villet, H. (2022). Dimensions of Learning Organization: Implications for Human Resources Effectiveness in Commercial Banks. *Management Science Letters*, 12, pp. 117–124.

Bejinaru, R. (2018). Assessing Students' Entrepreneurial Skills Needed in the Knowledge Economy. *Management & Marketing, Challenges for the Knowledge Society*, 13(3), pp. 1119–1132. https://doi.org/10.2478/mmcks-2018-0027.

Crites, G. E., McNamara, M. C., Akl, E. A., Richardson, W. S., Umscheid, C. A., & Nishikawa, J. (2009). Evidence in the Learning Organization. *Health Research Policy and Systems*, 7, p. 4. https://doi.org/10.1186/1478-4505-7-4.

Digital Europe Program (2022). https://digital-strategy.ec.europa.eu/en/activities/digital-programme (accessed on 21.7.2022).

Dwyer, F. R., & Tanner, J. F. (2002). *Business Marketing: Connecting Strategy, Relationships, and Learning*. McGraw-Hill.

Eom, S.-J., & Lee, J. (2022). Digital Government Transformation in Turbulent Times: Responses, Challenges, and Future Direction. *Government Information Quarterly*, 39, https://doi.org/10.1016/j.giq.2022.101690.

European Commission (2022). https://ec.europa.eu/regional_policy/en/newsroom/news/2022/05/05-06-2022-discover-the-100-cities-selected-for-the-cities-mission (accessed on 21.7.2022).

European Committee of the Regions (2021). *The State of Digital Transformation at Regional Level and COVID-19 Induced Changes to Economy and Business Models, and Their Consequences for Regions.* European Union.

Filos, E. (2006). Smart Organisations in the Digital Age. In Mazgar, I. (Ed.), *Integration of ICT in Smart Organisations* (pp. 1–38). Hershey, PA: Idea Group Publishing.

Gajowiak, M. (2016). High-Tech SMEs in the Concept of Intelligent Organizations: The Reconstruction of the Approach in the Light of Empirical Research. In Kosała, M., Urbaniec, M., & Żur, A. (Eds.), *Entrepreneurship: Antecedents and Effects* ("Przedsiębiorczość Międzynarodowa", vol. 2, no. 2) (pp. 165–177). Kraków: Cracow University of Economics.

Gertler, M. S. (2005). Tacit Knowledge, Path Dependency and Local Trajectories of Growth. In Fuchs, G., & Shapira, P. (Eds.), *Rethinking Regional Innovation and Change. Economics of Science, Technology and Innovation,* vol. 30. New York: Springer, https://doi.org/10.1007/0-387-23002-5_2.

Grudzewski, W. M., & Hejduk, I. K. (2004). *Zarządzanie wiedzą w przedsiębiorstwach.* Wydawnictwo Difin S.A.

Gupta, A. (2013). Environment & PEST Analysis: An Approach to External Business Environment. *International Journal of Modern Social Sciences,* 2(1), pp. 34–43.

Hovlid, E., Bukve, O., Haug, K., Aslaksen, A. B., & von Plessen, C. (2012). Sustainability of Healthcare Improvement: What Can We Learn from Learning Theory? *BMC Health Services Research,* 12(1), pp. 1–13.

Hussein, N., Mohamad, A., Noordin, F., & Ishak, N. A. (2013). Learning Organization and Its Effect on Organizational Performance and Organizational Innovativeness: A Proposed Framework for Malaysian Public Institutions of Higher Education. *Procedia – Social and Behavioral Sciences,* 130, pp. 299–304.

Jasińska, M. (2020). Synergy – an Enhancement of Learning Organisations Undergoing a Change. *Entrepreneurship and Sustainability Issues,* 7(3), pp. 1902–1920.

Jerman, A., Pejić Bach, M., & Bertoncelj, A. (2018). A Bibliometric and Topic Analysis on Future Competences at Smart Factories. *Machines,* 6(3), pp. 1–13.

Krugman, P. (1991). Increasing Returns and Economic Geography. *Journal of Political Economy,* 99, pp. 483–499.

Krugman, P. (1994). *Peddling Prosperity.* W.W. Norton.

Lenart-Gansiniec, R. (2019). Organizational Learning in Industry 4.0. *Problemy Zarządzania – Management Issues,* 17(2)(82), pp. 96–108. https://doi.org/10.7172/1644-9584.82.4.

Lopez-Robles, J. R., Otegi-Olaso, J. R., Porto Gomez, I., & Cobo, M. J. (2019). 30 Years of Intelligence Models in Management and Business: A Bibliometric Review. *International Journal of Information Management,* 48, pp. 22–38. https://doi.org/10.1016/j.ijinfomgt.2019.01.013.

Maier, H. T., Schmiedbauer, O., & Biedermann, H. (2020). Validation of a Lean Smart Maintenance Maturity Model. *Technical Journal,* 14(3), pp. 296–302. https://doi.org/10.31803/tg-20200706131623.

Matheson, D., & Matheson, J. E. (2001). Smart Organizations Perform Better. *Research Technology Management,* 44(4), pp. 49–54.

Mishra, B., & Bhaskar, A. U. (2010). Empowerment: A Necessary Attribute of a Learning Organization? *Organizations and Markets in Emerging Economies*, 1(2), pp. 48–70.

OECD (2020). Digital Transformation in the Age of COVID-19: Building Resilience and Bridging Divides, Digital Economy Outlook 2020 Supplement, OECD, Paris, www.oecd.org/digital/digital-economy-outlook-covid.pdf.

Ogrodnik, K. (2020). Multi-criteria Analysis of Smart Cities in Poland. *Geographia Polonica, 93(2), pp. 163–181.*

Olejniczak, K., & Śliwowski, P. (Eds.) (2014). *Jak diagnozować mechanizm uczenia się w organizacjach rządowych.* Warszawa: Wydawnictwo Naukowe Scholar.

Ostrovska, H. Y., Sherstiuk, R. P., Tsikh, H. V., Demianyshyn, V. H., & Danyliuk-Chernykh, I. M. (2021). Conceptual Principles of Learning Organization Building. *Naukovyi Visnyk Natsionalnoho Hirnychoho Universytetu*, no. 3. https://doi.org/10.33271/nvngu/2021-3/167.

Papamichail, K., & Rajaram, V. (2007). A framework for assessing best practice in decision making, 29th International DSI Conference – Bangkok.

Poppe, E. (2010). Rise of Mobility Programs in Germany Due to Globalization. In *Proceedings of the International Conference on European Policies on Business Development*, Iaşi, Romania, 26–27 October.

Saraei, M. H., & Hajforoush, S. (2018). Assessment and Prioritizing "Indicators Social and Legal of Learning City" in the Areas of Yazd City. *Revista de Direito da Cidade*, 10(3), pp. 1692–1712.

Schilling, M. (2013). *Strategic Management of Technological Innovation.* Fourth Edition. McGraw-Hill.

Schutte, N., & Barkhuizen, N. (2014). Creating Public Service Excellence Applying Learning Organisation Methods: The Role of Strategic Leadership. *Mediterranean Journal of Social Sciences*, 5(4), pp. 159–165.

Sousa, T. B. D., Yamanari, J. S., & Guerrini, F. M. (2020). An Enterprise Model on Sensing, Smart, and Sustainable (S^3) Enterprises. *Gestão & Produção*, 27(3), p. e5624. https://doi.org/10.1590/0104-530X5624-20.

Szczygielska, A. (2015). Methods and Technologies Supporting Information and Knowledge. *Foundations of Management*, 6(2). https://doi.org/10.1515/fman-2015-0013.

Vasileva, E. (2018). Application of the PEST Analysis for Strategic Planning of Regional Development. *49th International Scientific Conference Quantitative and Qualitative Analysis in Economics, Economic Faculty in Nis*, pp. 223–229.

Wodecka-Hyjek, A. (2014). A Learning Public Organization as the Condition for Innovations Adaptation. *Procedia – Social and Behavioral Sciences*, 110, pp. 148–155.

Part 2

Smart organization in a local government – institutional context

1 Smart organization in self-government – institutional and knowledge base context

II.1 Institutions and the new institutional economy

Understanding the essence of institutions is necessary to indicate their role in shaping a smart organization. Institutions are very important to the functioning of the economy because of their influence on the selection processes. Thanks to them, our actions become predictable, and the created rules and ways of people's behavior toward each other facilitate human life and shape relations with the social environment. Social institutions are often created in a long process of historical social changes, the effect of which are rules that regulate, select, and direct the activities of both local and national contemporaneity in a relatively permanent manner. That is why institutions often have a very long, centuries-old history (Wilkin, 2016). Therefore, a question may be asked: where are the institutions? The easiest way, as Wilkin said, is to realize that institutions are in people's heads.

The key to understanding institutions is realizing that they have an immaterial dimension and that their social character is revealed by taking roots in the human mind. This influences humans' behavior and decisions. It programs their behavior in relation to the environment in which they are located, as institutions are assigned to the place where a person lives. Changing surroundings often requires us to change the rules of conduct, because place and communities create a specific cultural and institutional environment. Therefore, we are not able to follow this process, but we can recognize its results, most often as regular, repetitive human behavior, and decisions.

Institutions require universal approval. If the public does not agree to the rules of conduct, it will prevent them from influencing its decisions. It is difficult to talk about institutions in a social sense if they do not take root in the human mind. Therefore, legal systems and various types of organizations that do not regularly and permanently influence people's behavior are dead as social institutions (Wilkin, 2016).

An attempt to explain economic processes through institutions is made by the new institutional economics (NIE). The key role in it is played by non-economic factors (historical, legal, social, political) that influence

DOI: 10.4324/9781003265870-7

economic phenomena. Institutions are therefore a broad, holistic concept that uses the achievements of other scientific disciplines in the field of law, political science, sociology, and organization theory. The NIE is an economic perspective that attempts to extend the economy by focusing on the institutions (that is, the social and legal norms and principles) that underlie economic activity and analysis that goes beyond the previous institutional and neoclassical economics (Rutherford, 2001). Contrary to neoclassical economics, it also considers the role of culture and classical political economy in economic development (Maridal, 2013).

The difficulty in studying institutions is that they are invisible. They take many forms and are sometimes shared as tacit knowledge as opposed to overt forms that are clearly articulated and written. Therefore, researchers are faced with a fundamental problem of how to recognize the presence of institutions in a region or local units. Lack of understanding of social embedding, local informal rules, norms, and culture results in incomplete understanding of the mechanisms of local resource flow and shaping of the local economy. For example, physical structures such as buildings, roads, transmission networks, and spatial changes are visible almost immediately and are relatively easy to observe. On the other hand, rules are immaterial (invisible) structures, the manifestations of which we can recognize as regular behaviors. For example, infrastructural investments that are made within the framework of social cohesion building programs often do not bring the assumed results and do not increase the activity of the population and social capital. Another example is the digitization of public services and the circulation of information and documents. Despite the technical amenities in the form of access to the Internet, computers, and the rules of using Electronic Platforms of Public Administration Services, a large part of the society still does not use these opportunities.

The approach to defining them is also problematic in the study of institutions. Especially when scientists treat this term widely and assign it many meanings. They often treat institutions as organizational units, such as a city hall, business company, political party, or family. Other academics use the term to refer to societal policies, norms, and strategies that facilitate interactions and provide a framework for relationships between organizations. Institutions relate to rules, norms, and strategies that people use in repetitive situations. Principles should be understood as common rules (must, cannot, or may) that are mutually understood and enforced in a predictable manner in specific situations by agents responsible for monitoring conduct and imposing sanctions (Crawford & Ostrom, 1995). Standards are considered to be regulations that are known and accepted by the majority of market participants, the effect of which are the costs and benefits. Whereas, strategies are plans that, through the prism of rules, norms, and expectations regarding the probable behavior of others, are constructed on the basis of physical and material conditions.

Institutions exist at different analytical levels and geographic ranges. Therefore, it is important to distinguish and isolate the different types of structures needed to analyze both communities and individuals. This also applies to the regional (NUTS 2) and local (LAU 2) approach.[1] An example may be country-level macro-scale analyzes (NUTS), which focus on the constitutional level of analysis, while decisions made at this level have a collective dimension, as they influence the operational decisions of individuals (Firmin-Sellers, 1996; Agrawal, 1999; Gibson, 1999). Another level of analysis may concern smaller local communities with specific historical and cultural conditions that influence their decisions. Often there may be overlapping systems of principles and values, which may work by reinforcing or generating conflicts. Finding ways to communicate in different ways on structural and geographical levels is a key theoretical and practical challenge for institutional researchers.

Studying an institution also requires looking at the configuration and relationships between the rules and policies that apply in a given community. They often influence each other by creating a network of relationships. The effect on the incentives and behavior of one type of rule is not independent of the configuration of other rules. The research challenge is the skillful breakdown of the studied phenomenon into prime factors, and then their synthesis and capturing the connections between them. The impact of changing one of the current rules, which is part of the national strategy for regional development and integrated territorial investments, depends on what other rules also apply to renewable energy, transport, or emission standards. Additionally, in accordance with the constitutional principle of the hierarchical structure of the system of sources of law, acts of local law must comply with all generally applicable acts. Another factor may be informal social rules regarding resource management, an approach to saving and respect for material goods. As a result, local communities can adapt to a varying degree to the new regulations regarding energy transformation or waste segregation. Therefore, in the case of institutional analysis, a multi-faceted approach is important, which will take into account all these elements. Researchers must be aware of them and, for the purposes of partial analysis and excluding some of them from the analysis, use the *"Ceteris paribus"* principle.

Institutions are created through two different processes. Most often they are the result of many years of interaction and the formation of bonds between people within a given community. Hence, it is often considered that the process of institutional formation is usually spontaneous and evolutionary as well as invisible, just like institutional structures. Institutions can also be created by states, supranational organizations, and large economic entities with an international reach. The rules and principles they create become mechanisms for regulating economic, political, and social life. James Coleman called the phenomenon of replacing informal institutions shaped in an evolutionary way with created institutions "rational reconstruction of society" (Coleman, 1993).

Eric Berne (1968), in his book "Games People Play", describes the phenomenon of social programming that also applies to institution creation. This is due to the observation of the mechanisms of social relations that are shaped from the first years of human life, and which we often call "good manners". It is the knowledge of customs and social forms, rules of conduct in life, and coping with various difficult situations that are passed from a parent to a child. Behavioral forms include conversation skills, kindness to people, courtesy, tolerance, and the important ability to control emotions. We observe these processes all over the world, however, an important criterion for social programming is their acceptance in the local social environment. They allow building social capital, relationships, and social communication. Importantly, some of these behaviors can be found in many communities because they are universal, while some of them are unique and assigned to a place, which makes them local (Berne, 1968, p. 11).

Institutions appear in many areas of human life and fulfill various functions, which makes defining them not easy. The phenomenon *of institutions* has become widespread in the social sciences through the increased acceptance of institutional economics and the use of the concept of institutions in several other disciplines, including philosophy, sociology, politics, and geography. The term has a long history of use in the social sciences, dating back at least to Giambattista Vico in his *Scienza Nuova* of 1725 (Hodgson, 2006). However, even today there is no unanimity in the definition of this concept (Table II.1).

To explain the multidimensionality of institutions and the nature of their changes, Williamson (2000 distinguishes four levels of their analysis (Figure II.1). The highest level is the level of social embedding, which includes norms, customs, traditions, and religion, which plays a large role at this level. Institutions evolve spontaneously and change very slowly. This process may take centuries or millennia, and thus scientists are asking what mechanisms of informal restraints have an impact on the long-term nature of economies. By identifying and explaining the mechanisms by which informal institutions are created and maintained, we can better understand slow changes and the lasting impact on the way society behaves.

The next level is the institutional environment. It is made up of structures that, although formed in the process of evolution, can be designed and shaped consciously. These are formal rules articulated in the form of a constitution, a system of property rights, binding legal regulations, and public and social regulations. Within this level, we can talk about project instruments that cover the executive, legislative, judicial, and bureaucratic functions of the government, as well as the division of powers at various levels of delegation of power, including local government. Changes at this

Table II.1 Definitions and various aspects of institutions. Own work

No.	Key characteristics of institution	Author (s)
1	It connotes a way of thought or action of some prevalence and permanence, which is embedded in the habits of a group or the customs of a people. In ordinary speech it is another word for procedure, convention, or arrangement; in the language of books it is the singular of which mores or the folkways are the plural. Institutions fix the confines of and impose forms upon the activities of human beings. The world of use and wont, to which imperfectly we accommodate our lives, is a tangled and unbroken web of institutions.	Hamilton (1932)
2	Institutions are the rules of the game in society or, more formally, are the humanly devised constraints that shape human interaction. In consequence, they structure incentives in human exchange, whether political, social, or economic. Institutional change shapes the way societies evolve through time and hence is the key to understanding historical change.	North (1990)
3	Institutions are the humanly devised constraints that structure political, economic, and social interaction. They consist of both informal constraints (sanctions, taboos, customs, traditions, and codes of conduct), and formal rules (constitutions, laws, property rights).	North (1991)
4	Institutions are sets of common habits, routines, established practices, rules, or laws that regulate the relations and interactions between individuals and groups.	Edquist and Johnson (1997)
5	Institutions are fundamentally shared concepts; they exist in the minds of participants and sometimes are shared as implicit knowledge rather than in an explicit and written form. One of the problems facing scholars and officials is learning how to recognize the presence of institutions on the ground. [...] Unlike physical structures that are immediately visible on the horizon, rules are invisible structures that can be deeply buried under the regularities of observed behavior.	Ostrom (2008)
6	The fundamental nature of institutions is systemic and sustainable constraints on types of admissible strategic choices of players (including man-made organizations) approximate to equilibrium strategies of a game played in the economy. Institutions may serve to reduce costs of information, implementation, and enforcement, as well as costs of disequilibrium.	Aoki (1966)
7	An institution is self-sustaining, salient patterns of social interactions, as represented by meaningful rules that every agent knows and are incorporated as agents' shared beliefs about how the game is played and to be played.	Aoki (2007)

level take place relatively over a long period of time, from decades to centuries. Sudden events, such as pandemics or the outbreak of war, as well as social revolutions, etc., may be an exception to this. Social and economic effects are the consequence of decisions and implemented policies. This is examined by social choice theory that provides a theoretical framework for analyzing the combination of individual opinions, preferences, interests, or well-being in order to reach a collective decision. Examples of such collective decisions are enacted laws or a body of laws under the constitution.

The lower level is governance, i.e. the rules of the game applied by the state government, market entities or network actors. At this level, laws, norms, authority, or social rules are used to build relationships and make decisions at the family, community, formal and informal levels, or, at a larger scale, territory and between territories. The involvement of the community in the participatory process of making collective decisions allows for changes in the norms of social institutions and development policy. Therefore, changes at this level occur much faster than at higher levels and cover the period from one to ten years. This is due to the need to respond to the changing environment, which determines the need to

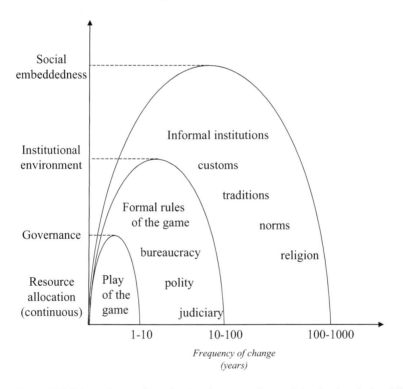

Figure II.1 Dimensions of institutional economics and institutional durability. Own work.

change the approach to management and the rules associated with it. The relationships that arise between actors on the market require the creation of an order that will help counteract shocks, recessions, and conflicts, as well as lead to risk reduction and mutual benefits.

Other activities related to the market game, capital location, and investment decisions are a continuous process because they are subject to constant changes that take place in the market.

II.2 Institutional environment of smart organization (concepts and definitions)

Smart organizations in local governments operate according to specific principles and rules resulting from legal provisions and acts on the functioning of central and local government administration. Their main goal is to shape and implement a policy aimed at improving the quality of life of residents within their assigned competences, i.e. rules and legal provisions resulting from statutes. According to the prevailing policy, actions taken by local governments should fit in with the concept of sustainable development, while caring for the local natural environment in which local communities live and work. Effective solutions are still being sought to streamline this process and optimize the decisions made. They will make it possible to use local potentials and create a framework for sustainable and resilient local development. In this context, the concept of smart organizations offers a number of new, groundbreaking solutions that blend in with the multi-threaded functionality of the entire local and supra-local management system. It should be clearly emphasized that the changes that are triggered and will take place in the future raise the problem of compatibility of local and supra-local systems with different levels of organizational intelligence. Therefore, actions taken by local governments must be territorially and administratively coherent, as only then will the full synergy effect of smart solutions be achieved at the level of the country and the world economy.

The development of a knowledge-based economy where smart individuals work together at all administrative and economic levels is a challenge facing the European Union and other countries in the global economic system. That is why looking at the supra-local functioning of smart organizations in local governments is an important theoretical and practical problem. Going beyond the administrative framework of local governments will allow obtaining a broader cognitive perspective of the institutional environment, i.e. the conditions that accompany modern processes of adapting information technologies in many areas of local social and economic life.

First of all, a smart organization must effectively manage information and innovation. This is manifested in the creation of modern information technologies and the architecture of the network of relations in order to efficiently communicate with the environment in order to implement public tasks and control local development processes (Godlewska-Majkowska & Komor, 2019). Diffusion, absorption, and creation of knowledge become the key processes that determine sustainable development and establish the competitive advantages of smart local governments. The uniqueness of such systems lies in the mechanisms of reacting to the changing environment and the effective creation of innovative solutions. The answer of smart organizations to emerging shocks and changes is innovative solutions that prove the resilience of the local economy and the ability to build sustainable development. Therefore, it is important that organizations are rooted in local and regional innovation systems, become active participants in them, and collectively use knowledge bases and strategic flows of knowledge and innovation.

Initially, researchers dealing with the subject of smart organizations focused mainly on cooperation, the use of technology, big data resources, and the involvement of citizens in creating more socially, economically, and ecologically sustainable development (Tomor, Meijer, Michels & Geertman, 2019). However, later on, an increasing number of scientists began to pay attention to the importance of context in understanding smart management processes. Experience from research on typologies of regions and communes provides evidence that there are significant differences in the conditions in which local governments operate, especially in terms of investment and development potential (Godlewska-Majkowska, 2018, Zarębski, Kwiatkowski, Malchrowicz-Mośko & Oklevik, 2019). It should be expected that a closer look at smart organizations in local governments in the context of their institutional environment will reveal various mechanisms and determinants of their functioning. The observed differences in development potentials caused researchers to search for different development paths depending on the context of a given place. A critical approach to the use of a uniform cognitive framework and reasoning devoid of in-depth analysis of the area-specific features began. The formal and informal institutional environment has become an important cognitive perspective in understanding smart processes that take place in local governments.

The influence of institutions on organizations began to be perceived in the diversified potential of a place of an economic, social, political, legal, and regulatory nature. Therefore, the study of smart organizations in local governments requires the use of a contextual approach. This is confirmed by studies that prove that good practices of smart management of one local government may not bring the expected results in another (Meijer, 2016). The individual context of each commune shapes its technological, organizational, and political conditions (Nam & Pardo, 2011). Unique conditions assigned to a place determine development and its dynamics. Therefore, one should look for individual solutions that relate to the specific conditions of the place in terms of current strategies, human resources policy, information policy, and undertaken actions. Examples from the literature show that smart solutions in local governments are implemented in various ways (Raven et al., 2019). Understanding the specificity of a place at the local level and the mechanisms of relations between organizations allows for a better understanding of the geography of changes toward sustainable development (Hansen & Coenen, 2015).

Smart management in local governments is usually focused on their functional areas, which result from statutory competences. Local governments are responsible for their own tasks for the benefit of local communities, for the implementation of which they create relationships with various organizations in the field of information transfer, as well as acquiring and implementing modern methods and information technologies. Information activities of local governments include, among others, promotion in terms of investment attractiveness or the image of the commune, building relationships and effective communication with residents, and acquiring innovative sources of financing and knowledge by improving the education of public administration employees and their skills. Smart management also means the ability of local governments to react in an innovative way to external shocks and the ability to adapt to new management conditions. This process is strengthened by building relational capital and establishing cooperation between local governments and institutions of various levels and geographically.

Why should we study smart organizations in the context of the institutional environment? Research on the institutional environment is derived from the institutional theory. Its main research issue is the influence of the institutional environment on the functioning of the organization. Researchers investigating this trend argue that institutional solutions can have profound long-term effects on states and regions. The institutional environment is created by regulations, customs, and accepted norms prevailing in states, societies, professions, and organizations (Swaminathan & Wade, 2016). Together, these factors influence the economy of the region through formal and informal institutions. An institutional environment characterized by well-developed institutions, and respect for property rights and rules achieves long-term results in the form of higher productivity and economic growth (North, 1971; North & Thomas, 1973).

Institutions are limitations created by man. Their goal is to achieve order and organize relations in the area of politics, economy and social relations. Institutions can become informal, in the form of behavioral norms, taboos, customs, traditions, and codes of conduct. The formal dimension of the institution is represented by consciously and formally created rules, such as constitutions, statutes, and property rights. In the history of the development of civilization, man created institutions to facilitate economic processes, thanks to which the uncertainty in exchange relations was reduced. Institutions shape the direction of economic changes and may influence growth, stagnation, or decline (North, 1991). They have an impact on the functioning of many organizations and legal systems, as well as economic and social environments. However, this is not a one-way street. Recently, researchers have suggested that the institutional environment is not just an exogenous force that shapes and constrains organizational activities and policies. Numerous examples of research show that organizations can take steps to shape the institutional environment in which they are embedded (Dimaggio, 1988).

The current direction of research presented in the literature indicates the need to pay more attention to the institutional context. Especially to what extent institutions support or constitute a barrier to the creation and development of smart organizations in local governments. Studying the institutional environment and its role in creating smart organizations can lead to a better understanding of cooperation models of local governments, e.g., why some communes establish relationships within networks and partnerships and how this affects their sustainable development and resistance to external shocks. There is a noticeable lack of adequate theoretical and empirical research on the relationship between the institutional environment and smart management in local governments. Therefore, a question arises about what it is and what dimensions the institutional environment of local governments assumes.

II.3 Dimensions of the institutional environment of local governments

The central element of the institutional environment is the state, due to its superior status and ability to generate and enforce laws, rules, and practices through formal and informal means (Swaminathan & Wade, 2016). However, the state should not be considered a unitary entity, as it may be composed of many entities and jurisdictions among which power is unevenly distributed (Meyer, Scott & Strang, 1987; Carroll, Goodstein & Gyenes, 1988).

In Poland and European countries, only some local and regional tasks are carried out by government administration agencies, which directly (hierarchically) report to the Council of Ministers, the Prime Minister, or individual ministers. The main part of the administrative tasks, having no national significance, is performed by the local government. This is done by local government bodies that are subordinate to the appropriate local (commune, poviat) or regional (provincial) community and which represent its interests.

Due to the diverse nature and purpose of various organizations, we can assume that the environment in which they are rooted is unique and assigned to them in terms of the specific functions they perform. Organizations interact with those elements of the environment that are indispensable and constitute a strategic element of their functioning. The overriding strategy is therefore the identification of the environment in order to initiate the transfer of information and knowledge necessary to build a competitive advantage and establish relationships. However, in the case of the public administration environment, the category of uniqueness has a different meaning and a smaller scope. It results from the principles of functioning of local governments, which are subject to the same legal norms and regulations. As a result, it is necessary to operate within the same competences and to apply the same structural, organizational, and objective solutions by local governments. It is particularly visible in the case of communes, poviats, voivodeships, municipal social welfare centers, tax offices, etc. There are more common features in the surroundings of local governments than in the surroundings of private organizations.

The institutional environment of self-government consists of regulations, customs, and generally accepted norms in force in countries, societies, professions, and organizations that affect the functioning of the organization. Typically, this environment results from the legal and administrative scope of competences that the local government has in the performance of its basic functions. The management area is therefore delimited by the administrative boundaries of the local government. The geographical scope of the public administration environment, in a general sense, will therefore be the same as operating in a specific area: local, regional, national, European, and international. Unlike private organizations, which are free to choose their location and organizational environment, the public sector no longer has this option. The location of the local government is unchanged, and its features determine its functioning.

The environment of the organization creates a complex and multi-element, comprehensive system within which phenomena occur, and its elements influence each other or are interdependent. A network of connections and relations between the local government and the environment is being created, which is necessary for it to carry out its tasks. Management of the environment becomes necessary in order to efficiently respond to unforeseen events related to economic as well as social and natural aspects (economic crises, pandemics, disasters, catastrophes, etc.). The process of globalization, which shapes the social and economic order in the world, also affects the scope of public administration, significantly increasing its organizational environment. In this context, one can speak of the emergence of European, EU, and international public administration.

The relations of local governments with the environment may take on a smart dimension on many levels. In relation to each of the elements of the environment, we can distinguish smart behavior of a public organization in the areas of:

- communication intelligence – the ability to quickly obtain information and use it efficiently in the process of managing a city, commune, or region;

- ecological intelligence – high awareness and care of residents and authorities for the state of the natural environment, taking measures to reduce pollution emissions, waste segregation, use of public transport, ecological transport, use of technology to produce renewable energy;
- technological intelligence – the use of modern information, communication, energy, and transport technologies to improve the quality of life of residents;
- social intelligence – the ability to create good relations with residents, the ability to conduct dialogue; sensitivity to social problems, building local identity and social bonds; and
- innovative intelligence – acquiring and implementing innovative solutions, creativity of residents and public administration employees and their active participation in creating innovation and acquiring knowledge.

It follows from the above that the environment of a local government unit is not homogeneous, it can take various sizes, forms, and spans, which means that it reaches a level of high complexity, rich in relations between actors, which are regulated by networks of various formal and informal character (Figure II.2). In addition, the dynamics of changes in the environment and the development of its elements cause it to become more and more multithreaded, and the processes taking place in it are difficult to predict. The aforementioned smart behaviors of the organization derive from the resources of the environment. In the context of smart management, the complexity of external phenomena determines access to knowledge and information and shapes learning processes. Additionally, difficulties in the flow of knowledge and information may result from the specific structure of the public administration system. The complexity of the public administration environment also results from the delegation of powers and functions in the field of meeting social needs, which affects the number and variety of elements that this environment is composed of.

The demographic and social environment of local governments seems to be the most important due to its dual role in the process of smart management. First of all, it determines human capital that can be involved in management processes in various dimensions. It influences the age structure of public administration personnel directly involved in the management processes and constitutes a potential for various non-governmental organizations, associations, and social activities. Another dimension of the demographic environment determines the behavior of residents and the needs of individuals and communities, which affects the implementation of tasks by public administration. The aging of the society and the development of the silver economy also impose additional obligations on local governments. There was a need to increase the number of nursing homes, residential homes, and community nurses. Demographic and

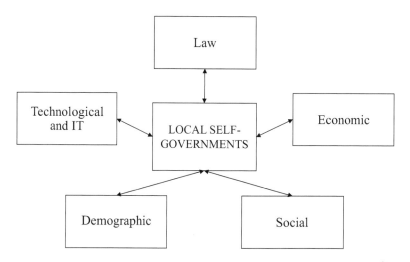

Figure II.2 Institutional environment of local self-governments. Own work

health trends, the extension of time and quality of life are also associated with the need to activate the elderly, who, despite their age, still want to be active in the labor market and social life. This is done by creating appropriate conditions that encourage people to resume work or to extend their professional activities. The social environment reports to the public administration infrastructure needs in the form of roads, public transport, generally accessible transportation infrastructure, social facilities for culture, sport, health, education, and intangible needs related to building local ties, opportunities for meetings and integration, social assistance and building security, and cohesion and local identity.

The current technological and environmental changes force the inhabitants of communes to acquire new digital skills and the ability to segregate waste. The responsibility for teaching these skills rests, inter alia, with local governments and their subordinate institutions. There is a feedback loop between the public administration and the social environment, as well as the exchange of information, which makes it possible to identify needs, make decisions, and control activities. New technologies may prove helpful in solving many problems and creating social innovations. An example of how IT technologies can support local governments in solving these problems is the "Dobre Wsparcie" (Good Support) phone application. It is a system designed by the non-governmental organization "Fundacja Nauka dla Środowiska" (Science for Environment Foundation) from Poland, with care services in mind, as a response to the rapidly progressing problem of an aging society in Europe and as means to relieve and support the activities of local governments in the implementation of their basic tasks related to social assistance (see appendix). Thanks to the application, residents can communicate with each other and with employees of local social welfare and medical aid centers. The system creates social networks through which information is sent, it is possible to monitor the demand for social services and smart management of social services by the commune.

The economic environment is a source of a lot of information for local governments. It is directly related to the degree of meeting the needs and a guide in making decisions and determining the type and scope of tasks to be performed. An example is economic crises that trigger a system of support and guarantees for meeting basic needs. There is a growing demand for public administration activities related to, inter alia, social security and activation of the unemployed. Another effect of the crisis is a decline in the economic condition, a reduction in income, and thus a decline in revenues to local self-government budgets. The consequences of the economic crises are felt in the budget policy and include, in the first place, a decrease in social spending and the implementation of activities for the benefit of the inhabitants. The opposite situation, i.e. economic growth and increasing budget revenues, allows local governments to implement a broader social policy and meet the needs of culture, sports and land development, expansion of parks and playgrounds, and improvement of the aesthetics and quality of public space to a greater extent.

The legal environment of public administration consists of an entire range of normative regulations of various order, which define the framework and conditions for the functioning of the organization. The rules of local self-government are defined by the European Charter of Local Self-Government (*European Charter of Local Self-government*), which is a document of the Council of Europe regulating the status of local governments in relation to the authorities of a given state and in relation to the authorities of other countries and the local governments operating in them.[2] In the document, the concept of local self-government is defined as: "*the right and the ability of local authorities, within the limits of the law, to regulate and manage a substantial share of public affairs under their own responsibility and in the interests of the local population*".[3] The European Charter of Local Self-Government contains a catalog of principles essential for the proper functioning of local self-government and indicates that local self-government is the main element of the democratic system. This means that citizens are involved in creating democracy where they live. This imposes an obligation on local authorities to consult local communities on all matters directly affecting them, including the change of the boundaries of administrative division units. In terms of cooperation between local and regional self-governments, including cooperation with communities of other countries, the European Charter of Local Self-Government grants local self-governments such rights with reference to the legislation of individual countries.

The combination of various dimensions of the local government environment creates a competitive environment that can be considered in the context of migration and investment attractiveness. In the first case, local governments compete with each other to attract or retain new residents. Many factors determine the attractiveness of migration, however, in a general sense, it can be said that it is an opportunity to achieve high standards of quality of life, access to work, attractive public spaces, and a clean environment that does not threaten health. Migration processes around the world show that the main directions of migration are large agglomerations with above-average migration values mentioned above, mainly economic. The phenomenon of migration causes large disparities in population density in many countries and creates areas with a high level of depopulation. The competitiveness of the local government is also evidenced by the investment attractiveness, which should be understood as the local government's ability to attract investors and investments. Investment attractiveness is created by the location advantages of a place for launching an investment and starting a business. Some of these values, e.g. natural, are independent in nature, especially energy resources or values for the development of tourism, such as seaside beaches, lakes, mountains, etc. (Zarębski, Kwiatkowski, Malchrowicz-Mośko & Oklevik, 2019). Besides local development policy, spatial planning and development, and technical infrastructure, other values may change their value under the influence of local authorities. They also have an impact on shaping human capital through the education system they manage, especially in the area of creating education courses tailored to the needs of the labor market.

The superior institution for local governments is the state, which is responsible for the broadly understood security and development opportunities of citizens. Thus, the activity of local governments concerns only certain fragments of public affairs and must be subject to national law and the interests of the citizens of the state as a whole. Therefore, only some of the matters are delegated to local governments as their own tasks for which they are fully responsible. The government administration conducts those matters that must be regulated in the same way throughout the country on the basis of equality of all citizens.

The self-government performs a significant part of public tasks on its own behalf and under its own responsibility. Self-management means that the local community makes all decisions in its own interest, but also under its own responsibility. This unbreakable combination of rights and responsibilities is the key to understanding the essence of self-government.

Within local government units, the addressees of institutionalization processes are residents of local government communities. The laws defining the local government system unequivocally define that a commune, poviat, and voivodship are communities of inhabitants living in these territories. This means that the institutional development of a commune, poviat, or voivodeship is the formation of permanent formal or informal patterns of behavior of the inhabitants of a given community.

II.4 The institutional environment of the European Union as a territorial source of resources for smart organizations

The current theoretical discourse related to regional development is radically different from classical economic theories. The researchers' attention is more focused on the territory that creates dynamics and provides its own autonomy to development processes. Region (territory) is not only a physical category, described in traditional theories of economic location as a development factor in the context of land, labor, and transportation costs. The region is no longer only a place of location and accumulation of resources and capital, but it can be perceived as a form of organization reducing uncertainty and risk, constituting a source of information, accumulation, and transfer of knowledge and skills (Nowakowska, 2011). In this approach, a resource-rich space that "produces" economic dynamics will be a place for digital and technological change and modernization, geared toward smart organizations.

Various definitions of smart organization can be found in the literature, examples of which were presented in the earlier chapters of the book. Most often, however, it is emphasized that a smart organization is distinguished by a unique focus on resources and processes related to human capital management, learning, and gaining new knowledge. The strategic area of competence of such an organization includes, above all, the ability to obtain, process, and use information better than other organizations (Godlewska-Majkowska & Komor, 2019). Therefore, the process of transformation of a traditional organization toward a smart organization requires, first of all, its employees to constantly acquire knowledge and skills, as well as use them for the development of the organization. Knowledge and knowledge institutions are therefore a resource necessary for the proper functioning of smart organizations. The concept of smart growth based on knowledge and innovation has been recognized by politicians and implemented into European strategies, initially becoming one of the priorities of the Europe 2020 strategy (European Commission, 2010) and now playing a key role in strategies aimed at digital transformation and creation of European Green Deal.

The common ground and point of reference for these changes and implemented policies is the territorial approach to the development of the regions of the European Union. A territory is a specific social structure based on history, culture, knowledge, and skills common to a given community. On the one hand, these factors constitute a specific resource, while, on the other hand, they are a product of this development (Jewtuchowicz, 2016). The rich theoretical achievements on this subject made it possible to look at the development in individual EU Member States anew and, as a consequence, contributed to fundamental reforms relating to the principles of shaping the development policy in the entire European Union. Since 1975, the European Union has been paying attention to the regional approach to creating development policy, which was initiated with the creation of the European Regional Development Fund. In the following years, there have been created documents that strengthened the need to support harmonious development, the aim of which was economic and social cohesion.

The policy of the European Union adopted in this form aims to reduce the disproportions in the levels of development of various regions and to reduce the backwardness of less-favored regions. Regional policies had to evolve along with the processes of globalization and economic crises and adapt to new conditions. Adoption of the direction of equalization of opportunities, the task of which was to support relatively less developed regions so that they could achieve faster economic growth, turned out to be insufficient. For this reason, more attention was paid to the individual conditions and potentials of individual territories. In 1994, the Committee of the Regions was established and a new instrument was created – the Cohesion Fund, allocated at the level of the Member States, vested in the so-called cohesion countries, focused on supporting a set of large infrastructure investments in the sphere of transport and the natural environment.

The goals accompanying the policy of the European Union are aimed at the development of a modern economy that achieves a lasting and sustainable socio-economic development. Debates in various political and scientific circles have highlighted that this can only be achieved by paying greater attention to regional and spatial aspects. This debate led in 1999 to the adoption of the European Spatial Development Perspective (ESDP), which contributed to many important initiatives, such as the INTERREG transnational cooperation programs and the creation of the European Spatial Planning Observation Network (ESPON).

In the following years, attention was drawn to the need to strengthen global competitiveness and balance all European regions by identifying and mobilizing their territorial potentials. In 2007, the Territorial Agenda of the European Union was adopted by the ministers responsible for regional development. The basic process of the adopted policy was to be *territorial governance*, i.e. communication and information flow as an intense and constant dialogue between all actors of territorial development. Integration and networks of relations were to include the economic sector, the scientific community, non-governmental organizations, and the public sector.

The discussion on the issues of regional diversity resulted in paying more attention not only to natural and cultural resources but also to other features and resources of a given area, which may constitute its development potential and create a specific "territorial capital". Building territorial cohesion through the synergy effect favors the strengthening of this capital, and thus increases the resources of individual regions. It allows starting bottom-up development processes based on unique local and regional capitals assigned to a given place. Thus, diversity becomes an asset and an important competitive advantage, as well as triggers comparative processes and increases the flexibility of public development policies and regional specialization.

In 2008, a Green Paper on territorial cohesion was created. The document defines territorial cohesion as the harmonious development of all places and guarantees that their inhabitants will be able to make the best use of the characteristic features of these areas. Cohesion is also an integrated approach to problem-solving at different territorial levels, which may require the cooperation of local, regional, and even national authorities.

With the entry into force of the Lisbon Treaty in 2009, territorial cohesion has become a political goal for the EU. In June 2010, the Europe 2020 Strategy became the basis of all EU policies that stimulate positive changes in the EU economy and society in the current decade. It identifies the most important challenges facing the regions in the perspective of 2020, such as globalization, demographic problems, climate change, and energy supply.

In his report, Barca (2009) proposed a new approach to the conduct of the European Union's cohesion policy, which in the years 2014–2020 had an impact on the shape of the implemented policy. In his opinion, the Place-based Approach best suits the contemporary challenges of conducting development policy. Both economic and social development can take place in almost any place of space by combining institutions and public investments that are tailored to the needs of the place, defined by interactions between local and supra-local elites (e.g. national or EU level). The essence of this approach is a dialogue, for which the public authority should ensure conditions; it should also stimulate debate and build a development policy based on its results. Such an approach means adopting multi-level development management, in which special attention is paid to local conditions and reducing the risk of centralization and uniformization of policies (Szlachta & Zaucha, 2014). A prominent issue that requires a solution within European and national policies is the determination of the scale and scope of aid and building cohesion through investments and redistribution of funds at the local level. This applies in particular to places with low or no development potential condemned to decline (Gorzelak, 2021).

The experience from previous development programs shows that there is no single universal policy for the development of smart organizations in local governments that could be successfully applied in all regions of the European Union. The complexity of the processes and factors necessary for sustainable development based on innovation means that each region should discover its own development path, which includes the transformation and diversification of several types of knowledge and its flows (Zarębski, Czerwińska-Jaśkiewicz & Klonowska-Matynia, 2022). Current European Union program, "Horizon Europe", goes a step further and, referring to the work of Mazzucato (2016), explicitly uses the concept of "mission" to meet widespread societal challenges. Mission orientation is what connects these activities within the framework of the innovation policy of the European Union (Kattel & Mazzucato, 2018). The experience in implementing the Europe 2020 development strategy, the key elements of which were smart specializations and regional development opportunities based on endogenous (local) potentials (Foray, Mowery & Nelson, 2012), have become the basis for mapping the new framework for innovation policy. The new approach assumes that the task of innovation is to stimulate growth and economic activity by actively facing global challenges.

By combining the core goals of smart growth, social inclusion, and sustainable development, innovation policy thus gains a clear direction with specific, measurable, and achievable missions that respond to urgent global challenges. To address these challenges, the European Green Deal action plan has been developed. It aims to help transform the EU into a fair and prosperous society, with a modern, resource-efficient, and competitive economy, with no net greenhouse gas emissions in 2050 and significantly less resource-dependent economic growth.

The "Cities" mission is part of an EU initiative – one of the main novelties of the "Horizon Europe" program. Missions, rooted in research and innovation, are designed to meet the societal challenges of today. The new EU mission for climate neutral and smart cities ("city mission") aims to mobilize local authorities, citizens, businesses, investors, and regional and national authorities to achieve the following goals (European Commission, 2021):

1 Achieving at least 100 climate-neutral and smart cities by 2030.
2 Ensuring that these cities act as centers of experimentation and innovation to enable all European cities to follow suit by 2050.

The European Union already dedicates a range of programs at regional, national, European, and global levels for cities. The importance of the "Cities" mission is that it adopts a cross-sectoral and demand-driven approach, creating synergies between existing initiatives. The mission will support different sectors in working together on smart, digital, and other types of solutions to help achieve climate neutrality.

To summarize, it should be stated that the institutional environment is responsible for the creation of territorial and international cooperation, the need of which was revealed by the economic, pandemic, and energy crises. The resources needed by smart organizations in local governments are not only assigned to a place, but together with relational and institutional mechanisms they create a territory, i.e. a specific structure conditioned by history, culture, human capital and relational, and research and innovation capital. The common ground for implementing new concepts of smart cities and smart villages is the territorial approach to the development of the regions of the European Union. Such an approach to creating policy and institutional frameworks allows using the potentials of the regions to a greater extent and to create integrated networks of cooperation, joint problem solving, and creation and implementation of broadly understood innovations tailored to the individual needs of local communities and economies. The territory becomes a resource base for smart organizations, thanks to which local governments strengthen their resilience and implement the concept of sustainable development.

Notes

1 The current NUTS 2021 classification is valid from January 1, 2021, and lists 92 regions at NUTS 1, 242 regions at NUTS 2 and 1166 regions at NUTS 3 level. The NUTS classification (Nomenclature of territorial units for statistics) is a hierarchical system for dividing up the economic territory of the EU and the UK for the purpose of: The collection, development, and harmonization of European regional statistics Socio-economic analyses of the regions: NUTS 1: major socio-economic regions, NUTS 2: basic regions for the application of regional policies, NUTS 3: small regions for specific diagnoses. Until 2016, two levels of Local Administrative Units (LAU) existed: The upper LAU level (LAU level 1, formerly NUTS level 4) was defined for most, but not all of the countries. The lower LAU level (LAU level 2, formerly NUTS level 5) consisted of municipalities or equivalent units in the 28 EU Member States.
2 The Charter was adopted on October 15, 1985, in Strasbourg by the Standing Conference of European Municipalities and Regions at the Council of Europe. It entered into force on September 1, 1988. Poland ratified the Charter in 1994, as one of the few countries, it ratified it in its entirety.
3 Art. 3 sec. 1 of the European Charter of Local Self-Government, drawn up in Strasbourg on October 15, 1985 (Journal of Laws of 1994, No. 124, item 607).

References

Agrawal, A. (1999). *Greener Pastures: Politics, Markets, and Community among a Migrant Pastoral People*. Duke University Press.
Aoki, M. (1996). Towards a Comparative Institutional Analysis: Motivations and Some Tentative Theorizing. *The Japanese Economic Review*, 47(1), 1–19. doi: 10.1111/j.1468-5876.1996.tb000.
Aoki, M. (2007). Endogenizing Institutions and Institutional Changes. *Journal of Institutional Economics*, 3, pp. 1–31. https://doi:10.1017/S1744137406000531.
Barca, F. (2009). An Agenda for a Reformed Cohesion Policy. A Place-Based Approach to Meeting European Union Challenges and Expectations Independent Report Prepared at the Request of Danuta Hübner. Commissioner for Regional Policy, Brussels.

Berne, E. (1968). *Games People Play: The Psychology of Human Relationships*, vol. 2768. Penguin UK.

Carroll, G. R., Goodstein, J., & Gyenes, A. (1988). Organizations and the State: Effects of the Institutional Environment on Agricultural Cooperatives in Hungary. *Administrative Science Quarterly*, 33(2), pp. 233–256.

Coleman, J. S. (1993). The Rational Reconstruction of society: 1992 Presidential Address. *American Sociological Review*, 58(1), pp. 1–15.

Crawford, S. E., & Ostrom, E. (1995). A Grammar of Institutions. *American Political Science Review*, 89(3), pp. 582–600.

Dimaggio, P. (1988). Interest and Agency in Institutional Theory. In Zucker, L. G. (Ed.), *Research on Institutional Patterns* (pp. 3–21). Environment and Culture. Cambridge: Ballinger Publishing Co.

Edquist, C., & Johnson, B. (1997). Institutions and Organizations in Systems of Innovation. In Edquist, C. (Ed.), *Systems of Innovation: Technologies Institutions and Organisations* (pp. 41–63). London.

European Commission (2010). Communication from the Commission Europe 2020: A Strategy for Smart, Sustainable and Inclusive Growth. Retrieved from: http://eurlex.europa.eu/LexUriServ/LexUriServ.do?uri=COM:2010:2020:FIN:EN:PDF.

European Commission (2021). European Missions: 100 Climate-Neutral and Smart Cities by 2030. Info Kit for Cities. Retrieved from: https://ec.europa.eu/info/sites/default/files/research_and_innovation/funding/documents/ec_rtd_eu-mission-climate-neutral-cities-infokit.pdf (accessed on 18.11.2021).

Firmin-Sellers, K. (1996). *The Transformation of Property Rights in the Gold Coast: An Empirical Study Applying Rational Choice Theory*. Cambridge University Press.

Foray, D., Mowery, D. C., & Nelson, R. R. (2012). Public R&D; and Social Challenges: What Lessons from Mission R&D; Programs? *Research Policy*, 41, pp. 1697–1702. https://doi.org/10.1016/j.respol.2012.07.011.

Gibson, C. C. (1999). *Politicians and Poachers: The Political Economy of Wildlife Policy in Africa*. Cambridge University Press.

Godlewska-Majkowska, H. (2018). Investment Attractiveness of Polish Municipalities in Relation to Local Entrepreneurship. *Olsztyn Economic Journal*, 13(2), pp. 103–122.

Godlewska-Majkowska, H., & Komor, A. (2019). Intelligent Organization in a Local Administrative Unit: From Theoretical Design to Reality. *European Research Studies Journal*, 22(4), pp. 290–307. https://doi.org/10.35808/ersj/1510.

Gorzelak, G. (2021). Różnice regionalne–preferencje polityczne–sprawiedliwość społeczna. *Studia Regionalne i Lokalne*, 2 (84), pp. 117–127.

Hamilton, W. (1932). Institution. In Seligman, E., & Johnson, A. (Eds.), *Encyclopaedia of the Social Sciences* (pp. 84–89). New York: Macmillan.

Hansen, T., & Coenen, L. (2015). The Geography of Sustainability Transitions: Review, Synthesis and Reflections on an Emergent Research Field. *Environmental Innovation and Societal Transitions*, 17, pp. 92–109. https://doi.org/10.1016/j.eist.2014.11.001.

Hodgson, G. M. (2006). What Are Institutions? *Journal of Economic Issues*, 90(1), pp. 1–25.

Jewtuchowicz, A. (2016). Terytorium i terytorializacja w europejskiej polityce rozwoju regionalnego. *Studia prawno-ekonomiczne*, 98, pp. 221–235.

Kattel, R., & Mazzucato, M. (2018). Mission-Oriented Innovation Policy and Dynamic Capabilities in the Public Sector. *Industrial and Corporate Change*, 27(5), pp. 787–801.

Maridal, J. H. (2013). Cultural Impact on National Economic Growth. *The Journal of Socio-Economics*, 47, pp. 136–146.

Mazzucato, M. (2016). From Market Fixing to Market-Creating: A New Framework for Innovation Policy. *Industrial Innovation*, 23(2), pp. 140–156. https://doi.org/10.1080/13662716.2016.1146124

Meijer, A. (2016). Smart City Governance: A Local Emergent Perspective. In Ramon Gil-Garcia, J., Pardo, T. A., & Nam, T. (Eds.), *Smarter as the New Urban Agenda* (pp. 73–85). https://doi.org/10.1007/978-3-319- 17620-8.

Meyer, J., Scott, W. R., & Strang, D. (1987). Centralization, Fragmentation, and School District Complexity. *Administrative Science Quarterly*, 32, pp. 186–201.

Nam, T., & Pardo, T. A. (2011). Smart city as Urban Innovation: Focusing on Management, Policy, and Context. In *Proceedings of the 5th International Conference on Theory and Practice of Electronic Governance — ICEGOV '11* (p. 185). https://doi.org/10.1145/2072069.2072100.

North, D. C. (1971). Institutional Change and Economic Growth. *Journal of Economic History*, 31, pp. 118–125.

North, D. C. (1990). *Institutions, Institutional Change and Economic Performance.* Cambridge University Press.

North, D. C. (1991). Institutions. *Journal of Economic Perspectives*, 5(1), pp. 97–112.

North, D. C., & Thomas, R. P. (1973). *The Rise of the Western World*. Cambridge University Press.

Nowakowska, A. (2011). *Regionalny wymiar procesów innowacji*. Wyd. Uniwersytetu Łódzkiego.

Ostrom, E. (2008). Doing Institutional Analysis: Digging Deeper Than Markets and Hierarchies. In Ménard, C., & Shirley, M. M. (Ed.), *Handbook of New Institutional Economics*. Springer, Berlin: Heidelberg. https://doi.org/10.1007/978-3-540-69305-5_31.

Raven, R., Sengers, F., Spaeth, P., Xie, L., Cheshmehzangi, A., & de Jong, M. (2019). Urban Experimentation and Institutional Arrangements. *European Planning Studies*, 27(2), pp. 258–281. https://doi.org/10.1080/09654313.2017.1393047.

Rutherford, M. (2001). Institutional Economics: Then and Now. *Journal of Economic Perspectives*, 15(3), pp. 173–194.

Swaminathan A., & Wade, J. B. (2016). Institutional Environment. In Augier, M., & Teece, D. (Eds.), *The Palgrave Encyclopedia of Strategic Management*. London: Palgrave Macmillan. https://doi.org/10.1057/978-1-349-94848-2_608-1.

Szlachta, J., & Zaucha, J. (2014). Dorobek z zakresu polityki regionalnej, w: Krystyna Gawlikowska-Hueckel, Jacek Szlachta (red.), Wrażliwość polskich regionów na wyzwania współczesnej gospodarki. Implikacje dla polityki rozwoju regionalnego, Wolters Kluwer, Warszawa, s. 47–71.

Tomor, Z., Meijer, A., Michels, A., & Geertman, S. (2019). Smart Governance for Sustainable Cities: Findings from a Systematic Literature Review. *Journal of Urban Technology*, 26(4), pp. 3–27. https://doi.org/10.1080/10630732.2019.1651178.

Williamson, O. E. (2000). The new institutional economics: taking stock, looking ahead. *Journal of Economic Literature*, 38(3), pp. 595–613.

Wilkin, J. (2016). *Instytucjonalne i kulturowe podstawy gospodarowania: humanistyczna perspektywa ekonomii.* Wydawnictwo Naukowe" Scholar".

Zarębski, P., Czerwińska-Jaśkiewicz, M., & Klonowska-Matynia, M. (2022). Innovation in Peripheral Regions from a Multidimensional Perspective: Evidence from the Middle Pomerania Region in Poland. *Sustainability,* 14(14), p. 8529. https://doi.org/10.3390/su14148529.

Zarębski, P., Kwiatkowski, G., Malchrowicz-Mośko, E., & Oklevik, O. (2019). Tourism Investment Gaps in Poland. *Sustainability,* 11(22), p. 6188. https://doi.org/10.3390/su11226188.

2 The institutional environment of the European Union

Regional approach

II.1 Smart organization in regional innovation system

Innovation plays a key role in the functioning of a smart organization. The changing environment generates a constant need to adapt to changes and create new, often innovative solutions. An organization that wants to participate in the processes of creating, absorbing, and diffusing new technologies and solutions must participate in local and regional innovation systems (RIS). The effectiveness of smart management of an organization and coping with crisis situations will depend on this. Taking the perspective of innovation systems, its four main elements can be listed as follows (Nelson, 1993; Patel & Pavitt, 1994):

1 The institutional structures of a country, region, or sector. These structures co-create companies, universities, research and training institutes, standards, procedures, networks, financial organizations, and policies to promote and regulate technical change.
2 The incentive system of a country, region, or sector. These are systems that activate participants to learn and improve qualifications, transfer technology, create and absorb innovation, entrepreneurship, and professional mobility in and between organizations.
3 The skills and creativity of innovation and economic actors in a country, a region, or sector. Both between and within countries, and between companies within a country, there are large differences in the variety and quality of products and services, and opportunities for paving new development paths.
4 The cultural peculiarities of a country, region, or sector that determine the degree of acceptance and understanding of technology by users.

These elements have often been the main theoretical framework for models of innovation system. In many cases, heuristic models of innovation systems are built around the general institutional structures of countries, regions, or sectors (Warnke et al., 2016). However, there is no "ideal model" for innovation policy, as innovation activities vary greatly between

DOI: 10.4324/9781003265870-8

central, peripheral, and old industrial areas (Tödtling & Trippl, 2005). RIS responds to spatial diversity. It is a system in which companies and other organizations are systematically involved in interactive learning through an institutional environment characterized by embeddedness (Cooke, Uranga & Etxebarria, 1998). Additionally, a (regional) innovation system consists of a production structure (techno-economic structures) and institutional infrastructure (political and institutional structures) (Asheim & Isaksen, 1997). The concept of RIS evolves from the assumption that innovation is a process that is based on various factors that are internal and external to the organization. It means that not only knowledge resources created by a single organization are important, but also the way in which organizations enter in interaction with themselves and the environment (Doloreux, 2002). Basically, the main elements of RIS are enterprises, institutions, knowledge infrastructure, and innovative policy. Enterprises perform multiple functions related to the generation and dissemination of knowledge through interactions with other enterprises and institutions. It was enterprises that were the first to spread knowledge about IT technologies and to implement these technologies in the public sector and local governments.

Institutions, whose task is to reduce uncertainty, coordinate the use of knowledge, mediate conflicts, and provide incentives, are of paramount importance in the system (Carlsson & Jacobsson, 1997). In other words, institutions shape activity in the area of innovation and provide a normative framework that is responsible for stable social relations. Institutional components depend on the national system, particularly in the areas of financing, organizational structure, and public resources, as well as political decisions. Industrial research and development, universities, governments, and other institutions are often mentioned in the literature as key actors that can influence the creation, development, transfer, and use of technology.

The knowledge infrastructure, which is part of the general framework of the knowledge system, includes not only physical elements, but also organizational skills in the field of production, financing, coordination, supervision, and evaluation of activities related to the use of knowledge in innovative processes. Knowledge in a system is created and transferred by both private and public organizations. Technology diffusion occurs through science parks or technology parks and technology incubators, which enable the development of new innovative and profitable activities. Knowledge is disseminated through public advisory agencies in the field of technology transfer and innovation. Their role is to provide technical support and information to knowledge-based companies. Another role in the system is played by research and development institutions such as universities, research institutes, and national laboratories, which produce and coordinate scientific and technological knowledge, as well as education, research, and development in technology. Infrastructure and knowledge flows can take many forms, and the same goes for their effectiveness. It depends to a large extent on social relations, trust, and rules of cooperation that are created by organizations in a given region and beyond.

Due to the adopted research area related to smart organizations, we will devote special attention to the institution of knowledge and innovation.

II.2 Mechanism of knowledge and information flow in regions

Knowledge and innovation play an important role in the functioning of smart organizations. Sustainable development based on innovation increases the competitiveness of local governments in the global economy. As research and discussion of innovation in the public sector develops, it is increasingly emphasized that a broader and more comprehensive view of innovation should be used as factors supporting smart processes in order to build competitive advantages of regions that are at different stages of economic development. In this part of the study, we will introduce readers to the importance of the institutional environment in RIS s, what we know about them, what mechanisms it creates, and what determines its effectiveness in the process of creating and diffusing knowledge for smart organizations.

The concept of RIS explains the mechanisms related to the emergence of innovation and the transfer of knowledge. The innovative performance of the economy depends on the innovative capabilities of enterprises and research institutions, as well as on how they interact with each other and with public institutions (Doloreux, 2002). The concept shows the multidimensional structures of the stakeholders and actors of the system, i.e. the broadly understood institutional infrastructure and the production system and then explains the mechanisms of relations that arise between them, based on the established rules and regional policy. Using the theoretical assumptions of the concept, it is worth considering how the institutional environment of RIS can support the functioning of smart organizations.

RIS are built on three pillars, the understanding of which is key to explaining the mechanisms of innovation development in regions. The first is the term "interactive learning", which denotes the process by which knowledge is transferred and then combined and, as a result, constitutes a knowledge base as a shared resource of various entities cooperating in the system. Knowledge is the basic factor used not only in the process of creating innovation, but also in the process of absorption of innovation and technology and building cognitive, organizational, and social closeness. The second element is the "institutional environment", which includes principles, norms, values, and human and material resources. It is a set of territorial conditions that create potential for functioning of system specific for a region. Economic relations are to some extent always embedded in a social context, so that social ties or relationships have an impact on economic performance (Boschma, 2005). Therefore, the concept also takes into account the phenomenon of "social embedding". This means that it is easier to run a business in an environment that knows, accepts, and integrates us into economic and knowledge creation processes and then duplicates that knowledge in enterprises and beyond. It should also be emphasized that the process of learning and absorption of innovation is often based on trust, therefore, social relations facilitate the exchange of tacit knowledge, which is by nature much more difficult to communicate and exchange through markets (Maskell & Malmberg, 1999).

The innovation system consists of institutions that play an important role in the process of knowledge transfer and innovation development. One of the first researchers who listed and explained the basic elements and mechanisms of such a system was Lundvall (1992). This author distinguished, inter alia, the internal organization of enterprises, relations between enterprises, the role of the public sector, the institutional structure of the financial sector, the intensity of research and development, and research and development organizations. Basically, the main elements encompassing RIS are enterprises, business environment institutions, knowledge infrastructure, and innovation policy.

The RIS concept assumes that innovation is a process in which enterprises use both internal and external resources of a material and institutional nature. The functioning of RIS depends not only on knowledge resources but also on the strength and structure of relationships, created networks that are the plane for information exchange. Innovations are not created in isolation on the internal resources of the organization alone, but rather are the result of a synergy of many factors and processes. The aforementioned environment can therefore be perceived as a network of organizations and institutions that cooperate with each other in the framework of innovative activities and conduct interactive learning with each other. In this way, the relationships between the actors of the innovation system can be defined in terms of knowledge and information flow, investment flow, networking, and other partnerships, which is the most important process of local systems (Doloreux, 2002). In conclusion, it should be stated that the RIS is primarily a social system that includes systematic interactions between various groups of private and public sector institutions. As part of the relationship between smart organizations, there are created channels supported by modern IT technologies in order to increase local opportunities for the flow of knowledge and information aimed at sustainable development.

II.3 Institutional environment mapping

II.3.1 Conceptual framework

In order to analyze the potentials of smart organizations in local governments, in diverse European regional ecosystems, we used the conceptual framework of RIS concept. In the light of the concepts in the regions, institutional capital, along with economic and social (network) capitals, are the key constructive elements that allow describing and explaining the mechanism of sustainable development. In the system, knowledge and innovation flow through various policies and informal behaviors of organizations and local communities. The overriding feature of local governments is their location and rooting in the socio-economic system. This means that smart organizations in local governments operate in a multidimensional institutional environment consisting of human capital, IT technology, innovation potential, relational capital, and a scientific and research base. The capitals and rules that govern them are often a critical mass without which the development processes would be impossible.

Smart organization in the structure of RIS can be represented by two subsystems embedded in a common institutional socio-economic and political environment (Autio, 1998). The system of application and exploitation of knowledge and innovation consists of organizations of the public sector and its environment, inhabitants, entrepreneurs, the natural environment, and social infrastructure as well as IT infrastructure. Local authorities, as a public sector, pursue social goals aimed at satisfying the needs of residents. They are also involved in shaping the public space in which the inhabitants of the commune live and work. Smart public sector organizations are connected by horizontal and vertical networks of relationships to exchange knowledge and information needed for efficient management of sustainable development. The second, main component of RIS, is the knowledge generation and diffusion subsystem. It is made up of various institutions that produce and disseminate skills and knowledge. These are public research institutions, organizations intermediating in technology transfer (technology licensing offices, innovation centers, research centers, etc.), as well as educational institutions (universities, universities of technology, vocational training institutions, etc.) and organizations that mediate employment and business contacts (associations of entrepreneurs, economic self-government, labor market institutions). Moreover, the diagram takes into account the regional policy dimension. Political actors at this level can play an important role in sustainable regional development, provided there is sufficient regional autonomy (legal competences and financial resources) to formulate and implement innovation policy (Cooke, Boekholt & Todtling, 2000). The ideal "model" situation in a system is the relationships within and between these subsystems that facilitate the continuous flow or exchange of knowledge, resources, and human capital. In reality, however, such systems have deficits in relation to organizations and institutions, and there are noticeable underdeveloped relational mechanisms within and between subsystems. In this study, we refer to the concept of the RIS and its subsystems. We assume that the central point of creating and managing sustainable development is a smart organization in the subsystem of knowledge absorption and innovation. The local government is therefore an important participant and beneficiary of

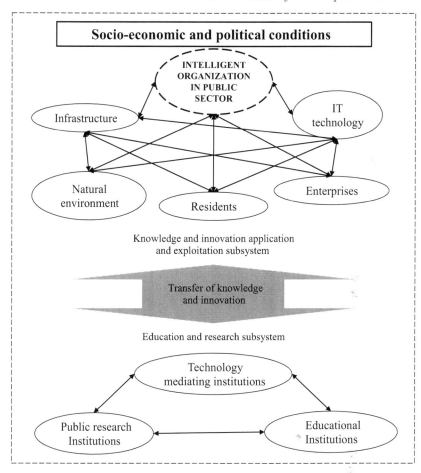

Figure II.3 A conceptual approach to smart organization research in RIS. Own work.

the knowledge and information exchange network and the implementation of innovations (Figure II.3).

Subsystems create a mechanism of knowledge and innovation transfer which, being a dynamic system, aims at socio-economic development and environmental protection. In the context of this theoretical framework, we propose an approach in which the five categories of capital – human capital, IT capital (digitalization), innovation capital, relational capital, and regional research capital – support the functioning of smart organizations in the public sector. In the diagram, arrows indicate the relationships between subsystem elements within the region. Research and innovation capital primarily influences the system's level of reactivity to sudden crisis situations, as well as the building of sustainable development. Regions equipped with their own research subsystem can create solutions that take into account the specificity of the region and optimize the use of potential. In this study, we first operationalized the potential of the five capitals based on empirical indicators and then performed an analysis for European regions to identify regional typologies and spatial patterns.

II. 3.2 Measuring conditions for smart organizations in public sector

In order to assess the conditions for the development of smart organizations in European regions, we used 10 indicators, each representing one of the five capitals: human, social, innovative, research, and relational (Table II.2). The potential for the development of smart organizations is a complex phenomenon, and measuring them requires the involvement of various indicators describing numerous phenomena. Territorial capital is a set of resources that determine the competitive potential of a territory (Mróz et al., 2022). The difficulty of measuring is to translate theoretical assumptions into measurable empirical indicators.

The concept of RIS describes the mechanisms that drive innovation in regions. The concept focuses on the institutional mechanism and social embeddedness that determine the method of operationalization of its basic components. The area we have chosen to build the capital potential model covers regions in Europe.

The study used data for 240 regions from 22 EU Member States, Norway, Serbia, Switzerland, and the United Kingdom at different NUTS levels.[1] The availability of data for NUTS levels varied, and thus the collected indicators cover 47 NUTS 1 regions, and 193 NUTS 2 regions. In the EU

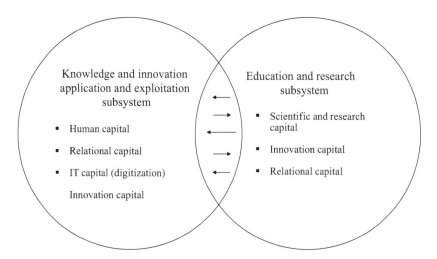

Figure II.4 Smart innovation system in the region. Own work.

Member States, Cyprus, Estonia, Latvia, Luxembourg, and Malta, NUTS 1 and NUTS 2 levels are identical to the country's territory, and therefore the national levels were taken into account. The aim of the study is to show the regional potential for the development of smart organizations in local governments. As was emphasized earlier, the problem of examining institutions results from their intangible nature. We observe the effects of the functioning of institutions and adopt policies and rules of conduct more often. The potential that is a result of the policy of innovation and the development of human capital and social networks will be explored in terms of improving digital competences and creating social networks based on advanced IT technologies. Thus, the selection of indicators took into account both the broadly understood potential of IT technology and innovation, as well as human potential and the possibility of implementing new technologies in social structures (Table II.2).

The rationale for all the ratios describing individual capitals used in the model is presented below. In particular, efforts were made to show the contextual value in relation to explaining the processes of the formation and functioning of smart organizations in local governments. Each of the described indicators brings cognitive value, and all of them together form a multidimensional construct, bound by mutual interdependencies, which additionally strengthen their role in influencing the studied phenomenon.

X1 Population with tertiary education. Knowledge and the ability to use it is a key element of human capital. From the point of view of sustainable development, a broad level of education is important not only in the field of science and technology but also in the service sector, where the vast majority of the population is employed. The implementation of IT technologies in many areas of the economy, including public service sectors, depends on a wide range of skills. The high level of education of the inhabitants creates greater opportunities for building a smart local economy based on knowledge and establishing a network of relations and effective communication between inhabitants and public organizations. Observation of the population aged 25–34 allows monitoring of smart solutions in education policy, leading to an increase in the number of university graduates.

X2 Lifelong learning. The change that accompanies most phenomena in the economy requires reaction and adaptation through continuous improvement of knowledge and acquisition of new skills. Nowadays, this applies in particular to the implementation of new technologies in social and economic life. The enormous technological progress that we observe in the world creates the need for education in the field of these technologies, creating new behavior algorithms and rules, especially in the group of people who have already completed the education process. Therefore, lifelong learning should fill this gap and include educational, formal, non-formal, or informal activities undertaken on an ongoing basis to improve the knowledge, skills, and competences of the population.

Table II.2 Determinants of smart organizations and their indicators. Own work

Capital	Indicator	Description	Year	Source of data and year
Human capital	X1 Population with tertiary education	Number of people with post-secondary education aged 25–34 in relation to the total number of inhabitants aged 25–34	2019	Eurostat, regional statistics 2019
	X2 Lifelong learning	Number of people aged 25–64 in households who participated in at least four weeks of education or training in relation to the age group 25–64	2019	Eurostat, regional statistics
IT capital (digitization)	X3 Digital skills	Number of people with over basic general digital skills in the areas (information, communication, problem solving, content creation) in relation to the age group 16–74	2019	Regional Innovation Scoreboard 2021
	X4 ICT specialists	Number of employed ICT specialists who are competent to develop, operate and maintain ICT systems and it is the main part of their work to the total number of employees	2019	Regional Innovation Scoreboard 2021
Innovation capital	X5 Product process innovators	Number of small and medium-sized enterprises (SMEs) that have introduced at least one product innovation in relation to the total number of enterprises	2018	Eurostat
	X6 Business process innovators	Number of small and medium-sized enterprises (SMEs) that have introduced at least one business process innovation that is either new to the enterprise or new to its market	2018	Eurostat
Relational capital	X7 Innovative SMEs collaborating with others	Number of SMEs operating under innovation cooperation. with other enterprises or institutions in relation to the total number of enterprises	2018	Eurostat
	X8 Public–private co-publications	Number of public–private scientific publications co-authors with both domestic and foreign collaborators in relation to the number of inhabitants	2020	Regional Innovation Scoreboard 2021
Scientific–research capital	X9 International scientific co-publications	Number of scientific publications with at least one co-author living abroad in relation to the number of inhabitants	2020	Regional Innovation Scoreboard 2021
	X10 Most-cited publications	Number of scientific publications among the 10% most cited publications in the world in relation to the number of scientific publications	2018	Regional Innovation Scoreboard 2021

X3 Digital skills of residents. The development toward a digital economy and the use of information technology in smart organizations and information management in local governments will primarily depend on the digital skills of the inhabitants. They will allow performing activities related to obtaining information, communicating using digital devices, solving problems with the use of programs and algorithms, and creating their own digital content by residents. Inhabitants can represent various skill levels of the above-mentioned activities. The basic level covers the use of devices for searching websites of public organizations, checking important terms, legal acts, forms, and official communications. The more advanced level includes activities related to digital editing of documents or using smart algorithms and creating own multidimensional queries. As public platforms develop, residents have the opportunity to use greater functionality of the e-office platforms, digitally fill them in with their own content, send information, solve problems, and use support in dealing with official matters using smart algorithms, which allows combining multi-level information, e.g. when setting up business activity or tax settlement.

X4 IT specialists employed at local companies. The smart revolution in cities and local governments was initiated by the dynamic development and use of digital technologies in private sector organizations. They largely contributed to the diffusion of these technologies and their implementation in various areas of local government functioning. The next stages of smart city development are the wider and deeper implementation of technologies in the socio-economic life. Without ICT specialists, this process will not be possible. The high participation and further increase in the participation of specialists in the occupational structure of regional economies will support and accelerate this process. Additionally, the creation of a cooperation network between the public and private sectors, as well as local government institutions, non-governmental organizations, and universities will facilitate the exchange of knowledge and innovations in the field of digital technologies.

X5 Product process innovators. Product innovation is the introduction of a new or significantly improved good or service to the market. In the context of smart cities and regions, innovations that allow countries to gain technological sovereignty, i.e. the ability to shape key IT technologies and technologies related to the production of renewable energy, are particularly desirable. EU policy supports the development of a decentralized energy system based on renewable energy sources. Transforming local urban systems toward clean energy use is a key challenge in initiatives to develop smart cities and create climate-friendly and sustainable urban areas. A development policy oriented in this way needs enterprises that introduce IT technologies and innovative energy technologies to the market, which significantly increases the region's income and its investment potential. Innovative enterprises create important competitive advantages in international trade, thanks to which the regions have relatively high GDP per capita and favorable parameters of sustainable development.

X6 Business process innovators. Many companies innovate not by improving new products, but by improving business processes. Business process innovations include marketing and organizational innovations. An example of applied innovations that support business processes is artificial intelligence, which supports doctors, manufacturers, and sellers in online stores. In the public sector, AI can predict traffic, help optimize employment, and aid the efficient deployment of social infrastructure. Systems based on artificial intelligence have the ability to analyze millions of user activities simultaneously, in real time, which is an important support for public sector organizations and other service companies whose activities are based on the ability to recognize needs and adapt services to them. Business processes are also supported by fifth-generation mobile devices and technologies (5G networks) belonging to the Internet of Things. The success of these technologies depends on the data being processed quickly enough to provide useful information. The development of smart cities, smart transport, and smart buildings in the near future will depend on the development of these technologies and IT processes.

X7 Innovative SMEs collaborating with others. Acquiring knowledge and collective learning will bring many benefits in smart cities. Technologies alone without active social networks will not be able to provide relevant information for smart management. For the communication process to take place, players need to know the benefits of information sharing and have the will to cooperate. One of the areas of such cooperation is innovations that involve various institutions and organizations, both in the private and public sectors, within local systems. The rules of cooperation are defined within informal relationships, which are the result of social embedding and mutual trust. Formal relations are created, inter alia, by the policy of development and support for entrepreneurship and innovation. The tool of this policy is funds for the implementation of partnership projects that engage enterprises, universities, non-governmental organizations, and local governments to cooperate.

X8 Public-private co-publication. Apart from basic and theoretical research, science must have a practical dimension. This idea is guided by a different concept, the theoretical framework of which indicates the mechanism of cooperation of three main players: enterprises, universities, and local authorities. Building the resilience of the economy and sustainable development is based on such cooperation, or more precisely, the possibility of a quick response to the changing environment and the threats it entails. Therefore, local development management requires a quick response when various unexpected situations and shocks arise, caused by events beyond one's control, e.g. pandemics, wars, sudden natural crises, or energy crises. The response of the scientific community to these crisis states is quick support and joint development of solutions that can be implemented in practice. Examples of such direct actions during the COVID-19 pandemic were, for example, the production of respirators, disinfectant fluid, visors, and mask adapters, as well as sewing masks. Universities are also involved in other areas of combating the pandemic and its effects, such as research and support in the fight against stress, donating blood, supporting seniors, and e-learning for high school students. Many universities cooperated with hospitals, local governments, non-governmental organizations, and other entities, e.g. military universities and fire brigades supported the evacuation of, e.g., social welfare homes.

X9 International scientific co-publications. International scientific publications are an indicator of the quality of scientific research. Collaboration with scientists from many countries increases the diffusion of knowledge and opens the region to the influx of new ideas and innovations. The innovativeness of regions and their development does not take place only due to endogenous factors occurring in the region. The regional scientific potential is insufficient to successfully develop new technologies and ideas. Typically, the international scientific environment is an open system where knowledge and information are transferred without market and administrative constraints. The basic principles of the academic community are universal access to knowledge and exchange of experiences in the form of scientific publications, conferences, and joint international projects, the result of which are international scientific co-publications. That is why public funds are so important, as thanks to them research can be carried out. Countries where relatively the largest financial resources are allocated to research and development gain competitive advantages and are the most innovative economies in the world. These countries are also leaders in the development and implementation of digital technologies as part of the smart city concept.

X10 Most-cited publication. The number of scientific publications among the 10% of the most cited publications in the world indicates the quality and topicality of research carried out in the regions. Scientific achievements thematically position research centers in the structure of national and international research, which facilitates the emergence of regional smart specializations. These are the identified, unique assets and resources of the region, emphasizing its competitive advantage. In the case of smart specializations, it is emphasized that the existing scientific and business potentials in the field of R&D&I (research, development, and innovation) should be taken into account when determining them.

The values of individual capitals were used to develop a typology of European regions, which was based on the k-means classification method. When selecting the indicators, the assumptions of the concept of innovation systems and their institutional, social, and technological dimensions were taken into account. The ratios were standardized and then grouped, which made it possible to obtain synthetic ratios for each capital. Due to the purpose of the research, which is to determine the potentials of regions and spatial regimes, the same weights of model indicators were used. The process of preparing a typology of regions for smart development included the implementation of subsequent activities: determining capitals; selection of empirical features; standardization of variables; calculating zero unitarization sums for capitals; grouping the units of the surveyed population by capital groups; and assessing the durability of the indicator structure (k-means classification).

The capital level was assessed by the method of linear ordering of standardized sum data. The procedure begins with standardization by normalizing univariate variables according to the following formula:

$$x_{ij}' = \frac{x_{ij} - x_{minj}}{x_{maxj} - x_{minj}} 100,$$

where

j *next function number,*
i *next spatial unit number,*
x_{ij}' *normalized feature j in the spatial unit i,*
x_{ij} *the value of the feature j in the spatial unit i.*

If the nature of the variable is different, e.g. destimulants or nominants, then the stimulant substitution procedure should be used:

$$x_{ij}' = \frac{x_{maxj} - x_{ij}}{x_{maxj} - x_{minj}} 100.$$

II.3.3 Regional institutional potential for smart organizations

For easier interpretation, the indicators were grouped into four clusters, which are components of the model. The typology was carried out in the JASP 0.16.1.0 program (JASP, 2022) in which the k-means method is implemented. The k-means algorithm is a clustering technique widely used in numerous studies to classify input data into k-clusters. Neighborhood-based clustering methods. It is a partitioning algorithm that aims to divide data into several clusters where each observation belongs to only one group. The data is split in such a way that the degree of similarity between the two data observations is maximum if they belong to the same group, and minimum if not. The selection of the best clustering model is made by comparing the statistical parameters presented in Table II.3. The first column shows the number of clusters generated. The next N column shows the sample size. R^2: indicates the amount of variance explained by the model. The AIC is value of the model, lower values represent better clustering outputs. The BIC is value of the model, lower values represent better clustering outputs. The Silhouette is value of the model, ranges from −1 to 1, where 1 represents a perfect score. The comparison of the obtained parameters shows that the best option is a model with 4 clusters.

Table II.3 K – means Clustering Model Table – clustering variants. Own work

Clustering variants	N	R^2	AIC	TO BEAT	Silhouette
4	240	0.541	152.25	291,48	0.24
5	240	0.584	165.58	339.62	0.2
6	240	0.621	179.78	388.61	0.21
7	240	0.652	194.81	438.45	0.21

Table II.4 Cluster Information. Own work

Cluster	1	2	3	4
Size	43	70	43	84
Explained proportion within-cluster heterogeneity	0.161	0.264	0.202	0.373
Within sum of squares	11,649	19.048	14,600	26,954
Silhouette score	0.204	0.223	0.177	0.295
Center x1	0.627	0.407	0.855	0.434
Center x2	0.727	0.295	0.662	0.215
Center x3	0.834	0.548	0.783	0.365
Center x4	0.440	0.378	0.814	0.245
Center x5	0.480	0.603	0.773	0.369
Center x6	0.687	0.810	0.661	0.290
Center x7	0.762	0.631	0.638	0.262
Center x8	0.566	0.613	0.859	0.298
Center x9	0.621	0.619	0.888	0.361
Center x10	0.637	0.559	0.668	0.314

Note: The Between Sum of Squares of the 4-cluster model is 85.3 *Note*. The Total Sum of Squares of the 4-cluster model is 157.55.

Table II.5 contains the basic parameters of the model. The maximum cluster diameter in euclidean distance is 0.719. Minimum separation is the minimum cluster separation in euclidean distance is 0.160. Pearson's γ is the correlation between distances and a 0-1-vector is 0.521, where 0 means same cluster and 1 means different clusters. Dunn index is minimum separation/maximum diameter is 0.093. Entropy of the distribution of cluster memberships is 1.343. The Calinski–Harabasz index is the variance ratio criterion of the cluster memberships is 92.869.

Each type of region can be described according to the presence of the capital level. In order to clarify the structure of each type, the value of capital in a given type was determined and an appropriate symbol was assigned to it, which facilitates the interpretation of the obtained results. The capital value was estimated in relation to the mean M and the standard deviation SD of the entire study population according to the following classification:

Table II.5 Evaluation Metrics. Own work.

	Value
Maximum diameter	1.719
Minimum separation	0.160
Pearson's γ	0.521
Dunn index	0.093
Entropy	1.343
Calinski-Harabasz index	92,869

Note: All metrics are based on the *euclidean* distance.

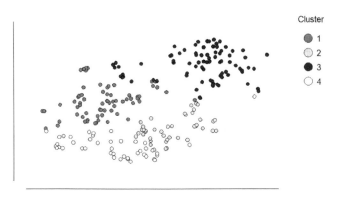

Figure II.5 Cluster density plots. Own work.

$M' > M + 0.7SD$	*very high (++++),*
$M' > M + 0.3SD$	*high (++),*
$M' > M + 0.3SD$	*medium (~~~),*
$M' > M + 0.7SD$	*low (-),*
$M' > M + 0.7SD$	*very low (----),*

where:

M' – *average capital value for a type,*
M – *average capital value for the entire set,*
SD – *standard deviation for the entire set.*

After applying the above formula, we obtain a matrix of assessments of individual capitals. A high level of equity value equilibrium occurs when obtaining comparable high values of all capitals that differ from each other by only one class. While the unsustainable type occurs in a situation of large disproportion in the assessment of at least one of the capitals in relation to the others (Table II.4).

The institutional environment of the European Union   109

Table II.6 Determinants of smart organizations and their indicators. Own work

Capital		Type			
		Average Value of the Cluster			
		1	2	3	4
Capital human	X1 Population with tertiary education	0.627 ++	0.407 -	0.855 ++++	0.434 -
	X2 Lifelong learning	0.727 ++++	0.295 -	0.662 ++++	0.215 ----
IT capital (digitization)	X3 Digital skills	0.834 ++++	0.548 -	0.783 ++++	0.365 ----
	X4 ICT specialists	0.44 ~~	0.378 ~~	0.814 ++++	0.245 -
Capital innovative	X5 Product process innovators	0.48 ~~	0.603 ~~	0.773 ++++	0.369 -
	X6 Business process innovators	0.687 ++	0.81 ++++	0.661 ~~	0.29 -
Capital relational	X7 Innovative SMEs collaborating with others	0.762 ++++	0.631 ++	0.638 ~~	0.262 ----
	X8 Public–private co-publications	0.566 ~~	0.613 ++	0.859 ++++	0.298 ----
Scientific–research capital	X9 International scientific co-publications	0.621 ~~	0.619 ~~	0.888 ++++	0.361 ----
	X10 Most–cited publications	0.637 ++	0.559 ~~	0.668 ++++	0.314 ----

Note: K-means clustering description: $k = 6$, item = 10, sum squared error (SSE) = 12.13355174. ★ symbol description of standardized value of centroids: ++++ very high (> $M + 0.7SD$), ++ high (> $M + 0.3SD$), ~~ medium (> $M + 0.3SD$), - low (> $M − 0.3SD$), ---- very low (< $M − 0.7SD$). ★ (the list of data used–see Table II.3).

II.4 European Union potential typology for smart organizations

The regions were grouped into 4 classes using the k–mean cluster analysis algorithm (Table II.6). The profile result tables present both data on the position of the center of gravity of individual types, as well as symbols for numerical values. In total, 240 European regions at the NUTS 2 level and smaller countries at the NUTS 1 level were included in the study. The research shows that the largest type 4, which represents 84 regions, covers about 35% of the surveyed regions. They are located mainly in the western and eastern parts of Europe. This is a group of regions that present very low capital values in almost all categories. Types 1 (43 regions) and 3 (43 regions) are the smallest groups, but with the highest capital potential. Each of them covers 43 regions, which is approximately 17% of the surveyed population. The last group of 70 regions is type 2 and accounts for 29% of the studied population. These are regions located mainly in the central part of the European Union.

The obtained results of the spatial distribution of the typology of capital for smart organizations can be related to the economic regions of Europe and the level of their development (Figure II.6). Types with relatively high and highest capitals are found mainly in the areas of operation of the main industrial districts of Europe, the United Kingdom, France, Germany, and Italy. Moreover, the highest values of capital were observed in large agglomerations and state capitals. Low potentials are clearly visible in the eastern and western regional peripheries of Europe, mainly in the post-communist countries.

II.4.1 Type 1 advantage of human and relational capital

This type is dominated by the regions of such countries as: the United Kingdom, France, the Netherlands, Norway, Sweden, and Finland, which are located in the northern part of the European Union, with a total of 43 regions. They are characterized by a high level of economic development, which translates into a relatively high level of GDP per capita and expenditure on research and development. At the same time, these are regions with a well-developed innovation potential. The competitive advantage of these regions is a very well-developed human capital, both due to the level of education achieved and the will to continue education throughout life. This results in the high digital skills of residents and the potential for the development of smart organizations, especially based on information and digital technologies. Moreover, in these regions, relational capital has developed very well in the context of cooperation between enterprises. It is conducive to the diffusion of knowledge and innovation, and to making decisions based on the experiences of other market participants. The scientific potential, on the other hand, is moderately developed. These are not leading research centers in the studied countries, which affects relational capital and the creation of joint scientific publications. Moderate deficits also occur in the field of ICT specialists and process innovators.

II.4.2 *Type 2 advantage of innovative capital*

This type includes 70 regions, mainly Germany, Austria, Italy, and Greece. They are located mainly in the central and southern parts of the European Union. The competitive advantage of these regions is the innovative capital of enterprises as well as entrepreneurship and a network of relations between entrepreneurs. Companies that introduce process and business innovations dominate. Economic traditions, innovation, and the level of economic development constitute the strength of these regions. However, the deficit of these regions is the low level of human capital, which is the result of two processes. The first is the aging of the European population and the increase in the share of the population over 65. Such people are in post-working age and are inactive in the labor market and, therefore, in the education market. Another phenomenon observed in countries with a high standard of living is the lack of willingness and need to study. Young people graduating from secondary school achieve a satisfactory standard of living and do not see the need for further education.

II.4.3 *Type 3 high potential*

It is a group of regions and cities with the highest potential for the development of smart organizations in all analyzed categories. These regions have balanced capitals, which means high comparable values in all analyzed categories: human capital, IT capital, relational capital, innovative capital, and research and development capital. This type is represented by 43 regions, mainly from Switzerland, the Netherlands, Germany, and Sweden. The rest of the regions that fall into this type are mainly state capitals and their functional areas. These are regions with high migration activity. People from other regions, as well as immigrants, are coming to capitals in the hope of a better job and a higher standard of living. As a result, these cities grow very quickly, and the urban space must be constantly adapted to population changes. Statistical forecasts indicate that cities will have to cope with structural demographic changes and thus the need to adapt their urban space and social infrastructure to the increase in the share of older people. The connection between high values of potentials for the development of smart organizations and the development of smart cities is clearly noticeable.

II.4.4 *Type 4 low potential*

The relatively weakest group of regions due to being equipped with development potentials for smart organizations. This type includes as many as 70 regions, mainly from post-communist countries such as Poland, Romania,

Table II.7 Classification of regions according to the types of potential for smart organizations. Own work

Type 1
Sjælland, Syddanmark, Comunidad Foral de Navarra, Åland, Center – Val de Loire, Grand Est, Pays de la Loire, Bretagne, Nouvelle-Aquitaine, Auvergne – Rhône-Alpes, Provence-Alpes-Côte d'Azur, Northern and Western, Southern, Friesland, Drenthe, Overijssel, Flevoland, Zeeland, Hedmark og Oppland, Sør-Østlandet, Agder og Rogaland, Nord-Norge, Småland med öarna, Norra Mellansverige, Mellersta Norrland, North East, North Wes, Yorkshire and The Humber, East Midlands, West Midlands, South West, Wales, Scotland, Northern Ireland, Ostschweiz, Nordjylland, Länsi-Suomi, Etelä-Suomi, Pohjois-ja Itä-Suomi, Occitanie, Limburg, Vestlandet, Övre Norrland

Type 2
Strední Features, Jihozápad, Severovýchod, Jihovýchod, Brandenburg, Kassel, Mecklenburg-Vorpommern, Lüneburg, Weser-Ems, Koblenz, Trier, Chemnitz, Sachsen-Anhalt, Attiki, Voreio Aigaio, Kriti, Kentriki Makedonia, Ipeiros, Ellada, Delfin Panonska Hrvatska, Grad Zagreb, Sjeverna Hrvatska, Liguria, Abruzzo, Molise, Campania, Provincia Autonoma Bolzano/Bozen, Marche, Belgrade, Bourgogne – Franche-Comté, Centro, Vzhodna Slovenija, Südösterreich, Westösterreich, Stuttgart, Fregion wall , Niederbayern, Oberpfalz, Oberfranken, Mittelfranken, Unterfranken, Schwaben, Bremen, Darmstadt, Gießen, Braunschweig, Hannover, Düsseldorf, Köln, Münster, Detmold, Arnsberg, Rheinhessen-Pfalz, Saarland, Dresden, Leipstein, Schleswig-Holstein, Schlese–Holing , Lombardia, Provincia Autonoma Trento, Veneto, Friuli-Venezia Giulia, Emilia-Romagna, Toscana, Umbria, Lazio

Type 3
País Vasco, Comunidad de Madrid, Cataluña, Budapest, Eastern and Midland, Warszawski stoleczny, Lisboa, Bratislavský kraj, London, South East, Ostösterreich, Région de Bruxelles-Capitale, Vlaams Gewest, Praha, Karlsruhe, Oberbayern, Berlin, Hamburg, Sostinés regionas, Zahodna Slovenija, Région lémanique, Espace Mittelland, Nordwestschweiz, Zürich, Zentralschweiz, Ticino, Hovedstaden, Midtjylland, Helsinki-Uusimaa, Île de France, Groningen, Gelderland, Utrecht, Noord-Holland, Zuid-Holland, Noord-Holland, Noord-Holland, Noord og Akershus, Trondelag, Stockholm, Östra Mellansverige, Sydsverige, Västsverige, East of England

Type 4
Strední Morava, Moravskoslezsko, Notio Aigaio, Anatoliki Makedonia, Thraki, Dytiki Makedonia, Ionia Nisia, Sterea Ellada, Peloponnisos, Régions ultrapériphériques françaises, Jadranska Hrvatska, Puglia, Basilicata, Aliaventas, Sardinia, Vojkata, Sardinia, Voronas, Sicarica, Sardinia, Šumadija and Western Serbia, Southern and Eastern Serbia, Galicia, Aragón, Castilla y León, Comunitat Valenciana, Normandie, Hauts-de-France, Norte, Severozapaden, Severen tsentralen, Severoiztochen, Yugoiztochen, Yugozapaden, Illes Yuzhen tsentralen, Severpadoentralen, Severpadoentralen Asturias, Cantabria, La Rioja, Castilla-la Mancha, Extremadura, Illes Balears, Andalucía, Región de Murcia, Ciudad de Ceuta, Ciudad de Melilla, Canarias, Corse, Pest, Közép-Dunántúl, Nyugat-Dunántúl, Dél-Dunántúl, –Magyarország, Észak-Alföld, Dél-Alföld, Valle d'Aosta/Vallée d'Aoste, Malopolskie, Silesian, Greater Poland, Zachodniopomorskie, Lubuskie, Dolnoslaskie, Opolskie, Kujawsko-Pomorskie, Warminsko-Mazurskie, Pom orskie, Lódzkie, Swietokrzyskie, Lubelskie, Podkarpackie, Podlaskie, Mazowiecki regional, Algarve, Região Autónoma dos Açores, Região Autónoma da Madeira, Nord-Vest, Centru, Nord-Est, Sud-Est, Sud – Muntenia, Bucuresti – Ilfov, Sud –Vest Oltenia, Vest, Západné Slovensko, Stredné Slovensko, Vachon Slovensko

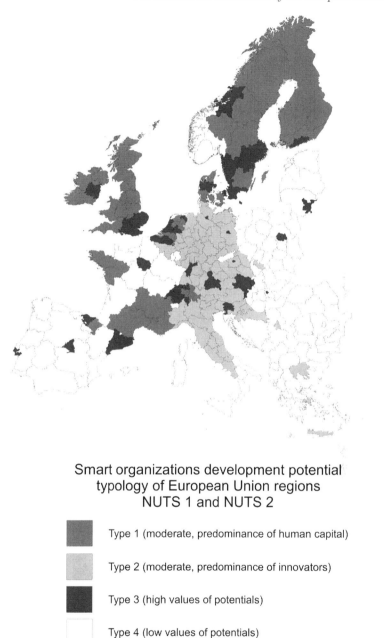

Smart organizations development potential
typology of European Union regions
NUTS 1 and NUTS 2

Type 1 (moderate, predominance of human capital)

Type 2 (moderate, predominance of innovators)

Type 3 (high values of potentials)

Type 4 (low values of potentials)

Figure II.6 Typology of European Union regions according to Smart Organizations development potential. Own work.

Bulgaria, and Hungary, and also from the western part of Europe, Spain, and Portugal. These are the most rapidly depopulating regions of Europe, for which demographic change poses a serious challenge. The internal EU migration to economically more developed regions is responsible for this process. Additionally, there is the phenomenon of brain drain, i.e. losing highly qualified human capital. As a result of permanent emigration, the "sending regions" are losing highly qualified people to the benefit of "receiving regions", which are more industrialized and economically developed. Another problem is the low fertility rate, which, with the increasing average age of life, causes European regions to age demographically.

II.5 Smart organizations in the context of the new EU mission-oriented strategy

The presented typology can be a starting point for a discussion on the role of missions that the EU has set for itself for the coming years in regard to the development of smart organizations. To achieve these goals, Europe is facing a process of transformation of socio-economic systems toward the implementation of missions focused on solving social problems (Hekkert, Janssen, Wesseling & Negro, 2020).

The planned activities are aimed at reducing policy fragmentation, interdisciplinarity, and cross-sector cooperation and increasing the participation of the public sector in this process by involving regional and local innovation systems. The "Horizon Europe 2021–2027" program takes into account the bottom-up nature of the mission, as well as the flexibility and broad involvement of citizens, which is a desirable approach to solving the problems of everyday life of urban and rural residents. The presented typology revealed the need to create individual regional strategies and thus an individual approach to creating local systems for smart organizations.

In the literature, one can find a proposal to create mission-oriented innovation systems (MIS). The authors of this proposal define them as a network of agents and a set of institutions that contribute to the development and implementation of innovative solutions in order to first identify social needs and then implement the social mission. In this approach, innovation systems gain new boundaries set by interactions, the direction of which is determined by the demand, and the solutions themselves combine technological and social aspects. The role of smart organizations in such systems may include various aspects and benefits outlined below.

First, as the typology of European regions has shown, smart organizations function in a different institutional and innovative environment. Regional disproportions and inconsistencies mean that the initial start-up capital for these organizations varies. This is especially true of human and innovative capital. Regions with high development parameters are already taking over the role of innovation leaders and achieve tangible results in the form of implementing new concepts of smart development. The question arises as to the other regions, how to deal with their capital deficits. Perhaps it is better to create institutional solutions that will provide a framework for cooperation for the flow of knowledge and information instead of investing in creating new capitals? But not as growth engines for which diffusion and spill-over development effects were expected. The missions proposed in the EU strategy involve everyone in the process of achieving the goal, which becomes a priority challenge for both leading and peripheral regions, and their participation in this process is directly proportional to their resources and endogenous potentials.

Second, the demand-driven approach to shaping the goals that sets the directions for action requires a bottom-up approach to current social problems. The concept of smart organizations in the public sector may become an ideal platform for the implementation of these missions. Grassroots initiatives will be more effective if the communication process is better organized based on modern IT solutions. The scale of society's acceptance of new technologies and the willingness to use them in everyday life will also be of key importance. It is therefore an attempt to create a multidimensional system based on feedback, where the flow of information will be two-way, with a high frequency of updating current social problems.

Third, smart organizations in local governments function in the system of social relations and, through developed rules and patterns of behavior, influence local communities. Local authorities shape the behavior and habits of residents through knowledge distribution systems and local politics. This is a very important factor that may decide about the implementation of 5 strategic missions of the EU. An example is the mission to create climate neutral and smart cities. It is intended that 100 European cities will receive support in their systemic transformation toward climate neutrality by 2030. It will be an example of a bottom-up approach to achieving city climate neutrality, through the participation of the entire local ecosystem and public authorities. The success of this project will depend on the social agreement to modernize the local energy model in which they have operated so far. It will be required to implement renewable energy sources in the homes of residents, and it will also be important to change the current behavior and habits related to energy saving, waste segregation, and the use of products in accordance with the idea of the circular economy. Communication patterns in social relations, the use of remote work from home and collective transport, electric vehicles, bicycles, and other vehicles with zero carbon dioxide emissions will also be changed. All this means that without the cooperation of various environments and smart management of these processes, the change of socio-economic systems may take a very long time.

Note

1 The NUTS (Nomenclature of territorial units for statistics) classification is a hierarchical system for dividing the economic territory of the EU that distinguishes three levels: NUTS 1 covers major socio-economic regions, NUTS

2 covers core regions for the application of regional policies, and NUTS 3 covers small regions to specific diagnoses.

References

Asheim, B. T., & Isaksen, A. (1997). Location, Agglomeration and Innovation: Towards Regional Innovation Systems in Norway? *European Planning Studies*, 5(3), pp. 299–330.

Autio, E. (1998). Evaluation of RTD in Regional Systems of Innovation. *European Planning Studies*, 6(2), pp. 131–140.

Boschma, R. (2005). Proximity and Innovation: A Critical Assessment. *Regional Studies*, 39(1), pp. 61–74.

Carlsson, B., & Jacobsson, S. (1997). Diversity Creation and Technological Systems: A Technology Policy Perspective. In Edquist, C. (Ed.), *Systems of Innovation: Technologies, Institutions and Organizations* (pp. 266–294). London: Pinter Publishers.

Cooke, P., Boekholt, P., & Todtling, F. (2000). *The Governance of Innovation in Europe: Regional Perspectives on Global Competitiveness*. Pinter.

Cooke, P., Uranga, M. G., & Etxebarria, G. (1998). Regional Systems of Innovation: An Evolutionary Perspective. *Environment and Planning A*, 30(9), pp. 1563–1584.

Doloreux, D. (2002). What We Should Know about Regional Systems of Innovation. *Technology in Society*, 24(3), pp. 243–263.

Hekkert, M. P., Janssen, M. J., Wesseling, J. H., & Negro, S. O. (2020). Mission-Oriented Innovation Systems. *Environmental Innovation and Societal Transitions*, 34, pp. 76–79.

Lundvall, B. A. (1992). *National Systems of Innovation: Towards a Theory of Innovation and Interactive Learning*. Pinter Publishers.

Maskell, P., & Malmberg, A. (1999). The Competitiveness of Firms and Regions: 'Ubiquitification' and the Importance of Localized Learning. *European Urban and Regional Studies*, 6(1), pp. 9–25.

Mróz, A., Komorowski, Ł., Wolański, M., Stawicki, M., Kozłowska, P., & Stanny, M. (2022). The Impact of Territorial Capital on Cohesion Policy in Rural Polish Areas. *Regional Studies*, pp. 1–14. http://doi.org/10.1080/00343404. 2022.2091774.

Nelson, R. R. (Ed.) (1993). *National Innovation Systems: A Comparative Analysis*. Oxford University Press on Demand.

Nelson, R. R. (1993). A Retrospective. In Nelson, R. R. (Ed.), *National Innovation Systems. A Comparative Analysis* (pp. 3–21). New York: Oxford University Press.

Patel, P., & Pavitt, K. (1994). National Innovation Systems: Why They Are Important, and How They Might Be Measured and Compared. *Economics of Innovation and New Technology*, 3(1), pp. 77–95. http://doi.org/10.1080/10438599400000004.

Tödtling, F., & Trippl, M. (2005). One Size Fits All?: Towards a Differentiated Regional Innovation Policy Approach. *Research Policy*, 34(8), pp. 1203–1219.

Warnke, P., Koschatzky, K., Dönitz, E., Zenker, A., Stahlecker, T., Som, O., ... & Güth, S. (2016). *Opening Up the Innovation System Framework towards New Actors and Institutions* (No. 49). Fraunhofer ISI Discussion Papers-Innovation Systems and Policy Analysis.

3 Resilience and collaboration of smart organizations

The role of institutions in times of uncertainty

II.1 Smart organization in times of uncertainty

The economies of the European countries are marked by numerous crises and uncertainty that has crept into many areas of social life. Difficult times, instead of slowing down development processes, have become a stimulus to increase activity in searching for new paths of development. Increasingly, attention is paid to the need to build resilience in many aspects of the functioning of socio-economic systems. Smart solutions may prove necessary in this process. Smart organization uses information and innovation management skills. It creates a modern architecture of social and institutional networks in order to efficiently communicate with the environment in order to acquire knowledge. Diffusion, absorption, and creation of knowledge become the key processes that determine sustainable development and determine the competitive advantages of smart local governments. The uniqueness of such systems lies in the mechanisms of reacting to the changing environment and the effective creation of innovative solutions. The response of smart organizations to emerging shocks and changes is new solutions that prove the resilience of the local economy and the ability to build sustainable development. Therefore, it is important that smart organizations are rooted in local and regional innovation systems with strong institutional structures and become active participants in these systems. That they collectively learned to respond to changes in the environment and made use of strategic flows of knowledge aimed at emerging shocks and threats. Therefore, the following questions arise: what builds the resilience of smart organizations in the context of innovation systems? Which mechanisms of innovation systems are responsible for it?

The concept of resistance can be defined in two ways, depending on the interpretation of the reference point to which the changes are compared. The first approach determines that a territory's resilience to shocks is a measure of its ability to recover. The weakness of this approach is that it does not take into account the natural evolution of economies and the changes taking place in the local, national, and global environment. Social and economic processes, which are the point of reference, do not stop or

DOI: 10.4324/9781003265870-9

weaken, which means that returning to the starting point will not be a positive phenomenon. Hence, many authors have started to attribute resilience to an evolutionary context that takes the approach that regions are not lonely islands but are immersed in a changing environment (Balland, Rigby & Boschma, 2015). Regions respond to changes in external factors and must adapt to them in order to sustain growth in the long term (Simmie & Martin, 2010).

The resilience of smart organizations can be considered in the context of regional potentials, such as networks, institutions, and the ability to conduct external adaptation and diversification of economic structures (Lee & Hamamoto, 2017). These are the mechanisms that are present in both the concept of resilience, as well as in the concept of regional innovation systems. There are, however, slight differences between them in terms of the direction of action and scope, which, in the author's opinion, are not an obstacle, but rather complement each other, creating more durable and resilient territorial structures.

Resilience is built through the interactions that occur between actors due to geographical proximity, which facilitates the flow of knowledge and information, and the creation of new solutions and innovations. However, not only the existence of entities in the region, but their cooperation within the system is of strategic importance for the supply of knowledge and functioning of smart organizations. The existing deficits in this area may be supplemented by innovation systems. Effective interaction will often be determined by social capital factors, such as trust, openness, the spread of knowledge and staff (Cooke, Uranga & Etxebarria, 1997), and the similarity in social and cultural standards (Maskell & Malmberg, 1999).

In the face of economic shocks and sudden events, institutions play a key role in the region and support smart organizations. It is the institutions that have the ability to promote learning, shape knowledge bases, and change the competence structure of the region (Balland, Rigby & Boschma, 2015). Institutions help to overcome these shocks by mitigating their effects and restoring the efficiency of the system. Institutions give shape and quality to complex systems of regulation and interaction. They use the knowledge and innovation redistribution tool to counteract emerging disruptions and to remedy their effects, as well as reduce their impact on local systems.

The resilience of smart organizations in a given region depends not only on the institution's ability to introduce changes and exert influence on external organizations in the region, but also on the ability to introduce changes in the institutions themselves (Davis, 2010). This may seem contrary to the logic of institutions, which by definition ensure the sustainability of processes and are not easily evolving. However, in the event of rapid and radical changes in the economy and functioning of society in uncertain times, institutions must evolve to adapt the existing rules to the new situation, which in the long term should bring tangible results and sustainable development of regions.

Regional innovation systems are created in order to create regional structures for the exchange of knowledge and innovation, as well as to stimulate their flows. They are based on social and institutional networks that can be disrupted by natural or unnatural factors that inhibit cooperation. The role of institutions in the system is to ensure an appropriate level of relations so that entities can cooperate sufficiently and effectively in order to achieve the maximum level of system innovation. The presence of institutions in regional innovation systems supports the processes of interaction between system actors for effective cooperation (Sweeney, 1995).

Institutions responsible for innovation processes at the regional level are institutions whose activities result in creating a learning environment, diffusion of knowledge, supporting production activities, and providing financial security for projects (Cooke, Uranga & Etxebarria, 1977). Most often, researchers in the group of these institutions mention universities, research-development and research institutes, consultants, training centers, and chambers of commerce (Cooke, 2001; Doloreux & Parto, 2005).

The presence of many actors in the region who cooperate with each other and exchange knowledge requires solid social grounding and building relationships based on trust. Institutions with rules and policies have the ability to promote trust. They guarantee the durability and reliability of cooperation, reducing the uncertainty that often accompanies projects in which many actors are involved (Doloreux & Parto, 2005).

The cooperation structures created by institutions within the framework of regional innovation systems are at the same time a support for smart organizations and help to organize the innovation potential in the region in uncertain times. It is the existence of a culture of cooperation that Porter (1990) recognized as a strong factor guaranteeing the creation of local competitive advantage. The condition for creating cooperation is not only the presence of entities, but also their closeness, which enables interaction. Institutions are therefore responsible for the efficiency and resilience in creating and implementing innovations in the region, through the cooperation of local governments with each other and with agglomerations with development potential. In practice, the functioning of innovation systems and smart organizations in territorial terms can be traced on the example of the functioning of smart cities, which are more commonly appearing on the map of the European Union.

II.2 Smart cities' location in European Union regions

Worldwide, the population of cities is growing, and it is predicted that by 2030, more than 60% of the world's population will live in cities (United Nations, 2014). Cities play a key role in achieving climate neutrality. They occupy only 4% of the EU's land area but are home to 75% of EU citizens. This figure in Europe is expected to increase to 85% by 2050. Worldwide, cities account for over 65% of energy consumption and over 70% of CO_2 emissions. The objectives of the European Green Deal, which envisages reducing CO2 emissions by 55% by 2030 and then transforming Europe into the first climate-neutral continent by 2050, will be impossible to achieve without coordinated modernization efforts and technological and social transformation of cities (European Commission, 2021).

Cities are also considered as hubs of innovation that drive the world's economic development (Currid, 2006). They are the dynamic heart of the regions that typically generate the highest income. Losing control of a dynamically developing urban economy may have a negative impact on the environment and its inhabitants (Annez & Buckley, 2008). The European Union has recognized that the projected growth of cities is a challenge for sustainable development and has adopted the direction – Mission on Climate-Neutral and Smart Cities.

The quality of life of citizens and the effectiveness of actions taken in cities will depend on the spatial planning policy, waste management, and local energy solutions (Degbelo et al., 2016).

The combination of new smart technological solutions with social sensitivity and attitude to care for the natural environment contributed to the formulation of the concept of intelligently sustainable cities (Ahvenniemi, Huovila, Pinto-Seppa & Airaksinen, 2017). A smart sustainable city is an innovative city that uses information and communication technologies (ICT) and other means to improve the quality of life, efficiency of operation and urban services and competitiveness, while ensuring that it meets the needs of present and future generations with regard to economic, social, environmental, and cultural aspects (UNECE, 2015).

Improving the living conditions in cities is a multifaceted challenge that requires a holistic view of urban space, examining its sustainable development and the effectiveness of actions taken in various dimensions.

Researchers and various organizations provide a lot of research and analysis that allows you to create smart city rankings. They serve as planning and evaluation tools for politicians, city officials, and town planners to compare different alternative projects and policies (Akande, Cabral, Gomes & Casteleyn, 2019). They help understand how the processes of globalization and urbanization are changing cities (Grant & Chuang, 2012). They create a knowledge base and a set of good practices on how cities have dealt with different dimensions of sustainability compared to other cities. They help identify deficits and problem areas requiring intervention.

For the purposes of the study, an attempt was made to map smart cities in the EU. This required adopting a procedure for selecting cities that can be considered smart. In the mapping process, it was decided to use the city ranking (Smart City Index Report, 2021), developed by the International

Institute for Management Development (IMD). The Smart Cities Index is a holistic attempt to capture the various dimensions of how the implemented smart solutions contribute to the development of cities in five areas: health and safety, mobility, conditions for spending free time (activities), opportunities for learning and employment, and quality in public authorities (governance). It is, above all, a grassroots view of citizens on their city, where they live and work. The index is structured to provide a realistic view of cities under the assumption that not all cities start at the same level of development, nor with the same potential for the development of smart organizations. In this context, "smart city" is defined as an urban environment that applies technology to increase the benefits and reduce the shortcomings of urbanization for its citizens. The indexes were determined for 118 cities in the world, and in each of them an interview with 120 residents was conducted. For the purposes of the comparative analysis, examples of 43 EU cities were used (Table II.8). In the geographical context, they show a strong concentration in selected European countries, such as Great Britain (six cities), Germany (five cities), Spain (four cities), France (four cities) and relatively smaller in terms of area and demographics, such as Switzerland (three cities) and the Netherlands (three cities). The highest-rated cities are Zurich in Switzerland (AA), Oslo in Norway

Table II.8 Regional potential and smart city location. Own work

Types of regions		Smart cities	
Typology	Number of regions	Cities	Number of cities
Type 1	43	Newcastle (BBB), Leeds (BBB), Manchester (BBB), Bordeaux (BB), Lyon (BB), Glasgow (BB), Birmingham (BB)	7
Type 2	70	Dusseldorf (BBB), Hanover (BB), Kiel (BB), Bologna (CCC), Athens (C), Rome (C)	6
Type 3	43	Zurich (AA), Oslo (AA), Lausanne (A), Helsinki (A), Copenhagen (A), Geneva (A), Bilbao (BBB), Vienna (BBB), Amsterdam (BBB), London (BBB), The Hague (BBB), Stockholm (BBB), Rotterdam (BBB), Madrid (BB), Hamburg (BB), Gothenburg (BB), Dublin (BB), Berlin (BB), Brussels (BB), Barcelona (B), Paris (B), Warsaw (CCC), Prague (CCC), Lisbon (CC), Bratislava (CC), Budapest (CC)	26
Type 4	84	Zaragoza (BBB), Lille (BB), Krakow (CCC), Sofia (C)	4

(AA), Lausanne (A), Helsinki in Finland (A), Copenhagen in Denmark (A), and Geneva in Switzerland (A).

Geolocalization of smart cities shows a relationship with the regional potentials identified earlier in the study (Figure II.7). According to the ranking, as many as 26 highly rated smart cities are located in type 3 with the highest potentials (Table II.8). This is, of course, a simple observation that does not reveal the exact mechanisms of this relationship. In the light of previous theoretical assumptions, an attempt can be made to explain this phenomenon. The creation of smart cities is influenced by the multi-dimensional institutional environment and the mechanism of influencing each other not only by technological capitals, but also social aspects related to the preparation of inhabitants for new technologies and the willingness to learn about them and use them in everyday life. This suggests that other regions that want to participate in the implementation of smart solutions will have to overcome not only technological barriers but also social ones. Mental changes of the inhabitants will in many cases be a serious challenge for local authorities responsible for implementing the smart strategy. Zurich, as one of the cities with the highest scores in this ranking, emphasizes in its strategy that "smart" means connecting people, organizations, and infrastructure. Effective city management is determined by dialogue and communication between the city administration and its inhabitants. This leads to joint city management and the creation of grass-roots initiatives in the form of civic budgets, strengthening participation, and direct democracy. This is what appears to be the main challenge in the coming years of digital transformation.

In order to investigate the resilience of cities in uncertain times, changes in the ranking of smart cities were compared to the regional potentials of smart organizations. Changes in the ranking were set for the years 2020–2021. Changes in the positions of cities in the ranking were compared to the synthetic indicator of potentials, which was calculated as the average of the standardized values of individual indicators included in the study (Table II.8).

The summary of the obtained results shows a group of cities whose position in the ranking has not changed or has changed to a small extent, namely, Oslo, Helsinki, Zurich, Copenhagen, London, and Stockholm. The above-mentioned cities also have the highest potential values. We can therefore conclude that equipping regions with potentials for smart organizations has contributed to the sustainability and resilience of these cities. It also proves effective decisions and skillful use of these potentials for the development of smart organizations. The highest-rated cities are those from the Scandinavian region of Northern Europe. Stockholm, Oslo, Helsinki, and Copenhagen have very strong environmental policies and focus on improving the quality of life of their citizens (Lindström & Eriksson, 1993).

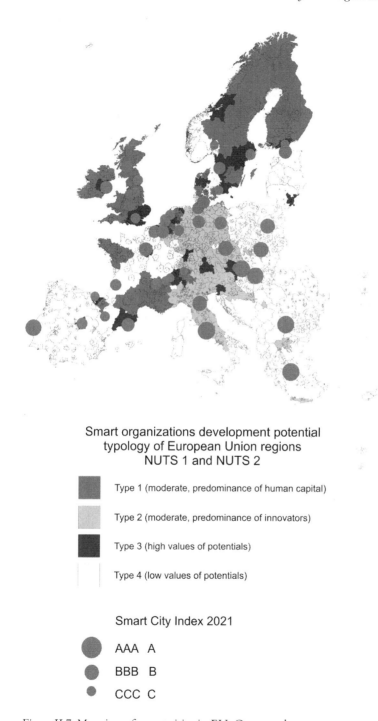

Figure II.7 Mapping of smart cities in EU. Own work.

The comparison also shows a certain regularity, namely, that the lower the potential of the regions, the greater the spread in the change in the ranking of cities. The comparison was revealed by six Eastern European cities: Sofia, Krakow, Warsaw, Bratislava, Budapest, and Prague, which recorded the highest decrease in the ranking (Figure II.8). Similar observations can be found in the works of the European Union, in which, thanks to comparative analyzes, disproportions in development between Western and Eastern European cities were observed (European Commission, 2014).

These cities belonged to the former Communist Bloc and are an example of dependence on the development path, shaped by the model of centrally planned economy. In this model, the primacy of the industrialization policy and the development of heavy industry was clearly visible, even at the expense of the natural environment and human health (Serbanica & Constantin, 2017). In Central and Eastern Europe, the collapse of the communist regime initiated profound changes in the sphere of production and the restructuring of the industry toward the servicisation of the economy (Hamilton, Dimitrowska-Andrews & Pichler-Milanovic, 2005). New economic processes contributed to a change in urban spaces. The increase in entrepreneurship and the wealth of citizens, as well as the increase in the number of vehicles owned, resulted in changes in the use of urban areas, increasing the area of roads and parking lots at the expense

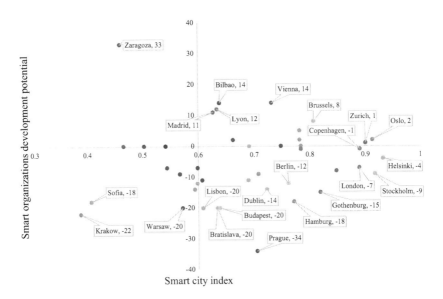

Figure II.8 Smart city development and the potential for smart organizations. Own work.[a] Own work.

[a]Comparison of the change in the smart city ranking in relation to the development potential of smart organizations. For the purpose of comparison, a synthetic index of the region's potential for smart organizations was calculated as an average of standardized index values.

of green areas. The form of use of premises also changed, and they were more and more often turned into shops, eateries, and entertainment venues (Hirt & Stanilov, 2009).

The three cities of Bilbao, Zaragosa, and Vienna deserve special attention due to the dynamic growth in the ranking position with significantly different potential.

Bilbao, a city in Spain, has gained world recognition for its economic regeneration known as the "Bilbao Effect" (Patterson, 2022; Wouters, 2022). In the 1980s, the city experienced an economic downturn that was the result of a significant reduction in shipbuilding, a dramatic flooding in the historic city center, and high levels of pollution. In order to counteract the negative effects of these events, a number of actions were taken, which included a system-wide urban planning strategy, housing programs, vocational training programs, the use of local culture, the banking system, and a long history of technical ingenuity and Basque determination. The results of the interventions and the decisions made were later referred to as the "Bilbao Effect". The city has seen its unemployment rate drop to one of the lowest in Spain. New businesses have sprung up in the city center, including offices, research firms, and retailers. Tourism has grown more than tenfold, and the city has regularly hosted national and international conferences. The smart growth of the city made the Basque Region once again the main source of economic growth in Spain. The effectiveness of these activities was awarded the European City of the Year award in 2018.

On the other hand, another historic Spanish city of Zaragoza, despite its low development potential, is an example of using social potential and implementing the strategy of a culture of involvement and participation of citizens in local development. Its example shows the shift from a technology-driven smart city vision to a citizen-centered vision and citizen-driven innovation. In 2012, with the new Saragossa Open Government Strategy (Ayuntamiento, 2012), the city began the process of involving citizens in the city's innovation system. Zaragoza's performance in terms of urban innovation was recognized in 2017, when the city received the European Digital Green Card (GDC) award for citizen participation and impact on society.

Vienna is an example of a city that, since 2014, has been holistically implementing a smart strategy in three main categories: quality of life, resource efficiency, and innovation (Fernandez-Anez, Fernández-Güell & Giffinger, 2018). It involves stakeholders from different city departments and various experts in the city. Most digital technology initiatives are very well suited to short, medium, and long-term goals. At the same time, the initiatives involve sponsors and pilot programs that strengthen the city and the economy. The implementation of the strategy is the responsibility of a specially established Smart City Agency, which employs experts who have technical and social competences, as well as competences that allow coordinating the divergent interests of the city, the government, and service providers.

Finally, it should be noted that the comparison of the results of changes in the ranking of cities with their regional potential for the development of integral organizations shows the scale of mismatches and development gaps. This means that not all cities fully use the regional potential, and the scale of their development toward smart has not fully developed and requires appropriate interventions. The region as a territory should activate endogenous development processes based on the flow of knowledge and innovation. Relations, the development of social participation and citizens as innovators should be the basic mechanism. Another problem is the very scale of regional potentials, which does not maintain spatial cohesion. There are large disproportions of conditions between regions, which favor development trends. There is a problem of how to raise the regional potential, with what investments and tools. Another solution may be the development of cooperation between regions and local governments within the framework of integrated programs and territorial investments. This requires a change in institutional capital and a shift to new rules for building relations between cities and regions. The diffusion of knowledge and smart potentials may become a key challenge in the policy of sustainable development.

II.3 The importance of institutions in shaping a smart organization

The main function of an institution is to shape the communication process and regulate relations between people and groups of people within organizations, as well as between organizations and beyond. The measurable benefit of communication and obtaining information is making rational decisions relative to the level of knowledge. The institutional structure influences the internal and external system of communication and interaction of smart organizations. The development of smart city results from, inter alia, interactive learning processes and the implementation of innovations, which are conditioned by the institutional structure.

Links between smart organizations and institutions are frequent and exist at many levels. They exist at the level inside the local government (city, municipality), where institutions influence the relations between employees of various organizational units and departments, e.g. strategic and spatial planning, education, municipal waste, investments, social welfare, culture, and sports. These are relationships that are created by formal and informal networks and have a strong impact on the implementation of smart solutions to the city or commune management system.

There are also relations at the external level within the administrative boundaries of the city or commune. They occur between public organizations, schools, community centers, social welfare centers, road, and communication authorities, as well as residents and social organizations.

At this level, of a great importance are the principles and rules according to which we deal with a feedback mechanism of residents' reactions to innovative social programs, new communication technologies, the social infrastructure being created, the creation of green space, and communication and energy solutions. This level binds the public space functionally, creating a socio-economic system with the natural environment. It is at this level that the effects of sustainable development of cities or municipalities are often measured.

The higher level is regional systems that require organizational order and efficient methods of creating integrated activities between local government units. It is at this level that cities and municipalities conclude agreements, creating joint projects across administrative divisions. Due to the fact that regions are equipped with endogenous scientific and research potential, it is at this level that one can influence the creation of innovations. This is the effect of the synergy of the potentials of the science, business, and public administration sectors that are present in the region. The relations between them are the result of social entrenchment and the institutional framework strengthened by the policy of innovation development, as well as the policy of smart development and implementation of digital technologies. Regional mechanisms of creating and diffusing innovation make it possible to understand how local governments located peripherally in relation to large economic centers can benefit from the transfer of knowledge and innovation. In the regions, it is precisely the networks of cooperation and communication in the context of smart development that are shaped by the institutional structure and achieve a territorial dimension.

In order to better understand the role of institutions in the development and functioning of smart organizations, we can describe the process of sustainable development of cities and municipalities in the context of various specific functions of institutions. Referring to literature sources, we can list three such functions (Edquist & Johnson, 2005):

- reducing uncertainty by providing information,
- conflict management and cooperation, and
- providing incentives.

They are general in nature, however, later in this chapter, they will be presented in the context of their specific roles in relation to smart organizations. It is especially worth noting that institutions decide about the distribution and use of potentials for smart sustainable development. Institutions can also generate barriers or support smart organizations.

II.3.1 *Institutions provide information and reduce uncertainty*

Public organizations that operate in a complex and constantly changing environment are looking for opportunities to reduce the uncertainty that appears in relations with residents and other organizations. Uncertainty is reduced by providing information or reducing the amount of information needed. Examples include popularity polls, contests, or voting opportunities organized by local authorities through internet websites as an expression of local democracy. On the other hand, an example of limiting the need to obtain information is the possibility of using ready-made databases describing residents, in which various information is collected by means of specific rules and regulations. Communication systems and the rules governing them provide the necessary knowledge in the decision-making process, reduce the information burden and, relative to the acquired knowledge, affect the rationality of decisions made.

Another example of the role of institutions in the development of smart organizations is support for the design and implementation of innovations, which is associated with a high level of uncertainty and the need to launch venture capital. Institutions appear in the field of research and universities, the effects of which are also known in crisis situations, as exemplified by the work on the COVID-19 vaccine. Many innovative solutions from the world of science power the technological potential of smart cities. That is why it is so important for the scientific community to cooperate with the regional self-government environment and provide support in creating practical solutions for smart local governments. This is favored by political solutions, the tools of which are programs that finance not only basic research but also implementation projects based on cooperation between science and business practice.

Another issue is the creation of solutions in the field of technological safety, both in the area of service support, as well as the supply of components and the production of devices. Without security and technological sovereignty, current and future projects in the area of smart cities and municipalities will be threatened by the lack of continuity and lack of maintenance of the required level of infrastructure. Therefore, institutions support both human capital in the field of IT specialists, as well as uninterrupted access to technology and components. It is a strategic goal of national and European Union scope and is more and more often reflected in the created development policies.

Smart organizations that use innovation also need a range of patent and intellectual property rights solutions and regulations to help reduce uncertainty about appropriation. This applies to innovations in the field of communication devices, as well as the software of these devices, utility applications, and business processes. These are all elements that distinguish smart organizations and are used in smart cities and smart villages.

Institutions also become a guarantor of energy security and support the implementation of solutions in the field of renewable energy and the principles and regulations of energy conservation in public spaces. This is closely related to the sustainable development policy, the fight against smog in large cities and the reduction of exhaust gas and CO_2 emissions. Green cities are a vision in which a balance is sought between social and economic needs and care for the condition of the natural environment and the health of residents. It should be noted that in the case of local governments, it is difficult to find universal solutions for the energy system. Therefore, when making decisions about the choice of diversification of energy sources, local authorities must take into account the differences in the development and population density of urban and rural spaces. The local and regional energy, solar, wind, biomass, and geothermal potentials are also important.

The processes of change that we observe in the area of digital technologies development and their implementation into smart organizations in the public sector are a big challenge. As the examples above show, technologies become useful when they are applied in everyday life, improve the quality of this life and, most importantly, are accepted and adopted by the society. Therefore, in the entire process of transformation to the digital economy, institutions will play a key role as a regulator and guarantor of the correctness of this process.

II.3.2 Institutions manage conflicts and cooperation

Institutions introduce an important element to the processes of sustainable development related to conflict management and building relationships in the area of cooperation between individuals and groups. It can even be assumed that without the institutions regulating conflicts, the survival of many social forms would be difficult and even impossible. Conflicts that we observe at various organizational levels of society, ranging from production organizations, local governments, and the state, mean that the lack of cooperation translates into poor functioning of the economy, economic and energy crises, and negative changes in the natural environment. In the case of smart organizations in local governments, conflicts may arise in both internal relations of the organization as well as relations with the environment.

For example, in the city hall, the communication system and established patterns of cooperation between the departments of strategy and development, education, transport, waste management, social affairs, and investment and promotion, which usually participate in the implementation of smart solutions and technologies, are disrupted by conflicts and lack of trust. The department responsible for development and strategies may be more focused on the long-term effects of sustainable development and less focused on the current costs and problems of the city's functioning and social infrastructure management. In the department of social affairs, they may be more oriented toward the needs of residents and less on investment capacity, fundraising, and energy management. On the other hand, external conflicts arise as a result of poor communication between local authorities and residents and entrepreneurs. The scale and frequency of such hidden conflicts are largely the result of the adopted norms and rules of cooperation, management style and informal rules of behavior in the workplace, and other institutional factors.

Conflicts and resistance also arise in the process of implementing innovations and new digital technologies. The process of users' adaptation to new forms of work requires modernization efforts, increased activity, and training and learning how to use devices. This applies to both public administration employees and residents who contact and send documents via websites and applications.

Digital modernization and the development of smart solutions in organizations is a phenomenon that currently affects the entire socio-economic system. We see it both in the manufacturing and public sectors, as well as in the homes of urban and rural residents. Digital transformation is changing the distribution of economic forces. Companies in the IT sector are developing dynamically, while other sectors remain stagnant or collapse. The change caused by the introduction of new technologies is changing economic structures, especially where algorithms and smart solutions replace traditional areas of services or production. It also changes consumer behavior and creates new markets. The possibilities of digital data storage have changed, for example, the music market. With the advent of new formats for storing music files on computer hard disks, mobile phones, or in the data cloud, sales of traditional analog discs and CDs have dropped significantly. The situation is similar in the bookstore market, where traditional paper printing has been replaced with digital text. These are just some examples of the transformation that has taken place in recent years and has contributed to radical changes in access to information and its possible use in everyday life. The costs of these changes burden the society, which is often associated with dissatisfaction, frustration, and aversion to new technologies.

The old order changes, new rules of life emerge, and old skills and competences become obsolete. The restructuring of the economy also affects some professional groups, the decline in their income and the inability to find employment. The social inequalities that arise as a result of these changes can provoke opposition and conflict. The role of institutions in such a situation is to provide regulations and social security, in particular guarantees of access to education and training, which will allow them to adapt to the changing conditions of work and social life. Institutions, including local governments, become responsible for the nature and scale of such conflicts and for reducing resistance to change. Local and regional self-governments, which through institutional structures effectively manage the costs of these changes and create support systems, also support the fast pace of implementation and development of smart cities and villages.

II.3.3 Institutions provide incentives

Smart organizations in local governments will not function efficiently without a smart environment and an appropriate level of implementation of new technologies. This means that for the process of communication and information exchange to run smoothly, all participants of the local system, including entrepreneurs, residents, and non-governmental organizations, must be active users of local information networks. However, it requires many changes and incentives so that both employees employed in organizations and inhabitants of towns and villages want to make the effort to modernize and start using new technologies.

In the organizational environment of self-government, incentives among employees may appear as salaries and wages, a reward system, and incentives may arise through the creation of a friendly atmosphere and appropriate conditions. First of all, it is important to understand and accept the failures and difficulties in acquiring new knowledge by employees. Additionally, incentives can support engagement in learning and competence development.

Smart solutions increase the competitiveness of local governments in many areas of their operation. There are migrations in the world to cities that are not only characterized by the highest economic results but are also certified as cities with the highest standard and quality of life. The current migration movements show that the disproportions in the distribution of the population are deepening in favor of large urban agglomerations, while peripheral areas, as well as medium and small towns, especially rural areas with a predominant agricultural function, are emptying. Smart cities, due to the solutions they apply in the area of sustainable development and care for the quality of life of residents, record a rapid population growth.

The implementation of new solutions and technologies is also associated with risk. This is especially taken into account and calculated in decision-making processes by local government leaders responsible for sustainable development programs. Investments related to the implementation of emission-free transport, city bikes, electric buses, modern energy systems, transport and communication systems, and utility applications are cost-intensive and require good budget management and local government finances. With many investments and unexpected crises that have recently occurred in the global economy, there is a real threat of loss of financial liquidity and an increase in excessive indebtedness of local governments.

Another threat is the lack of technological sovereignty associated with the technologies being introduced. Smart organizations may be exposed to the loss of constant supplies of components and technological services, as shown by the recent pandemic and war crises. This applies to the rules of foreign trade, the situation of dependence on external technology suppliers from other countries outside the European Union. Other sources of risk may be software failures and errors, incompatibility, and common standards. Risk may also be caused by the lack of energy sovereignty, low diversification of energy sources, and a low share of renewable energy sources, which can cause blackouts. All this means that risk aversion will hinder the creation of radical strategies for the development of smart organizations in local governments and the implementation of the smart concept in cities and rural areas.

Institutions will more and more often create incentives for territorial projects, because collective actions of local governments can benefit from communication, cooperation and jointly coping with challenges, creating integrated investments in the area of their functionality. These incentives can be created by cooperation standards, learning practices, access to territorial information, etc., and by incentives in the form of financing joint territorial projects and investments.

In the case of managing regional funds and using tools to stimulate development in the region, a conflict may arise due to individual incentives for only selected local governments while omitting the others. This situation can harm trust and the sharing of information and knowledge. This will have a negative impact on the implementation of joint projects based on mutual trust and willingness to cooperate.

II.3.4 Institutions direct their resources to the development of smart technologies

Institutions influence not only the process in which smart organizations are created, but also decide on the amount of resources allocated for development in the context of creating innovations and technologies used in smart local governments. It should be noted that the innovation and development policy of individual countries is highly diversified. There are countries that allocate more resources to research and development than others, and also in regions, some companies hold a greater share of spending on development and innovation in their turnover than others. Decisions to fund R&D investments can take many forms. The best-recognized factor in this matter is grants and expenditure on programs aimed at both research and scientific institutions, as well as directly at enterprises. The scale and direction of financing depend on the policy at the European Union level, as well as on the national policies of individual countries. For this reason, the allocation of resources for the development of smart solutions takes place to some extent as a result of well-thought-out decisions made by politicians in the form of government support for specific programs. However, also in this case it is important to make a diagnosis and to recognize the conditions well, so that the allocation of resources is not random.

The sustainability policy tool is largely supported by research and development focused on smart solutions. This is done through formal institutions such as tax regulations and government subsidies. There are also informal norms and traditions of government involvement at national and regional levels in allocating resources to universities, research institutes, libraries, and other organizations involved in learning and knowledge transfer.

The informal nature of resource distribution may also be determined by the current discourse in the development of soft theories that explain the functioning mechanisms of modern economies. In these considerations, the role of society is particularly emphasized, which in response to constant changes in the environment must be an information society. The competitive advantages of such communities consist in the ability to build knowledge capital through a flexible approach to re-education and acquiring new knowledge adequate to the digital revolution.

II.4 Summary

We have already emphasized that innovative activities are uncertain and threatened with conflicts, therefore they need strong institutional support and guarantees thanks to which they can be financed and implemented into the economy. Institutions, as entities, introduce stability and guarantees into the socio-economic system, which may, however, in some cases lead to a lack of flexibility in relation to changes in the economy caused by digital transformation and implementation of smart solutions. As we have already shown in Figure II.1, institutional changes take time and are slow, which may result in them lagging behind technical changes. In the case of local governments, such concerns may relate to changes in community touting and adaptation to new rules and the acquisition of digital skills.

Problems of administrative employees and residents with adaptation and mismatch to the new situation may affect the development of smart organizations in local governments. In this case, the emergence of new technologies is insufficient, as institutional barriers that prevent the implementation of innovative solutions may appear. What is needed are changes in everyday habits, rules, and the development of skills and competences, which in turn triggers the need to create a system of promotion and training, as well as rules and regulations. It is clear that institutions cannot change constantly as this will be contrary to the role they should play. Therefore, it can be assumed that their durability may be a certain threat, a hindrance to introducing changes toward a smart digital economy. However, the institutions will have to evolve and adapt the rules to the new situation as much as possible. Nevertheless, the history of civilization shows that institutions are changing and, after these changes, they are still the entities responsible for stable patterns of behavior in communities. Thus, if we look at the institutional potential and its role in the development of smart organizations in this way, we must recognize that institutions can both have a supportive influence and be a barrier to introduced changes.

Individual countries in the EU and in the world, through their historical, social, cultural, and organizational conditions, achieve different effects in striving for a balance between social and economic stabilization and the need to introduce changes. In shaping the development policy based on smart solutions and digital technologies, it should be borne in mind that there will be tensions between radical changes in the field of digital technologies, green energy, and the institutional structure, which may lead to temporary economic stagnation. This situation will continue until new institutions and institutional changes introduce regulations between digital institutions and technologies that contribute to the goal of sustainable development.

Thus, what is the relationship between institutions, smart organizations, and sustainable development? The analysis and the arguments provided show that the economy's ability for sustainable development depends on its ability to generate technological changes based on innovation, digital, and energy, while meeting the condition of adapting and renewing institutions based on social innovations that support this development.

References

Ahvenniemi, H., Huovila, A., Pinto-Seppa, I., & Airaksinen, M. (2017). What Are the Differences between Sustainable and Smart Cities? *Cities*, 60, pp. 234–245. https://doi.org/10.1016/j.cities.2016.09.009.

Akande, A., Cabral, P., Gomes, P., & Casteleyn, S. (2019). The Lisbon Ranking for Smart Sustainable Cities in Europe. *Sustainable Cities and Society*, 44, pp. 475–487.

Annez, P. C., & Buckley, R. M. (2008). *Urbanization and Growth: Setting the Context*. https://doi.org/10.1596/978-0-8213-7573-0.

Ayuntamiento, Z. (2012). *Open Government Strategy in the Digital City 2012–2015* Received from: https://www.zaragoza.es/contenidos/sectores/tecnologia/Estrategia-Ciencia-Tecnologia-en.pdf.

Balland, P. A., Rigby, D., & Boschma, R. (2015). The Technological Resilience of US Cities. *Cambridge Journal of Regions, Economy and Society*, 8(2), pp. 167–184.

Cooke, P. (2001). Regional Innovation Systems, Clusters, and the Knowledge Economy. *Industrial and Corporate Change*, 10(4), pp. 945–974.

Cooke, P., Uranga, M. G., & Etxebarria, G. (1997). Regional Innovation Systems: Institutional and Organisational Dimensions. *Research Policy*, 26(4–5), pp. 475–491.

Currid, E. (2006). New York as a Global Creative Hub: A Competitive Analysis of Four Theories on World Cities. *Economic Development Quarterly*, 20(4), pp. 330–350. https://doi.org/10.1177/0891242406292708.

Davis, L. S. (2010). Institutional Flexibility and Economic Growth. *Journal of Comparative Economics*, 38(3), pp. 306–320.

Degbelo, A., Granell, C., Trilles Oliver, S., Bhattacharya, D., Casteleyn, S., & Kray, C. (2016). Opening Up Smart Cities: Citizen-Centric Challenges and Opportunities from GIScience. *ISPRS International Journal of Geo-Information*, 5(2), p. 16. https://doi.org/10.3390/ijgi5020016.

Doloreux, D., & Parto, S. (2005). Regional Innovation Systems: Current Discourse and Unresolved Issues. *Technology in Society*, 27(2), pp. 33–153.

Edquist, C., & Johnson, B. (2005). Institutions and Organisations in Systems of Innovation. In Edquist, C. (ed.), *Systems of Innovation: Growth, Competitiveness and Employment* (pp. 41–60). Edward Elgar Publishing.

European Commission (2014). *The Urban Dimension of EU Policies – Key Features of an EU Urban Agenda, 12.* Retrieved from: https://www.housingeurope.eu/file/203/download.

European Commission (2021). *European Missions: 100 Climate-Neutral and Smart Cities by 2030. Info Kit for Cities.* Received from: https://ec.europa.eu/info/sites/default/files/research_and_innovation/funding/documents/ec_rtd_eu-mission-climate-neutral-cities-infokit.pdf (accessed on 18.11.2021).

Fernandez-Anez, V., Fernández-Güell, J. M., & Giffinger, R. (2018). Smart City Implementation and Discourses: An Integrated Conceptual Model. The Case of Vienna. *Cities*, 78, pp. 4–16.

Grant, K. A., & Chuang, S. (2012). An Aggregating Approach to Ranking Cities for Knowledge-Based Development. *International Journal of Knowledge-Based Development*, 3(1), 17. https://doi.org/10.1504/IJKBD.2012.045558.

Hamilton, F. E. I., Dimitrowska-Andrews, K., & Pichler-Milanovic, N. (2005). Introduction. In Hamilton, F. E. I., Dimitrowska-Andrews, K., & Pichler-Milanovic, N. (Eds.), *Transformation of Cities in Central and Eastern Europe: Towards Globalization.* The United Nations University Press.

Hirt, S., & Stanilov, K. (2009). Twenty Years of Transition: The Evolution of Urban Planning in Eastern Europe and the Former Soviet Union 1989–2009. *Human Settlements Global Dialogue* Series, No. 5. Retrieved from: https://unhabitat.org/sites/default/files/download-manager-files/Twenty%20Years%20of%20Transition%20The%20Evolution%20of%20Urban%20Planning%20in%20Eastern%20Europe%20and%20the%20Former%20Soviet%20Union,%201989-2009.pdf

Lee, P. C., & Hamamoto, R. (2017). The Role of Resilience in Regional Innovation System. In *2017 Portland International Conference on Management of Engineering and Technology (PICMET).* IEEE.

Lindström, B., & Eriksson, B. (1993). Quality of Life among Children in the Nordic Countries. *Quality of Life Research*, 2(1), pp. 23–32. https://doi.org/10.1007/BF00642886.

Maskell, P., & Malmberg, A. (1999). Localised Learning and Industrial Competitiveness. *Cambridge Journal of Economics*, 23(2), pp. 167–185.

Patterson, M. (2022). Revitalization, Transformation and the 'Bilbao Effect': Testing the Local Area Impact of Iconic Architectural Developments in North America, 2000–2009. *European Planning Studies*, 30(1), pp. 32–49. https://doi.org/10.1080/09654313.2020.1863341.

Porter, M. E. (1990). *The Competitive Advantage of Nations.* The Free Press.

Serbanica, C., & Constantin, D. L. (2017). Sustainable Cities in Central and Eastern European Countries. Moving Towards Smart Specialization. *Habitat International*, 68, pp. 55–63. https://doi.org/10.1016/j.habitatint.2017.03.005.

Simmie, J., & Martin, R. (2010). The Economic Resilience of Regions: Towards an Evolutionary Approach. *Cambridge Journal of Regions, Economy and Society*, 3(1), pp. 27–43.

Smart City Index (2021). The Institute for Management Development; Singapore University for Technology and Design (SUTD): Singapore. Available online:

https://www.imd.org/smart-city-observatory/home/#_smartCity   (accessed on 1.8.2022).

Sweeney, G. (1995). *National Innovation Policy or a Regional Innovation Culture.* Birmingham Business School, Research Centre for Industrial Strategy.

UNECE (2015). *Key Performance Indicators for Smart Sustainable Cities to Assess the Achievement of Sustainable Development Goals, 1603* ITU-T L.1603.

United Nations (2014). *World Urbanization Prospects: The 2014 Revision, Highlights* (ST/ESA/SER.A/352). New York. United States of America. https://doi.org/10.4054/DemRes.2005.12.9.

Wouters, M. (2022). Reinventing Bilbao, the Story of the Bilbao Effect. In Piselli, C., Altan, H., Balaban, O., & Kremer, P. (Ed.), *Innovating Strategies and Solutions for Urban Performance and Regeneration. Advances in Science, Technology & Innovation.* Springer, Cham. https://doi.org/10.1007/978-3-030-98187-7_4.

Part 3

Results achieved by smart organizations in local government units during the Covid-19 pandemic

1 Developmental effects of smart organizations in local government units in the age of digitization

The essence and the basis of the analysis

III.1 The essence of sustainable local development in the age of digitalization

The starting point for considerations regarding the impact of smart organizations in local government units (LGUs) on local development in the era of digitization is determining the way of understanding key phenomena (defining them), and the method of their analysis (metrics, spatial scope, time scope, analyzed dependencies).

Therefore, the first question is: what is the contemporary socio-economic development of regions/areas? The concept of socio-economic development evolves according to the needs of social groups and the ability to satisfy them. Nowadays, regional/local development is most often identified with sustainable development.

The idea of sustainable development of a region in spatial terms is widely known and defined by many institutions and organizations. Sustainable development is a specific compromise between environmental, economic, and social goals that represent the well-being of current and future generations. The economic aspect of sustainable development means not only meeting the needs of today but also securing the resources needed to meet the needs of future generations (man-made natural and physical capitals, as well as intellectual and social capitals). The ecological aspect means setting the limits of the natural system and not exceeding them by human activities, while the social aspect is identified with education and acquiring the ability to solve the most important social problems, as well as participation in the development processes of the whole system (Cegis, Ramanauskiene & Martinkus, 2009).

According to Hawkes, instead of the traditional three (environmental, social, economic), there can be distinguished four elements: cultural vitality, social equity, environmental responsibility, and economic viability (Hawkes, 2001). The social factor is therefore represented by selected elements of social life. Nevertheless, this approach omits many important demographic problems, which are, especially nowadays, exacerbated by the migratory movements of the population, aging, and the feeling of loneliness in the modern world.

DOI: 10.4324/9781003265870-11

In the contemporary approach to the essence of sustainable development, there is often a lack of reference to the specificity of development in the conditions of spontaneous development of high technologies, especially ICT, which revolutionizes life in many regions of the world through the digital revolution and, consequently, brings about the phenomenon of increasingly widespread use of modern communication technologies, but also the negative phenomenon of digital exclusion. Thus, in our opinion, it is appropriate to mention the first proposed definitions in the context of the digitalization of public life that is currently taking place. It is therefore worth indicating that smart regional development is based on the idea of region-specific skills, competences, and knowledge that can lead to new innovations, products, and services (Tennberg, Lempinen & Pirnes, 2020, p. 8).

There are also considerations of smart local development in the context of smart city or metropolitan development. This involves a scale that goes beyond a local unit of government. However, the way the relationship between digitization and the nature of spatial development is perceived is an interesting reference point for the research problem we are addressing.

Smart spatial development is seen as the sustainable, inclusive, and prosperous development of metropolitan areas that promotes a people-centered approach based on three components: a foundation dedicated to the smart development of regions, information and communication technology, and smart institutions and laws. The foundation goes beyond the administrative boundaries of the city and includes the elements of mobility between urban centers that make up the metropolitan region. Therefore, LGUs are considered part of a larger functional whole. Regional foundations, institutions, and laws, as well as ICT, are the pillars of the seven other dimensions of the smart metropolitan region: Infrastructure Development, Environmental Sustainability, Social Development, Social Inclusion, Disaster Exposure, Resilience, and Peace and Security (Vinod Kumar, 2019, p. 246).

In the case of an agricultural region, the process of smartification is linked to the promotion of knowledge transfer and innovation in agriculture, forestry, and rural areas. Other important objectives are the improvement of the livelihood and competitiveness of all types of agriculture in all regions and promotion of innovative agricultural technologies and sustainable forestry.

According to the literature, smart regional development requires smooth and continuous interaction between the SME network and regional communities (Pirnau, Ghiculescu & Marinescu, 2018). This is achieved through the creation of new/regional innovation systems and cluster structures (Triple Helix, Four Clovers or Five for everyone, etc.). The specificity of local communities is also important (Smart Community, Creative Organic Community, etc.).

Smart regions should use innovation in all possible areas by employing the SME network and cluster organizations to create regional and local competitive advantages and support the natural environment.

Another approach to smart regional development is based on the appropriate use of regional resources that are important for the modern economy. It is the approach that promotes knowledge-based development through continuous learning of human resources as an integral part of regional resource development, especially by promoting harmonization between protected and development areas under the national development planning system. This leads to effective and efficient development of the regional economic sector supported by appropriate technologies up to high technology as a result of continuous learning (Sutriadi, 2018).

In examining the smart development paradigm, at least four common elements were found to underlie the various associations with smart development:

First, the centrality of technological innovation and the growing potential of ICT.

Second, the role of networks linking ICT infrastructure with intangible assets is related to knowledge-based innovative services (KIS), knowledge organization, and cultural activities.

Third, the importance of the economic organization of knowledge – especially transferable knowledge – and human capital – including soft skills – in fostering innovation.

Fourth, the bottom-up approach that leverages the vocation of the individual components of the system and the communities involved (Antonelli & Cappiello, 2017, p. 2).

Focusing on sustainability also means recognizing the critical role of the local dimension, understood as a complex of socio-economic relationships based on the relationships between communities, private individuals, and local authorities in policy development.

In the age of digitalization, local development should therefore be more than just sustainable, i.e., meet ecological, economic, and social goals. It should also include the digital dimension, which depends on the communication and information infrastructure, knowledge flows, and technological innovations adopted and developed by all local stakeholders.

III.2 Methodological dilemmas of identification of development effect of smart local units

Modern socio-economic development should be based on smart solutions of complex strategic problems to ensure human functioning, and as such, it requires much more from modern organizations and their environment than just the presence and operation of smart devices, ICT, convergence strategies, and government support. It must be built on a solid foundation of forward-looking soft innovations such as social justice, rule of law, transparency, accountability, coherent collective human wisdom, sustainable development, social cohesion, and shared visions and goals. Against this backdrop, people's knowledge and information become the new currency. People use networks and devices, through human interactions or machine interfaces, to create value by generating massive amounts of data, which are then processed and analyzed (Adamik & Sikora-Fernandez, 2021, p. 4). It is important at all spatial levels of socio-economic development, from the global, through international, national, regional, and local perspectives.

In order to identify the developmental effects of smart local units, it is necessary to clarify the method of their analysis (metrics, spatial scope, time range, considered dependencies). The starting point for measuring the level of economic development should be the definition of its goals and the method of measuring the achieved effects in accordance with the set goals. Starting from the most general goals of sustainable development, one can refer to the most basic document, adopted on September 25, 2015, in New York by a resolution of the United Nations General Assembly. The agenda defines 17 sustainable development goals and 169 targets related to them. The 17 goals include no poverty, no hunger, good health and well-being, quality education, gender equality, clean water and sanitation, affordable and clean energy, decent work and economic growth, industry, innovation and infrastructure, reducing inequality, sustainable cities and communities, responsible consumption and production, climate action, life below water, life on land, peace, justice and strong institutions, and partnerships for goals (United Nations, 2015).

Not all of them should be considered at the regional and local level, not only because of the lower range of competences assigned to these levels, but also because of specific conditions of development, regional identity, and unique features. This diversity of regions translates into different bundles of goals, expressed in development strategies. Haarstad (2017; see Haarstad, 2016) indicates that the issue of sustainable development is poorly represented in EU documents on the smart city policy. Using the example of the Norwegian city of Stavanger, the author shows that the "supposedly ubiquitous smart city discourse" is in fact more specifically constructed depending on actors, policy levels, and context.

Assuming that ecological, economic, and social goals are equally important in accordance with the idea of sustainable development, in order to include the smart component, it may be necessary to indicate technological goals to be achieved, assuming that new technologies are a source of satisfying the needs of regional or local society.

A proposal that meets the holistic approach to measuring the level of socio-economic development in accordance with the realities of the twenty-first century is the DPSIR method (Driving Forces-Pressures-State-Impact-Responses). It was developed in the late 1990s and proposed by the Organization for Economic Co-operation and Development (OECD, 2003) as a means of structuring and organizing environmental indicators in a way that could be understood by policymakers. It is recommended for the assessment of smart and sustainable development, as it includes the assessment of the effects of decisions made by decision-makers.

The DPSIR model defines the relations between various sectors of human activity and the environment as a causal chain of connections and helps to define the interdependencies between them:

1 Driving forces – areas of public life that may have an impact on the environment,
2 Pressure is the level of human impact on the environment,
3 State is the condition of the natural environment in the context of human activity,
4 Impact – the final effect of human long-term impact on the functioning of ecosystems and the consequences for their regeneration capacity, and
5 Response is taking measures to reduce the negative effects of human beings on the environment.

The DPSIR model was developed to show the cause-and-effect relationships between environmental protection and humans. However, it can be used to measure the level of development of smart-sustainable regions. Of key importance is the selection of adequate partial indicators, which, on the one hand, illustrate social, economic, and natural goals, and on the other, allow indicating the degree of achievement of technological goals.

The proposal to measure the level of regional development formulated by Dorel Nicolae Manitiu and Giulio Pedrini (2016) includes proposals for individual components describing specific aspects of sustainable and smart development. The study identifies a set of indicators for the three dimensions of environment, social, and culture. In particular, the multidimensional indicators are able to address short- and long-term aspects in three different areas of the smart city concept. Within each domain, the proposal considers pillars that are critical to achieving smartness and sustainability: demographics, pollution, mobility, health, education, crime, living conditions, and digital services.

The classification broadens and organizes the issues related to measurement presented in Chapter 3 of Part I of the monograph.

The natural component is assessed using the following partial variables belonging to the following groups:

– Driving Force: Rail accessibility; Multimodal accessibility; N. of cars per 1,000 inhabitants; N. of motorcycles per 1,000 inhabitants;
– Pressure: Water consumption (m^3 per annum) per inhabitant; Collected solid waste per inhabitant and year; Price of m^3 of domestic water;

- State: Number of days Pm10 exceeds 50 ug/m^3 per year, Annual average concentration of NO_2, N. of days ozone exceeds 120 pg/m^3 per year; Proportion of solid waste processed by landfill;
- Impact: Mortality rate for people over 65, Mortality rate for people aged 65 and upwards due to heart diseases and respiratory illnesses; Number of deaths in road accidents per 10,000 inhabitants; Number of persons seriously injured in road accidents per 10,000 inhabitants;
- Response: Length of public transport network divided per land area; number of stops of public transport per km^2; Length of public transport network per inhabitant (Antonelli & Cappiello, 2017, p. 160).
- Social factors, in turn, are described by the following partial variables broken down into the following main components:
- Driving Force: Share of population aged 75 and upwards; Demographic dependency; Share of inhabitants aged 0–4, Female to male ratio; non-EU nationals as a share of population; Number of persons per household;
- Pressure: Population change over one year; Population changes over five years; Share of nationals that have moved to the city during the last two years; Share of non-EU Nationals that have moved to the city during the last two years; Share of non-EU Nationals and citizens of a country with a medium or low human development index (HDI); Share of companies gone bankrupt;
- State: Unemployment rate (1999–2002); Share of working age population qualified at level 1 or 2 ISCED endowment (1999–2002); Share of dwellings lacking basic amenities (1999–2002); Share of overcrowded households (1999–2002);
- Impact: Number of recorded crimes per 1,000 inhabitants; Number of domestic burglaries per 1,000 inhabitants; Number of car thefts per 1,000 inhabitants;
- Response: Employment in public administration, health, education; Children 3–4 in day care per 1,000 inhabitants; Children 0–2 in day care per 1,000 inhabitants (Antonelli & Cappiello, 2017, p. 160).
- The cultural indicators, in turn, were constructed from the following variables:
- Driving Force: Share of inhabitants aged 15–64; Share of inhabitants aged 25–34; Share of inhabitants aged 20–24; Share of inhabitants aged 15–64 qualified at tertiary level (ISCED 5–6);
- Pressure: Students in tertiary education per 1,000 inhabitants; Students in higher education (ISCED 5–6) per 1,000 inhabitants aged 20–34; Change in the proportion of inhabitants aged 25–34; Share of female students in higher education (ISCED level 5–6);
- State: Share of employment in trade and restaurant industry; Share of employment in culture and entertainment industry; Share of employment in financial intermediation and business activities;

- Impact: New business registered; Local units providing ICT services per 1,000 companies; Available beds per 1,000 inhabitants;
- Response: Women elected city representatives per 1,000 inhabitants; Libraries per 1,000 inhabitants; Digital services offered by local authorities; Administrative forms that can be submitted electronically (2003–2006); Daily internet visits on the official site (do. 163)

However, this model is very complex and contains many partial variables describing mainly the level of smart city development/region, which does not always translate into developmental effects. With respect to cultural sustainability, the dataset does not include a possible measurement of social capital, which plays a crucial role in the development of a diversified and knowledge-based local economy. This approach also ignores governance issues to some degree. Cultural sustainability measures would need to include indicators of democratic urban pluralism to incorporate this aspect into the DPSIR model.

The problem of data comparability and data availability for different regions is also visible, as the variables included in this summary are not widely available. Moreover, the division of cultural and social factors is blurring, while very narrowly considering the technological factors related to the latest phases of technological development.

Using this method, all the factors influencing a given phenomenon can be mapped, however, their consequences can be assessed to a lesser extent. Too large agglomerates of partial indicators may also cause chaos related to mutually exclusive developmental effects – e.g., economic effects may be achieved at the cost of exceeding the capacity of natural ecosystems.

Therefore, it is sometimes better to use generally available and recognized indicators, such as the HDI, supported by measures describing the level of development of technological entrepreneurship and the quality of life using more extensive indicators than those included in the HDI.

Another issue is determining the spatial scope of the analysis of the impact of a smart organization on the developmental effects of regions/areas. The biggest problem is the selection of spatial units in such a way that they reflect the actually existing spatial structures, i.e., objectively existing regions, and not only statistical regions. Therefore, when considering the links between smart organizations in LGUs and the development of smart-sustainable regions, it is important to capture this phenomenon, based on real structures, if possible.

Hence, on the one hand, it is worth analyzing smart cities as smart economy carriers, and at the same time as statistical units corrected in administrative and statistical division according to management needs. Examples of this include adjustments to the administrative and statistical breakdown or the emergence of public-public partnerships.

Another methodological difficulty is the heterogeneous nature of the spatial development of larger units of local self-government (city or urban complex), due to its fragmented and discontinuous nature. This is visible not only in metropolises but also in regions with a less polarized socio-economic structure. On a local scale, there can exist, for example, the interweaving of old decapitalized housing combined with relics of industrialization and islands of the smart city being created based on science-technology parks or a new generation of housing estates based on the latest achievements of science.

A further issue is the adoption of a specific time perspective for the analysis of the impact of a smart organization on the developmental effects of regions/areas. This can be approached in the long or medium term. The longer the time perspective, the more universal regularities in local development can be discerned. However, in the case of smart organizations, this is not possible, as the smartification of the economy is a new phenomenon, noticed only in 2000, when the definition of a smart city was first introduced (Hall, 2000). On the other hand, too short a time perspective may be burdened with a cognitive error resulting from the atypicality and discontinuity of economic processes. Phenomena such as the great financial crisis of 2004–2007, hitting the regions actively involved in globalization processes, or pandemics constitute incidents in the history of cities and regions, and in the medium term, they primarily provide information on how to increase resistance to stress caused by both external and internal factors (e.g., natural factors).

The period of the pandemic provided a lot of information about the coping of LGUs in the conditions of a sudden and massively manifesting phenomenon. Therefore, it is worth combining both approaches – long-term and medium-term. The short-term approach, limited to one year, is more operational, allowing the identification and assessment of technological/administrative/organizational solutions that can be applied in the region.

The last methodological issue is the selection of relations/mechanisms describing the impact of a smart organization on the developmental effects of regions/areas. The basic theoretical framework is the concept of diffusion of innovation, which runs hierarchically (from the centers of space to the periphery) and according to the spatial key determined by the distance from the centers of the birth of innovation, especially in the field of ICT.

This is what Albert Hirschman pointed out. According to him, economic development is uneven and concentrated in the so-called geographical growth centers. Later, however, development naturally spreads from the centers to the neighboring areas. Therefore, Albert Hirschman recommends strengthening the development of the central regions and supporting the subsequent development diffusion by building, for example, communication infrastructure. Regional development goals should aim to create complementarities and linkages to connect technological infrastructures, competence centers, large or small innovation clusters, companies, and talent groups (Hirschman & Lindblom, 1962, pp. 211–222).

The explanation of the process of diffusion of innovations, which is still valid today, is the work of T. Hägerstrand. The beginning of the application of this approach is the work of T. Hägerstrand and his students in the 1960s, based on observations of the spread of innovative solutions in agriculture. Although many years have passed since then, some of the regularities discovered by the doyen of economic geography are still visible. In spatial models, space is treated as a resistance factor that inhibits the flow of information or people. There are three types of diffusion theory. The first is micro-scale contagion theory or individual-level communication theory, the second is macro-scale wave theory of social phenomena, and the third is hierarchical theory.

The first is based on the premise that "innovation is socially contagious. People who are already infected with the innovation infect others. The mechanism of innovation diffusion in T. Hägerstrand's model works only through personal contacts. It manifests itself in such a way that if the information has been heard, adoption of the innovation is certain" (Hägerstrand, 1967). This kind of assumption is, of course, only a theoretical solution, because the mere fact of hearing does not have to mean that the innovation will be adopted, and a new overheard solution will be applied. Whether a particular innovation is adopted depends on interpersonal communication. If there are no barriers to the diffusion of the innovation, it will be adopted. However, the situation is different when one of the hypothetical obstacles occurs: the superabsorbing obstacle when the source of the innovation is destroyed, the absorbing obstacle when the source is isolated, the reflecting obstacle when the innovation is returned to the source, and the distracting obstacle that merely causes the innovation to be passed on to another person who can adopt it.

The second theory uses the physical phenomenon of heat wave propagation for modeling. According to this model, the propagation pattern depends on the initial wave amplitude, the distance from the source, and the coefficient of resistance to the innovation. As stated by this model, waves propagate as a function of the openness of a given local environment to innovative solutions.

The third theory is based on the observation that diffusion is spatially discontinuous. Innovations spread in the hierarchy from larger cities to smaller cities. As in the previous models, distance is the inhibiting factor. However, when considering the hierarchical order of innovation diffusion, attention is paid to its perturbations. Individual cities at a given level of the hierarchy take up innovations differently. This is often related to the supralocal openness of spatial systems to the creation and absorption of innovations.

In socio-economic space, we are dealing with constant waves of diffusion of innovations. They form waves of varying lengths and speeds. Their course, duration, and scope depend not only on the nature of the innovation but also on the openness of societies to accept it and on the presence of objective obstacles that slow it down. This has significant implications for the regional development of smart and sustainable technologies and their manifestations in the form of the development of smart cities and regions.

In order to explain this phenomenon, one can use the theory of core and periphery. According to Friedmann, the production and service activities of the most competitive companies are located in the most developed regions, especially in the large metropolitan areas. At the same time, economic centers dominate their peripheries. Although they help determine the development path of these areas, it is subordinate to the central areas and service oriented. Moreover, the centers strive for dominance not only in the economic sphere, but also in the political and cultural spheres (Malizia, Feser, Renski & Drucker, 2020).

It is also important to consider the concept of path dependence, which explains why regions adopt innovations to varying degrees, causing them to take the shape of ripples traveling at different speeds through economic space. Policy choices not only influence the shape of today's institutions but also determine the range of possible institutional choices in the future. According to Douglass North, the mutual interactions between institutions, i.e., the rules of the game, and economic organizations and entrepreneurs, namely, the actors, shape the development of the economy (North, 2004).

Therefore, in order to understand how smart organizations can influence the stimulation of socio-economic development (smart and sustainable), one should see the forces stimulating or inhibiting the diffusion of innovation. Hence, the consideration of the impact of smart organizations in LGUs on developmental effects requires a spatial analysis of the phenomenon, taking into account the time factor.

The second important methodological approach is related to the understanding of endogenous forces influencing the creation of spatial developmental effects of existing smart organizations in LGUs. Therefore, it is helpful to use the concept of regional innovation systems and its development in the form of the concept of local innovation systems.

Regional innovation system is defined as a set of interacting private and public interests, formal institutions, and other organizations that function according to organizational and institutional arrangements and relationships conducive to the generation, use, and dissemination of knowledge (Ke Rong, Lin, Yu, Zhang & Radziwon, 2020). According to the concept of regional innovation ecosystems (or regional innovation systems), four interrelated elements are required: (1) science, technology, and research; (2) leading industrial and service clusters; (3) talented and innovative start-ups; and (4) territorial and urban quality.

In the theory of the local innovation system, it is assumed that the capacity to innovate is determined by the institutions operating for this purpose, which are linked to other institutions and organizations in each area. The links between institutions are determined by the resources available to them. The number and diversity of institutions that create local innovation systems vary according to the specifics of each area. Institutions implementing social innovation in rural areas primarily include local authorities, non-governmental organizations, local action groups, social economy enterprises, social cooperatives, and entrepreneurs (Rantisi, 2002).

According to these two concepts, the synergistic effects of the activity of local/regional stakeholders are a source of development incentives with resistance to shocks, and, at the same time, it is possible to obtain the benefits of diversity (diversification) and/or economies of scale.

III.3 Analyzing the development impact of local government units – how to use case studies as a research method

In order to analyze the impact of smart organizations on smart and sustainable regional or local development, one has to face the very complex nature of the interdependencies studied. Therefore, especially when a relatively new phenomenon in the socio-economic sphere takes place, it is worth specifying in-depth research based on case studies.

Case study methods, which currently relate to both single case studies and comparative studies, have several key advantages over statistical methods. First, qualitative research is equivalent or better to developing a valid theory. More complete and detailed contact with specific events and phenomena about which we want to generalize helps to accentuate the distinctions. It stimulates new concepts, typologies, and hypotheses. This is especially important when studying new phenomena occurring simultaneously for the first time or on an unprecedented scale. This is the case of smart and sustainable local development in the conditions of globalization of a pandemic in the world economy torn by unprecedented black swans.

There are many ways to use case studies. The approaches that are used in further analysis are indicated below.

The simplest form of case study is the descriptive case study – it aims to document an important event. The goal of the case study is to record history that can be used by later practitioners to avoid pitfalls and identify strategies that work (Odell, 2001).

A case study does not need to be limited to the presentation of facts.

The disciplined interpretive case study interprets or explains an event by applying a known theory to the new context. The risk of this method is selective reconstruction of the event to support a preferred theory by undervaluing evidence that contradicts the theory or supports an alternative. A control against this risk is to faithfully represent one or more of the strongest alternative theories and use the evidence to test each. In this way, an interpretive case study also becomes more disciplined.

J. S. Mill's method of differences (Mill, 1970) requires comparison of cases in which the phenomenon occurs with cases that are similar in other respects as well as those in which it does not occur. Following the method of differences, it is worth comparing specific smart cities or regions to examine specific national and urban settings where the smart city/region was, is, or should be a high priority according to specific actors and documents. These cities/regions can be selected to examine the relationship between global, local, and intermediate arenas of policymaking by focusing on specific places, which allows researchers to create "dense case studies" (Flyvberg, 2006, p. 238) with "rich ambiguity" (Flyvberg, 2006, p. 237).

A good example of the application of the case study method is an empirical analysis based on two realized smart cities: Amsterdam and Genoa. Amsterdam is the first European city to implement a smart program. Genoa is the leading city to receive funding under the recent EU call for smart initiatives.

What are the two cities doing? What are their goals? Who are the key actors and stakeholders involved in smart and/or digital city programs? The empirical study of the project portfolios in Amsterdam and Genoa is the tool to understand their strategy and the meaning of the terms "smart" and "digital". Contents, objectives, and actors are examined, compared, and evaluated to arrive at a theoretical definition of smart city and digital city, supported by empirical evidence from two best practices in Europe (Dameri, 2017).

When selected regions are analyzed, the focus can be put on identifying possibly different types of models describing the impact of smart organizations on smart and sustainable development. Selected case studies can be used to demonstrate the uniqueness of Smart City as a phenomenon with varying relevance, content, and impact depending on local conditions and history. In this way, a catalog of best practices and non-recommended solutions can be created to serve as a warning to successors.

Therefore, it is important to choose a criterion for selecting the researched spatial units appropriate for research purposes.

In this study, two keys for selecting regions were considered. The first was based on the selection of regions showing a similar level of socioeconomic development and the type of development level of smart organizations (the same class in terms of the level of development of smart organizations) and the type of economic region (capital-type region or post-industrial region, similarity natural conditions, etc.).

The second possible approach referred to the search for good solutions based on the best-ranked units, which are at the same time characterized by a similar level of economic development and the development of smart organization (Exner et al., 2018). Therefore, Stockholm, Helsinki, Oslo, and Vienna can be used as leading smart cities in the European Union for comparison.

III.4 Smart organizations as a source of potential benefits for smart and sustainable local development

According to the model proposed by the authors (see Chapter 1), the development of a smart organization is a source of benefits in decision-making and impacts on smart and sustainable local development. It is also possible that the developmental effects of decisions go beyond the local context.

When thinking about the outcomes of smart organizational decision-making, we should consider the following elements: stakeholder involvement in the decision-making process, response time to decisions, cost of decisions, consistency of local government decisions with the government's development strategy, and short- and long-term risks of the decisions made.

The next important question relates to the results of developing smart organizations at the local government level. The results of the development of smart organizations at a level beyond the self-government level and the regional level should be considered in terms of the economic, social, and environmental aspects of development.

With IoT, Big Data, and AI, cities can conduct continuous monitoring, issue disaster warnings, and make quick decisions (Zhu, Li & Feng, 2019). This is important, as spatial development requires noticing the need to maintain resistance to both external disturbances and those arising from the loss of development reserves in the face of increasing demographic pressure.

The use of smart devices in physical infrastructure leads to lower costs for regional development. For example, garbage can systems are electronically connected to a system that notifies authorities when they are full (Andrelini, 2019). This leads to a reduction in the time and cost of decision-making (Kummitha, 2020).

Technologies are used to inform people about decisions, find ways to solve important problems for civil society and involve them in decision-making processes. Decisions made by regional and local actors are more effective and based on people's real needs (Hollands, 2008; Komninos, 2008). Therefore, they lead to an increase in the quality of life of the regional community.

However, the impact of solutions typical for smart organizations on the decision-making process and their effects in the form of regional development are poorly documented in the literature. A theoretical tool in the form of Smart City Performance Dashboard, which was proposed to be used in Genoa (Dameri, 2017), was developed. The author proposes to develop a Smart City Performance Dashboard to measure and evaluate the ability of a smart strategy to improve quality of life. Based on the world's best-known urban indicators, this paper defines a five-step path to implementing a standardized but customized dashboard to support smart city investments and evaluate their performance, but mostly in terms of quality of life. However, the course and effects of the implementation of this instrument are not known.

In order to be able to use smart solutions to improve decision-making processes and thus induce the effects of regional/local development desired by the society, various risk factors should be noticed, such as, e.g., obtaining false readings from devices based on the Internet of Things, threats of cyber-attacks, or non-repeatability or uniqueness of decision situations that are unsolvable for artificial intelligence. Moreover, data from smart urban information systems are difficult to analyze due to the complex urban environment in which they are created and identified. Minor signs of an anomaly in the early stages are easy to misinterpret. In addition, anomalies sometimes occur in various municipal data sources (Zhang, Mingyang & Li, Tong & Yu, Yue & Li, Yong & Hui, Pan & Zheng, Yu, 2020).

Therefore, man as a decision-maker plays a key role in smart organizations in the regions. Assessment and decision-making skills are essential in any decision-making process. Of key importance is the issue of developing decision-makers' ability to make good and very good decisions, especially in conditions of uncertainty and limited information, as well as the inability to forecast both future demand for public services and the possibility of financing them. However, it can be argued that some extremely serious and unpredictable phenomena may accelerate changes in the ecosystem of cities, hastening their evolution toward smart. One of such challenges is the pandemic – the modern black swan. Extremely serious and unpredictable phenomena trigger new ways of thinking about making decisions, and thus sometimes change the existing development paths.

Although the literature on smart cities emphasizes that technologies help urban authorities address intractable social problems, the way Covid-19 has been handled underscores that the technology-driven approach does not directly lead to technological determinism, but rather provides decision-makers with a vector of options from which to choose as they see fit. As a result, the impact of smart technologies in smart cities is less effective than predicted in the literature (Hollands, 2008), because people use, interpret, manipulate, and communicate the trends selected by the IoT based on political and institutional needs (Kummitha, 2020).

Smart organizations created in LGUs can stimulate local development while maintaining the principles resulting from the implementation of social, economic, natural, and technological goals.

During the pandemic, smart organizations played a special role as natural integrators of pro-development activities with the use of information and communication technologies.

References

Adamik, A., & Sikora-Fernandez, D. (2021). Smart Organizations as a Source of Competitiveness and Sustainable Development in the Age of Industry 4.0: Integration of Micro and Macro Perspective. *Energies*, 14(6), p. 1572. https://doi.org/10.3390/en14061572.

Agenda for Sustainable Development United Nations (2015). *Transforming Our World: The 2030*. Retrieved from: https://sustainabledevelopment.un.org/post2015/transformingourworld/publication (accessed on 11.06.2022).

Andrelini, J. (2019). How China's Smart City Tech Focuses on Its Own Citizens. *Financial Times*, https://www.ft.com/content/46bc137a-5d27-11e9-840c-530737425559 (accessed 28.7.2022).

Antonelli, G., & Cappiello, G. (Eds.) (2017). *Smart Development in Smart Communities*. Routledge.

Cegis, R., Ramanauskiene J., & Martinkus, B. T. (2009). The Concept of Sustainable Development and Its Use for Sustainability Scenarios. *Inzinierine Ekonomika-Engineering Economics*, 2(68), pp. 28–37.

Dameri, R. (2017). *Smart City. Implementation Creating Economic and Public Value in Innovative Urban Systems*. Springer.

Exner, A., Cepoiu, L., Weinzierl, C., & Asara, V. (2018). Performing Smartness Differently – Strategic Enactments of a Global Imaginary in Three European Cities. SRE – Discussion Papers, vol. 5. Vienna: WU Vienna University of Economics and Business.

Flyvberg, B. (2006). Five Misunderstandings about Case-Study Research. Qualitative Inquiry, 12(2), pp. 219–245.

Hall, P. (2000). Creative cities and economic development. Urban Studies, Vol 37, No. 4, pp. 639-649.

Hägerstrand, T. (1967). *Innovation Diffusion as a Spatial Process*. University of Chicago Press.

Haarstad, H. (2016). Who Is Driving the 'Smart City' Agenda? Assessing Smartness as a Governance Strategy for Cities in Europe. In Jones, A., Ström, P., Hermelin, B., & Rusten, G. (Eds.), *Services and the Green Economy* (pp. 199–218). London: Palgrave Macmillan.

Haarstad, H. (2017). Constructing the Sustainable City: Examining the Role of Sustainability in the 'Smart City' Discourse. *Journal of Environmental Policy & Planning*, 19(4), pp. 423–437.

Hawkes, J. (2001). *The Fourth Pillar of Sustainability: Culture's Essential Role in Public Planning*. Melbourne: Cultural Development Network and Part of University Press.

Hirschman, A. O., & Lindblom, C. E. (1962). Economic Development, Research and Development, Policy Making: Some Converging Views. *Behavioral science*, 7(2), pp. 211–222.

Hollands, R. G. (2008). Will the Real Smart City Please Stand Up? *City: Analysis of Urban Trends, Culture, Theory, Policy, Action*, 12(3), pp. 303–320.

Komninos, N. (2008). *Intelligent Cities and Globalization of Innovation Networks*. Routledge.

Kummitha, R. (2020). Smart Technologies for Fighting Pandemics: The Techno- and Human-Driven Approaches in Controlling the Virus Transmission. *Government Information Quarterly*, 37(101481), pp. 1–11.

Malizia, E., Feser, E. J., Renski, H., & Drucker, J. (2020). *Understanding Local Economic Development*. Second Edition. London: Routledge. https://doi. org/10.4324/9780367815134.

Manitiu, D. N., & Pedrini, D. (2016). Smartness Indicators in the European Urban Framework. In Antonelli, G., & Cappiello G. (Eds.), *Smart Development in Smart Communities* (pp. 152–169). New York: Routledge.

Mill, J. S. (1970). Two Methods of Comparison. In Etzioni, A., Dubow, F. L. (Eds.), *Comparative Perspectives: Theories and Methods* (pp. 205–213). Boston: Little, Brown Company.

North, D. C. (2004). Institutions and Economic Growth: A Historical Introduction. In Frieden, J. A., & Lake D. A. (Eds.), *International Political Economy: Perspectives on Global Power and Wealth* (pp. 47–59). London: Routledge.

OECD (2003). Environmental indicators – Development, Measurement and Use. Report. Organisation of Economic Co-operation and Development, 37 pp. https://www.oecd.org/environment/indicators-modelling-outlooks/ 24993546.pdf

Odell, J. S. (2001). Case Study Methods in International Political Economy. *International Studies Perspectives*, 2, pp. 161–176.

Pirnau, C., Ghiculescu, D., & Marinescu, N. I. (2018). SMEs Creativity and Smart Regional Development, *MATEC Web of Conferences* 178, 07007, IManE&E 2018. https://doi.org/10.1051/matecconf/201817807007.

Rantisi, N. M. (2002). The Local Innovation System as a Source of 'Variety': Openness and Adaptability in New York City's Garment District. *Regional Studies*, 36(6), pp. 587–602. doi: 10.1080/00343400220146740.

Rong, K., Lin, Y., Yu, J., Zhang, Y., & Radziwon, A. (2020). Exploring Regional Innovation Ecosystems: An Empirical Study in China. *Industry and Innovation*, 28(5), pp. 545–569. doi: 10.1080/13662716.2020.1830042.

Sutriadi, R. (2018). *Defining Smart City, Smart Region, Smart Village, and Technopolis as an Innovative Concept in Indonesia's Urban and Regional Development Themes to Reach Sustainability*. IOP Conference Series: Earth and Environmental Science, Volume 202, 012047. https://doi.org/10.1088/1755-1315/202/1/012047.

Tennberg, M., Lempinen, H., &Pirnes S. (Eds.) (2020). *Resources, Social and Cultural Sustainabilities in the Arctic*. Routledge.

Vinod Kumar, T. M. (Ed.) (2019). *Smart Metropolitan Regional Development: Economic and Spatial Design Strategies*. Springer.

Zhang, Mingyang, Li, T., Yu, Y., Li, Y., Hui, P. & Zheng, Y. (2020). Urban Anomaly Analytics: Description, Detection, and Prediction. *IEEE Transactions on Big Data*, 8, pp. 809–826. https://doi.org/10.1109/TBDATA.2020.2991008.

Zhu, S., Li, D., & Feng, H. (2019). Is Smart City Resilient? Evidence from China. *Sustainable, Cities and Society*, 50, 101636.

2 Smart organizations in the COVID-19 pandemic

III.1 Pandemic as cause of developmental shock

A particular test of the resilience of regions is their ability to evolve under pandemic conditions. A pandemic is defined as a new disease that spreads rapidly across multiple countries and continents. It can be seen as the next version of the globalization process. Because of its unpredictable course and magnitude, a pandemic is considered a black swan – defined as an event with a low probability but large impact, such as a natural disaster, a pandemic, a financial crisis, a terrorist attack, or a completely new event for which there is no historical experience (Taleb, 2010).

The pandemic began in Europe on January 24, 2020, when the first case of the coronavirus was reported in France. EU countries are closely linked, mainly due to their geographical proximity and trade partnerships with China. For this reason, the Covid-19 pandemic could easily spread from China to major cities in these countries (Cohen & Kupfesrchmidt, 2020). The rapid, the abrupt character of the growing cases of infections, high mortality, and the lack of effective methods of preventing the disease or limiting its serious effects resulted in a massive lockdown.

Individual countries have adopted various measures to combat the pandemic (Kummitha, 2020). Nevertheless, the effects of the pandemic were visible both in the form of disturbance of the development dynamics of regions, especially deep in regions with exceptionally high dynamics and prevalence of infections. On the other hand, work practices have changed in terms of remote work, including working from home and digital communication platforms, the Internet and communication technologies (ICTs) (Del Rio & Malani, 2020).

During the pandemic, there were many limitations to the classical forms of contact. Moreover, these contacts changed because of reduced mobility, especially mobility of interregional flows. This led to increased interaction between members of local communities. The possibility of influencing jobs and supply in local markets opened the opportunity to develop original solutions to promote local development.

As a result of the pandemic, new local needs emerged, such as supporting people in quarantine or suffering from Covid-19, caring for people who

DOI: 10.4324/9781003265870-12

are lonely or temporarily isolated from the rest of the family, supporting access to electronic communications and thus reducing the exclusion of information for those previously unwilling to use basic services that come with modern technologies, or remote access to medical services and other rapidly growing types of e-commerce.

The unexpected nature of the threat, the need for urgent actions by the authorities of regions and cities to protect residents and other people staying in a given territory, the lack of planned measures for this purpose due to the inability to predict such needs, the necessity to make spontaneous, often one-person decisions regarding the functioning of the regions, areas and cities caused major perturbations in the management of local government units and the provision of public services (Godlewska-Majkowska, Legutko-Kobus & Sierak, 2022).

The situation was complicated by the collapse of local finances, due to the reduced inflow of taxes and the failure to include unexpected expenses in the budgets of local government units. Co-financing from non-local funds could support individual regions to an unequal degree, but it was possible when taking into account financial aid from EU funds and funds transferred by individual countries.

Economic development during the pandemic was also hampered by negative phenomena related to running a business. The collapse of supply chains, reduced mobility of people and freight due to lockdown, border closure, or border traffic restrictions translated into business disruptions and had an impact on the daily lives of residents, commuters, and tourists.

Limited mobility has also accelerated technological progress, especially in the field of remote communication and virtualization of access to public services, particularly in the field of education and the expansion of telemedicine.

Technology has also improved coping and recovery skills by increasing participation and social inclusion, improving physical and mental health, and supporting the functioning of educational and economic systems. This has been achieved through various solutions and technologies, such as social media, telemedicine, positioning and monitoring systems, sensors, location-based applications, and telework systems. These solutions and technologies were also used during the Covid-19 pandemic to improve community well-being and maintain urban functions.

Digitalization is bringing about major changes due to the accelerated transformation processes in all areas of society in the wake of the Covid-19 pandemic: home office, homeschooling, e-learning, streaming, impact on the labor market, and new requirements for digital services. Thus, it is also a cultural shift that affects a large part of the way we live and work. It has brought new forms of collaboration and increased trade and interdepartmental cooperation in local government.

However, the use of technologies can also have negative impacts, such as social exclusion, digital divide, violation of privacy and confidentiality, political bias and spread of misinformation, and inefficient remote work and training (Hassankhani, Alidadi, Sharifi & Azhdari, 2021).

There has also been a great effort by the world community to invent vaccines against Covid-19.

Intuitively, it can be argued that regions better prepared for digital transformation more easily coped with challenges such as reduced mobility of all stakeholders (residents, tourists, people working, and commuting). However, it should also be noticed that local governments were struggling with numerous previously unknown problems or already known difficulties, but not on such a large scale or with less complexity of problems to be solved.

The pandemic is one of many possible impacts that disrupt socio-economic development at various spatial scales. Extreme phenomena of natural or anthropogenic origin can be unpredictable, and their effects are catastrophic and difficult to remove. Therefore, it is important that local government units are able to monitor their territories and manage the risk of major development disruptions. Hence, the question about tools supporting crisis management, especially in large local units (e.g., large cities) under the influence of various types of stakeholders and local actors.

III.2 Innovative local shields as a tool for smart organizations to influence local development

The new realities of living in a pandemic provide the basis for finding new solutions that can help meet the needs of the local community while respecting its diversity. It concerns bundles of targeted interventions in response to the effects of a pandemic on the economy – e.g., innovative local shields (sets of targeted interventions oriented toward economic aspects of pandemic and lockdowns). They should take the form of innovative local shields, i.e., innovative solutions of a comprehensive nature that simultaneously create synergies, including community and business support, thanks to the initiatives of local authorities at the local level, local businesses, and non-profit organizations.

Such solutions can be the result of grassroots activities reported by the population, social groups, and local businesses, stimulated by the city or county government in the implementation of its own tasks, and delegated on the basis of agreements or commissioned by the state administration.

It should be emphasized that smart and sustainable local development depends on the cooperation of various actors, especially local governments, businesses, and social organizations. They all play an important role in all phases of local development, especially in urban areas.

Local innovation shields should be integrated into activities carried out within their own and delegated tasks. One factor that contributes to the creation of shields is a synergistic approach to different types of projects carried out by all actors operating in a given territorial unit.

In building shields, it is necessary to efficiently manage the flow of information, knowledge management, and the development of relational capital, not only within local government institutions, but also in collaboration with the local business environment, non-profit organizations, the education and training sector, and citizens who actively participate in shaping development processes. As the main drivers of local development, cities are of critical importance to the communities surrounding them. Cities become a testing ground for smart technology manufacturers, while local governments are co-producers of technologies that are sold to other cities. Innovative solutions help reduce cities' operating costs and improve residents' quality of life, but also offer the possibility of excessive invasion of residents' privacy and restriction of civil liberties. Hence the controversy over the scope and nature of modern ICT solutions.

On the other hand, there is a risk that strong business partners will impose solutions that create a larger market for the solutions they themselves offer than for the solutions that local communities really need. At this point, it is not clear whether smart technologies will actually have lasting material impacts beyond pilot projects, inflated expectations (or fears), or the label of catching up with technology standards already common in other cities, depending in no small part on the financial capacity of the municipality as a consumer and the resistance or public demand for smart technologies (Exner, Cepoiu, Weinzierl & Asara, 2018, p. 122).

Innovative local shields can be initiated by local governments, large employers in a given region, and local social organizations. Based on research conducted in Poland in 2021, we can confirm that Polish local authorities took a variety of initiatives that led to the creation of local innovative shields during the pandemic (Godlewska-Majkowska, Legutko-Kobus & Sierak, 2021).

The authors have tried to identify innovative solutions that have a comprehensive character and at the same time create synergies, such as supporting the population and the economy thanks to the initiatives of local authorities, local businesses, and non-profit organizations. The study included 18 cities of various sizes, which stood out in terms of the level of development of smart organizations in local government units. These were the cities awarded in the competitions for local governments, i.e., Pearls of local government (2020 edition), Innovative local government (2020 edition), and Smart commune worthy of A (in Polish: Gmina na 5!) (2021 edition). Moreover, reference was made to the (international) smart city certification, and the municipalities certified according to the ISO 371204 standard were indicated. On this basis, 18 cities were selected, 15 of which provided materials on actions taken during the pandemic. These were: Ciechanów, Gdynia, Głogów, Grodzisk Mazowiecki, Kielce, Kraków, Lublin, Łódź, Międzychód, Poznań, Rzeszów, Siemianowice Śląskie, Sosnowiec, Toruń, and Warsaw. The analyzed group of local governments is diversified in terms of the number of inhabitants: five of them are municipalities with less than 100,000 inhabitants, seven have more than 200,000 inhabitants, and three have between 100 and 200 thousand inhabitants.

Based on a detailed analysis of the cities selected for the study, it should be noted that in none of them there were identified fully developed innovative projects for local shields, in which a larger number of actors, especially a local government entity, would have a significant stake. The main initiator of activities for the benefit of the local environment was commune (city) offices. The study identified a total of 27 types of activities that were carried out by all municipalities, regardless of their nature and size. These were mainly solutions related to the provision of (and access to) public services, as well as entrepreneurial and labor market initiatives.

The municipalities participating in the study implemented different types of projects to achieve synergies between the initiatives of the different actors.

The local government was the initiator and integrator of these activities. This can be considered the initial phase for the creation of an innovative local shield.

As a result of the research, the following initiatives, involving at least two groups of local actors, were identified:

- Supporting the local economy and entrepreneurship development through local economic development, business consulting, and local patriotic activities;
- Popularizing the provision and use of electronic services to increase the availability of the e-economy;
- Equipping schools, including teachers and students, with distance learning devices;
- Providing social and psychological care for social risk groups (income) and IT;
- Innovative solutions related to leisure activities and cultural promotion; and
- Strengthening participatory management activities (including e-participation).

These measures have long-term effects. They can be used to create a coherent bottom-up development mechanism based on the civil society model, functioning in the conditions of increasing importance of informatization of all forms of human activities. Such solutions are the basis for building innovative local shields. Research conducted in Polish local government units showed that the main smart organizations were organizations established within the offices of these units. On the other hand, they were not of a comprehensive nature, so it is not possible to state the existence of a synergistic effect of these activities relating to all 4 dimensions of local or regional development.

III.3 Impact of smart organizations on the development of regional hubs – results of own research (examples from the EU)

In highly developed countries, the processes of adaptation to the new epidemiological situation resulted in the development of various types of activities and new solutions based on information and communications technology.

The practices, solutions, and applications developed by 25 European cities serving as regional capitals (hubs) classified in the Smart Cities Index (SCI) 2021 ranking (IMD World Competitiveness Center – Centre for Innovative Cities – IMD Smart City Observatory, 2021) are presented below. Categorization of the presented examples refers to the intended impact of the practice, solutions, and applications on decision-making process at self-government level, and technological, social, economic, and environmental development aspects. To the extent possible, we reflect upon scalability of the practice presented and possibility to deploy them in other locations, as well as upon sustainability aspects of the practices. The research approach for identification and analysis of the practices was electronic audit of official Internet landing pages of the investigated cities and a detailed review of data and documents revealed in September 2022 (Official internet portal   of city of Amsterdam – amsterdam.nl, Official internet portal of city of Berlin – berlin.de, Official internet portal of city of Bilbao – bilbao.eus, Official internet portal of city of Bordeaux – bordeaux.fr, Official internet portal of city of Brussels – brucity.be, Official internet portal of city of Copenhagen – international.kk.dk, Official internet portal of city of Glasgow – glasgow.gov.uk, Official internet portal of city of Gothenburg – goteborg.se, Official internet portal of city of Hamburg – hamburg.de, Official internet portal of city of Helsinki – hel. fi.

Official internet portal of city of London – london.gov.uk, Official internet portal of city of Madrid – madrid.es, Official internet portal of city of Rotterdam – rotterdam.nl, Official internet portal of city of Stockholm – international.stockholm.se, Official internet portal of city of Vienna – wien.at).

Practices looked for among organizations selected to our research were structured in several domains and derived from set of practices indicated in the literature as important for smart organization types. Examples of such practices were interorganizational learning (Anand, Brøns Kringelum, Øland Madsen & Selivanovskikh, 2021), collectivity aspects related to the creation of new knowledge (Bratianu, Prelipcean & Bejinaru, 2020; Osagie, Wesselink, Blok 2022), self-servicing aspects of services oriented toward certain types of recipients (De Florio, Bajhouya, Eloudghiri & Blondia, 2016).

Other, important aspects planned to identify and investigate related to enabling learning to external recipients, nurturing of learning culture, and capabilities enhancement were investigated (Eisenberg & Davidova, 2020). Learning partnerships as specific form of inter-organizational learning (Hesselgreaves, French, Hawkins & Lowe, 2021) were another example of specific organizational activities included in the search.

Technology solutions and decision-making processes (Gajowiak, 2016) were assumed as one of the key aspects to be looked for in reference to smart organizations practices. Particular types of technologies researched were IT technologies and modern IT solutions at smart organizations level (Łobaziewicz, 2016, 2019). Other phenomena indicated in the literature and assumed as reference point in the research performed were organizational practices of increasing job satisfaction, productivity, and engagement of employees for advancement and development of organization (Tuyen, 2021).

III.3.1 Social domain

In social domain of the investigated practices, solutions, and applications, particular attention was given to practices oriented toward provision and continued enhancement of capabilities of inhabitants through learning initiatives. Smart organizations at self-government level enable and promote access to initiatives supporting upgrade of skills relevant at the marketplaces and in the context of job transition. Practices fostering continued learning were promoted by self-governments in Bilbao, Gothenburg, Stockholm, and London.

On their official Internet websites, both Gothenburg and Stockholm revealed information about training initiatives by providing lists of educational institutions and available courses. However, what is not obvious in this type of practice is purposefully providing information on education available beyond primary, secondary, and tertiary education by detailing offers for adults and life-long learning initiatives. Both Gothenburg and Stockholm communicated these types of available offers and included special learning courses for immigrants. Cities have also offered support and adaptation by dedicated resource teams for prospective adult learners with individual difficulties and learning disabilities.

The offer of Bilbao included not only details of vocational training and courses, but also a special offer for employees of the public education sector, such as teachers. The latter initiative supports continued learning of those who teach others and are responsible for formal education of participants of primary and secondary education.

London's offer included support for teachers and lesson plans in the form of the "London Curriculum" initiative, aiming at ensuring that education in London is delivered at the highest possible standard. The city also provided a broad range of training sessions and courses for inhabitants, employees, and employers, as well as for training preparation and training delivery stakeholders, in order to enhance their capabilities in the training sector. Inhabitants of London had access not only to training and lifelong learning initiatives but also to incentives and rewards oriented on engagement into such initiatives. London's offer has been distinguished with a digital school atlas that presents all education institutions in London on a digital map "London Schools Atlas".

Practices oriented toward promotion of enhancing capabilities of human capital through learning initiatives exemplify the modus operandi of smart organizations. The aggregation of information on the educational offer of a given location on its official Internet website is scalable and an example worth following.

III.3.2 Economic domain

In the economic domain of smart organizations, the explored practices referred to aspects of transaction cost economics and lowering costs of conducting economic activity. A variety of solutions and promoted ways of work are oriented toward cooperation of various stakeholders for local development.

One of the most comprehensive practices related to the economic domain of smart organizations' activities was recognized in Hamburg under the DigITAll initiative for connection, digitization of different applications and processes related to infrastructure projects carried out by various entities, including public authorities. The DigITAll initiative improved the provision of information for effective communication and coordination activities. DigITAll is a part of the broader ambition of "Hamburg Digital City".

Hamburg was distinguished through series of projects and initiatives aiming at advanced digitization of public services. The digital city strategy of Hamburg and "Digital First" type of projects included launch of "Urban Data Platform" enabling cooperation and creation of applications based on data enabled by public sector institutions for both public and private stakeholders.

Another initiative in Hamburg – DIPAS – enabled digital participation in local development project planning through access to digitized maps, photographs, plans, models, and geographical data. DISPAS enabled inhabitants of Hamburg to localize planned infrastructural projects and to provide feedback on them.

A different undertaking, "Smart Delivery and Loading Zones", focused on the transportation and logistics domain of Hamburg, as well as optimization of urban traffic by virtual bookings, registration of planned deliveries and reservations of delivery zones to react to increasing delivery traffic, traffic jams, and CO_2 emission increase. The initiative introduced digital road signs channeling the traffic in the city, managing no-stopping zones, and streamlining the city traffic in possibly the most efficient manner. The area of transportation in Hamburg has also been included in a digital service for ship transport registration, with plans to include shipowners, notaries, and lawyers in documents exchange, in order to decrease the administrative efforts related to entering inland waterways.

Hamburg has been recognized with the award for "Best cooperation project 2022" at the eGovernment competition 2022 for its unique approach toward the continued, rapid development of digital applications, and process optimization services at lower costs compared to market standards.

Advanced digitization of public services and related practices lowers costs of data and information, as well as the time required to carry out economic activity. Digital services and ease of conducting business can contribute to investment attractiveness of a location. The scalability of these types of initiatives depends on the budget for investments and change management related to new ways of working.

III.3.3 Technological domain

The identified technological domain practices refer to a specific placement of open data initiatives enabled by smart organizations at self-government level and roles in local government structure responsible for digital transformation and planning. Smart organizations at self-government level streamline projects in digital advancement domain, set up adequate supervision models, and create and nurture broader coalitions of entities involved in technological advancement of their territories.

Brussels attracts attention due to its portfolio of projects oriented on transformation into smart city. One of such projects is IT master plan for Brussels detailing information technology architecture aspects needed to be set in place to enable harmonized and sustainable development in the digital domain. IT master plan defines reforms for IT hardware and software solutions used by the city's administration to enable the delivery of more accessible, simpler, and better-quality services for the citizens.

Berlin supervises technology-related projects, including digital domain, through a dedicated Chief Digital Officer role for Berlin, with mandate to advance Berlin's technological transformation with broader coalition of stakeholders. The focus of the Chief Digital Officer is on modernization of public administration and enablement of digital administrative services for the citizens of Berlin.

A similar approach is realized by London with the Chief Digital Officer role, in place since 2017, and Smart London council of various stakeholders involved in inclusive implementation mission of "Smarter London Together". The role of the council is to support the Mayor of London and Chief Digital Officer of London in the efforts to transform London into a smart city. "Smarter London Together" expresses ambition of transforming

London into the smartest city in the world through better digital services, open data initiatives, connectivity and digital inclusion, cybersecurity, and innovation. The ambition is structured with a set of missions, where each of them sets out series of initiatives and projects.

Multiple cities enable the creation of applications and solutions by leveraging data generated by public institutions through open data initiatives. For example, the "Bilbao Open Data" initiative, and other open data initiatives in Bordeaux, Madrid, or Stockholm. Madrid popularizes the open data concept and opportunities related to it through the open data days initiative, encouraging the adoption of data policies and data usage for the benefits of civil society. Bordeaux organizes interactive open data workshops to disseminate and enhance the usage of public data, share good practices, and ask questions on tools enabling effective usage of the data sets.

Stockholm regularly surveys inhabitants to learn their opinions on various aspects of digitization and services enabled through technology and to react appropriately with open data initiatives.

It is not easy to distinguish projects and initiatives carried out by cities oriented on technology from those oriented on digitization, as nowadays these domains interpenetrate due to high intensity of digitization activities enabled by technology. Creation of new applications and solutions based on the open data provided by cities can contribute to local development and creation of economic growth of individuals and enterprises. Multiple identified open data initiatives aim to foster technological advancement and prove that these types of initiatives are scalable.

III.3.4 Environmental domain

Environmental domain has been recognized as one into which smart organizations invest significant focus end efforts. The identified practices regard mobility, water management, waste management, environmental planning, and incentives aiming at modeling of environmentally friendly behaviors of inhabitants and enterprises. Practices in the environmental domain aim at reducing the industrial footprint on the environment and increasing energy and resources management efficiency, and they directly contribute to the sustainable development paradigm.

Waste management is a domain addressed by Kiel, where inhabitants can use a dedicated application to report areas polluted with waste, in order to trigger an intervention for waste elimination. This particular solution fits into the broader ambition of Kiel called "Zero Waste City", which also encompasses raising environmental awareness among citizens and initiatives related to recycling, food saving, and efficient energy usage by households.

Stockholm, in regard to the area of environment and climate protection, introduced in 2016 the concept of smart bins, an initiative cohesive with the brand promise of Stockholm – "The Eco-Smart City". Hundreds of waste bins in the city were fitted with solar-power mobile solutions and sensors, which reported waste containers utilization space, optimized the space of waste within the containers, and reduced the frequency of emptying. In the longer perspective, such approach can lower the costs of waste management and reduce waste emissions. Stockholm realizes its smart city concept through series of environment-oriented initiatives and projects elaborated in the "Environment program for the City of Stockholm", "Environment program 2020–2023", and "Climate Action Plan".

Natural resources management has been tackled by Glasgow, where first-of-its-kind construction in the form of the Glasgow Smart Canal for water management through technology was introduced. Glasgow Smart Canal set up a reference point in the digital surface water drainage management system. The solution is aimed at mitigating flood risk in the city and enabling the regeneration of the environment with the use of sensors and weather prediction technologies.

Other areas related to environmental prioritization are transport and mobility. In this area, Rotterdam regularly reports progress on of its attempts at achieving zero-emission mobility in the city. This is part of the broader goal of moving toward "Zero Emission City Logistics" in Rotterdam by 2025.

Similarly to Rotterdam, Madrid prioritizes public transport and mobility, thanks to investments into additional bike lanes, promotion of networked vehicles, vehicles sharing models, robust electronic vehicles charging infrastructure, and novel parking management solutions being part of "Madrid 360 Sustainable Mobility Plan".

In the area of transport and mobility, Vienna incentivizes alternative mobility options and provides support for the development of innovations in this area, as well as it creates instruments for balancing high costs of alternative fuel vehicles as part of "Urban Mobility Plan Vienna".

Practices oriented toward the protection of the environment contribute to the sustainable development paradigm. The wide range of actions in this domain includes scalable, low-resource-intensive initiatives, such as ecological awareness education.

III.3.5 Decision-making and governance domain

A separate category of practices related to the creation of cooperation and engagement needed for transformation of self-governments are practices in decision-making and city governance domain. These types of practices encompass instruments of involvement of local development stakeholders through enabling and facilitating public consultations, providing feedback and suggestions by inhabitants to local government authorities, and creating and nurturing of local neighborhoods and communities, also through dedicated tools like digital communication platforms.

Helsinki offers its inhabitants various forms of participation and being impactful on local development through a dedicated section on its official Internet website, which enables the presentation of early stage projects, participation in public dialogue, submission of feedback, endorsements, questions, and development suggestions. The city offers "The Participation Newsletter" and "Plan Watch" services on city planning, building, and maintaining urban infrastructure.

London enables dialogue related to early stage drafts of strategic documents the city hall is working on. The strategies and plans section on the official Internet website of London details documents on environment, health, housing, skills, economy, culture, food, sport, and fosters dialogue around them. City leads online communication channel in the form of a social medium with community discussing plans and local development policies as well as initiatives that the inhabitants and companies can join. The local social medium operating in the form of an online community is called "Talk London" and concentrates on dialogue that leads to better preparation of policies and plans within the "Let's make London better together" approach. There is also an initiative on partnering with the Mayor of London and participating in official events organized by the city hall in districts and neighborhoods covering the London area.

Brussels operates its own public, participation-oriented digital platform called "faireBXLsamen", which makes it possible to report problems and challenges identified in the city. The platform "faireBXLsamen" informs about events and meetings dedicated to city development projects people can discuss and consult. Projects are presented with reference to the existing or planned location on the map of Brussels and direct participants to their respective neighborhoods and communities. There is also a separate new projects submission form.

Copenhagen nurtures dialogue with citizens and enables reporting projects regarding these aspects of city development, which might require intervention in the social domain, governance, and traffic. This is done through an official Internet website.

The analyzed practices in decision-making and governance domain empower citizens to participate in local development and plans and projects related to it. Initiatives enabling collection of citizens' feedback enrich the decision-making process with perspectives of local development stakeholders and can contribute to more educated decision-making, trust, and cooperation. The multiple identified initiatives that enable dialogue indicate the scalability of this type of solution and their importance for participatory citizenship.

The above-mentioned solutions are universal tools that can be used not only in the conditions of epidemiological threats. Whereas their emergence or expansion of already existing solutions resulted from the transfer of many activities from the real world to the virtual world. In addition, tools dedicated to health care have also been developed. In this regard, one could mention the Polish solutions developed at the national level, which have been a great help in facilitating the digitization of medical services, e.g., the E-patient website or Stop Covid applications for mobile devices, which support the treatment process, documentation of treatment, and preventive medicine.

References

Anand, A., Brøns Kringelum, L., Øland Madsen, C., & Selivanovskikh, L. (2021). Interorganizational Learning: A Bibliometric Review and Research Agenda. *The Learning Organization*, 28(2), pp. 111–136. https://doi.org/10.1108/TLO-02-2020-0023.

Bratianu, C., Prelipcean, G., & Bejinaru, R. (2020). Exploring the latent Variables Which Support SMEs to Become Learning Organizations. *Management & Marketing. Challenges for the Knowledge Society*, 15(2), pp. 154–171.

Cohen, J., & Kupfesrchmidt, K. (2020). Strategies Shift as Coronavirus Pandemic Looms. *Globalization and Health*, 367, pp. 962–963.

De Florio, V., Bakhouya, M., Eloudghiri, D., & Blondia, C. (2016). Towards a Smarter organization for a Self-servicing Society. In *Proceedings of the 7th International Conference on Software Development and Technologies for Enhancing Accessibility and Fighting Info-exclusion*, pp. 254–260.

Del Rio, C., & Malani, P. N. (2020). COVID-19 – New Insights on a Rapidly Changing Epidemic. *JAMA - Journal of the American Medical Association*, 323(14), pp. 1339–1340. https://doi.org/10.1001/jama.2020.3072.

Eisenberg, A., & Davidova, J. (2020). Measurement and Analysis Issues in Research of Interrelation between Organizational Learning Culture and Organizational Citizenship Behaviour. *Rural Environment. Education. Personality*, 13, pp. 339–411. https://doi.org/10.22616/REEP.2020.047.

Exner, A., Cepoiu L., Weinzierl C., & Asara V. (2018). Performing Smartness Differently – Strategic Enactments of a Global Imaginary in Three European Cities. *SRE – Discussion Papers*, Vol. 5. Vienna: WU Vienna University of Economics and Business.

Gajowiak, M. (2016). High-Tech SMEs in the Concept of Intelligent Organizations: The Reconstruction of the Approach in the Light of Empirical Research. In Kosała, M., Urbaniec, M., & Żur, A. (Eds.), *Entrepreneurship: Antecedents and Effects (Przedsiębiorczość Międzynarodowa)*, 2(2), pp. 165–177.

Godlewska-Majkowska, H., Legutko-Kobus, P., & Sierak, J. (2021), *Innowacyjne tarcze lokalne – inicjatywy biznesu i samorządów.* In Chłoń-Dominczak, A., Sobiecki, R., Majewski, B., & Strojny, M. (Eds.) *Raport SGH i Forum Ekonomicznego 2021*, pp. 225–268.

Godlewska-Majkowska, H., Legutko-Kobus, P., & Sierak, J. (2022). *Inteligentne miasta w pandemii.* Elipsa.

Hassankhani, M., Alidadi, M., Sharifi, A., & Azhdari, A. (2021). Smart City and Crisis Management: Lessons for the COVID-19 Pandemic. *International Journal Environmental Research of Public Health*, 18, p. 7736. https://doi.org/10.3390/ijerph18157736.

Hesselgreaves, H., French, M., Hawkins, M., Lowe, T., Wheatman, A., Martin, M., & Wilson, R. (2021). New Development: The Emerging Role of a

'Learning Partner' Relationship in Supporting Public Service Reform. *Public Money & Management*, 41(8), pp. 672–675.

IMD World Competitiveness Center – Centre for Innovative Cities – IMD Smart City Observatory (2021). *Smart City Index 2021. A Tool for Action, an Instrument for Better Lives for All Citizens*. Retrieved from: https://www.imd. org/smart-city-observatory/home/ (accessed on 10.06.2022).

Kummitha, R. (2020). Smart technologies for Fighting Pandemics: The Techno- and Human-Driven Approaches in Controlling the Virus Transmission. *Government Information Quarterly*, 37, 101481.

Łobaziewicz, M. (2016). The Role of ICT Solutions in the Intelligent Enterprise Business Activity. *Federated Conference on Computer Science and Information Systems*, 8, pp. 1335–1340. https://doi.org/10.15439/2016F534.

Łobaziewicz, M. (2019). Data & Information Management in Decision Making Processes in an Intelligent Enterprise. *International Journal of Advanced Trends in Computer Science and Engineering*, 8(1.1), pp. 273–279.

Official internet portal of city of Amsterdam – amsterdam.nl.

Official internet portal of city of Berlin – berlin.de.

Official internet portal of city of Bilbao – bilbao.eus.

Official internet portal of city of Bordeaux – bordeaux.fr.

Official internet portal of city of Brussels – brucity.be.

Official internet portal of city of Copenhagen – international.kk.dk.

Official internet portal of city of Glasgow – glasgow.gov.uk.

Official internet portal of city of Gothenburg – goteborg.se.

Official internet portal of city of Hamburg – hamburg.de.

Official internet portal of city of Helsinki – hel.fi.

Official internet portal of city of London – london.gov.uk.

Official internet portal of city of Madrid – madrid.es.

Official internet portal of city of Rotterdam – rotterdam.nl.

Official internet portal of city of Stockholm – international.stockholm.se.

Official internet portal of city of Vienna – wien.at.

Osagie, E., Wesselink, R., Blok, V., & Mulder, M. (2022). Learning Organization for Corporate Social Responsibility Implementation: Unravelling the Intricate Relationship between Organizational and Operational Learning Organization Characteristics. *Organization & Environment*, 35(1), pp. 130–153.

Smart City Observatory. https://www.imd.org/smart-city-observatory/home/ (accessed on 12.05.2022).

Taleb, N. (2010). *The Black Swan: The Impact of the Highly Improbable*. Second edition. New York: Random House, ISBN: 978-1400063512.

Tuyen, B. Q. (20E21). Building a Learning Organization in the digital Era: A Proposed Model for Vietnamese Enterprises. *International Review of Management and Marketing*, 11(3), pp. 42–48.

3 Towards smart organizations in local government organizations

III.1 The impact of smart organizations on local development in the light of the analysis of the experiences of selected European cities

Smart organizations can influence local development directly, by strengthening the effectiveness and rationality of decisions made in accordance with the real needs of local communities. By rationalizing decision-making processes, they can contribute to stimulating local development in a comprehensive or selective manner, e.g., only by influencing public safety and improving mobility or quality of medical services.

Among the responses regarding the impact of smart organizations on the improvement of decision-making processes, the creation of open databases created in a structured manner based on the requirements related to smart city certification in accordance with the ISO 37122 standard and ISO 37123 (resilient city) should be especially recommended. In Poland, cities such as Gdynia, Kielce, and Warsaw are therefore changing in the manner of sharing data on various spheres of city functioning through open accession. It is especially important to create unique data relating to various spheres of socio-economic life on a local scale that otherwise would not be available. The certification process contributed to the collection of such data as, for example, the percentage of water loss due to technical and commercial reasons, the percentage of city residents covered by the regular solid waste collection service (households), the percentage of people commuting to work using means of transport other than their own car, the percentage of women elected to office at the level of municipal public administration among all those elected, the number of homeless people per 100,000 inhabitants, the percentage of women employed in the municipal administration, and so on. In total, in the open accession, there are 93 partial indicators with the ISO label, which are widely used as a source of knowledge for various stakeholder groups.

Currently, preparations are underway in Gdynia for the third certification process, which allows assuming that the databases will not only be developed but also improved in order to make them comparable with other open access systems in Poland and abroad.

DOI: 10.4324/9781003265870-13

The data collected for the purposes of smart city certification makes it possible to identify real development problems, their nature, scale, and direction of changes based on reliable and constantly verified data. Decisions based on the acquired data are more adjusted to the real needs of residents and other stakeholders. They can be the basis for identifying important development problems that have not been resolved so far.

The created unique indicators, however, are burdened with some imperfections related to the lack of an exhaustive definition of their substantive content, e.g., the indicator of technical infrastructure per 100,000 inhabitants, as well as the discontinuous nature of actions taken in the field of supplementing databases. This is the case, for example, in Kielce, which is the first in Poland to have obtained the ISO 37 122 certificate. However, the system of open access to public data is currently difficult to access, and it is not possible to assess its usefulness for external stakeholders.

A website dedicated to sharing public data has also been created in Wrocław. This website enables communication with residents about potential administrative decisions, and also, based on the above data decisions on innovative projects are made in the city. This takes place during meetings of a special group (the president's board), during which, on the basis of data and recommendations resulting from them, decisions are made while taking into account co-management on the implemented innovative projects. Moreover, the city provides open spatial data that can be used by businesses and scientists, which supports the sustainable development of Wrocław based on the needs of not only residents, but also other stakeholder groups. At the same time, a lot of emphasis is placed on cybersecurity, which is particularly important in the context of threats related to sharing open databases.

As already mentioned, smart organizations can also influence development effects, support the reduction of costs related to performing tasks of a given local unit, and affect the quality of life, especially in the sphere of public safety. An example of such use of open data is map services provided by the Warsaw City Hall, where, based on spatial information, it is possible to optimize operational processes related to the performance of tasks of a local government unit. Therefore, it is possible to optimize the use of council houses, reduce the costs associated with waste management, and rationalize the management of heat supplies. In Warsaw, a special smart information management system has been developed. It is the Warsaw 19 115 system, where about 100 people are employed. This system is a contact point with the residents, allowing simultaneous management of many processes, improving, and optimizing them.

The topic of data collection and its use to make decisions in virtually every aspect of life is also present in other cities studied. In Hanover, for example, data are collected on the city greenery as well as better use of infrastructure based on the Internet of Things.

Another example may be a solution developed by Katowice, consisting of a smart monitoring and analysis system. This system is based on cameras located in the city and artificial intelligence algorithms that detect crimes and dangerous situations, after which information is transferred to the crisis management center.

Another example is Rotterdam. The city pays great attention to having high-quality data that are used to support the implementation of tasks related to services, sports, culture, and health of its residents. Especially deserving of attention is the fact that the monitoring is supplemented with regular qualitative and quantitative research conducted by a group of about 60 to 80 researchers, thanks to which it is possible to observe the functioning of the city and make better decisions.

In Rotterdam, another very innovative solution that fits in with the idea of smart organization was developed. One of the key projects is Digital Twin, which consists in building a digital mapping of the city for simulation purposes. This project uses machine learning, which allows making more rational and effective administrative decisions. A similar solution is currently also being worked on in Gothenburg.

Comparable solutions have also been identified in Düsseldorf, where a specially created digitization department is responsible for internal process optimization and increasing digital competences among officials.

By collecting data, analyzing it, and recommending solutions, smart organizations contribute to the rationalization of costs and clerks' workload, reducing the number of errors, as well as increasing the quality of administrative duties. This aspect was emphasized, for example, in an interview in Wrocław.

Attention was also paid to the fact that it is not possible to unequivocally determine the impact of smart organizations on development effects in a given specific area. This is due to the fact that smart organizations have a multi-directional impact in relation to various elements of socioeconomic life. Therefore, there is no single measure by which one can derive a relation such as that 1 euro spent on the development of smart organizations translates, for example, into 2–3 euro of income generated in a given place.

On the other hand, at the level of individual projects that are substantively related to smart organizations, it is both possible and applied in practice to assign the planned effects of a given project. The KPIs defined for each project are an element that allows estimating the development effects of individual projects, the essence of which is information and knowledge management. Due to the fact that these projects translate into a higher quality of life in Wrocław, it was even said that the quality of life is the essence and key feature of a smart city. Therefore, the effects that are achieved in the sphere of quality of life thanks to the use of smart organizations are of particular importance not only in the short term but also in the medium and long terms.

An interesting example of using a smart organization to improve the quality of life is the construction of the city library in Düsseldorf. Thanks to the full digitization of the functioning of this building and, at the same time, the large scale of investment, this project assumed optimization of energy consumption and savings in labor costs thanks to the introduction of virtualization and automation of the service provided to the library users. At the same time, it was planned to ensure the availability of the library for the disabled, to prepare a place for workshops on new technologies, and to arrange space for teachers and students, businesses, and foundations of various associations, which would gain a place to conduct experiments in the use of new technologies.

In view of the developing energy crisis and the impoverishment of the population, these types of public utilities offering their services for free are of key importance in a situation where many people are subject to economic exclusion and suffer from the problem of loneliness. Therefore, shared public spaces with multifunctional use are an example of activities improving the quality of life, and at the same time achieving economies of scale thanks to the use of smart technological solutions (Dameri & Rosenthal-Sabroux, 2014).

III.2 Factors determining the impact of smart organizations on local development in the opinion of representatives of smart cities

As can be seen from the presented various examples of the impact of smart organization on local development, there are many factors influencing the possibilities of using smart solutions and their improvement. The interviews conducted among managerial staff of specialists and heads of selected cities indicated the most important conditions for the development of smart organizations and their impact on local development.

During the interviews, requests were formulated to indicate the most significant barriers to the development of smart organizations as a factor supporting local development. It was required that the answers were in accordance with the PESTEL method, thanks to which it is possible to take into account various reasons for the occurrence of difficulties in the development of smart organizations. Nevertheless, some barriers appeared more frequently in the responses than others.

The most frequently indicated barrier to the development of smart organizations is, in the opinion of the respondents, the financial barrier. It was pointed out that in local government units, there is much less flexibility in project management than in business. Projects based on information and communication technologies, on the one hand, have high process flexibility, due to the short life cycle of IT products, and on the other, public procurement procedures result in stiffening of all kinds of proceedings regarding the continuation of already started projects or the initiation of completely new projects that are not fully recognized at the time of commencement of the first works.

The representative of Rotterdam also pointed to a financial problem. The upcoming crisis is a big challenge. Therefore, according to the respondent, one should be agile and react to changes, which is very difficult in terms of public procurement. Also in Lisbon, there was a lack of investment funds for smart solutions, which hinders their development despite the undoubted benefits of using modern digital solutions. This problem is growing as a result of disturbances caused initially by the pandemic, then by the energy crisis, as pointed out by the representative of Wrocław.

The financial barrier may also be caused by the inability to carry out a reliable business analysis of capital-intensive projects implemented over a period of several years. An example of such a situation can be the implementation of a project focused on hydrogen solutions in Gothenburg.

Financial factors weakening the possibilities of developing smart organizations also include the problem of the inadequacy of allocation of development funds available at the local level to the actual development needs of large cities. This is the case, for example, in Warsaw. The representative of Warsaw drew attention to this problem on the example of the health service, which should be more strongly managed and supported at the central level than at the local government level. This problem is particularly important when we want to obtain durable permanent solutions, independent of the terms of office of the authorities.

This problem is related to the legal and administrative barriers. An important legal restriction may be too large legal limitations in undertaking experimental solutions, which was emphasized in the case of German cities (Hannover). It has been pointed out that in the Netherlands, for example, the legal framework is based on an experimental culture that does not work in Germany.

Significant barriers to the development of smart organizations as carriers of local development may also be of a social nature. This type of problem may be due to the aging of the administrative staff, as highlighted in Düsseldorf. On the one hand, people expect high-quality services, while on the other, the average age in the office is constantly increasing. Therefore, it is necessary to look for solutions for city management based on a much smaller number of employees, for example, through optimization solutions.

Smart organizations are often not established in the organizational structure of city offices. An example may be Gdynia, where a representative was appointed for the needs of the open data system, but without creating a human resources base at the same time. Such an important sphere is based on employees seconded from other departments, which does not translate into rationalization of the organization of their work. Excessive turnover of staff causes additional great difficulties in project management in the municipal office.

The social factor may also have a negative impact when there is no interest in smart solutions, which is related to a large mental barrier in the absorption of innovation, which was pointed out in Lisbon and Wrocław. The challenge is therefore to change the mindset of residents to make them aware of the need to use public transport, sharing, recycling, and other solutions related to ecology (Lisbon).

This problem is directly related to the digital exclusion of inhabitants who are less willing to adopt technological innovations. This is especially true for senior citizens. It is a very big problem in the implementation of solutions based on smart organizations in cities or their districts, where single-person households run by single senior citizens dominate. The representative of Verona and Warsaw indicated this problem.

In Gothenburg, attention was drawn to the reluctance of entities who treat specialist knowledge as a trade secret to share modern IT solutions. Therefore, there is a barrier to the dissemination of the concept of open innovation allowing for joining forces in the field of creative thinking and design thinking.

Technological barriers are also significant. They were also indicated by the respondent from Gdynia, who pointed to threats related to cybersecurity, as well as rapidly changing technologies, especially based on the Internet of Things. Their implementation faces many difficulties. Hence, for example, in Poland, they are less developed than in highly developed cities in Western Europe.

Another major technological challenge for cities is the dispersion of available data and the multithreaded nature of tasks carried out in individual departments. This problem was raised by the representative of Warsaw. The lack of common systems for departments makes it difficult to include separate databases, especially if it is accompanied by a diverse IT architecture of cloud solutions.

Difficulties in implementing smart solutions can also be political, as highlighted in Gothenburg. The main difficulty is the necessity to adapt long-term strategies to the changing four-year political terms of the municipal self-government, in particular the risk of changing priorities during the implementation of a long-lasting project. Hence, it is extremely important to maintain a common view of the city's future by councilors as important participants in political life in urban centers.

Sometimes a barrier to the development of smart organizations is the lack of a forum where residents could propose solutions for implementation. Such a situation takes place, for example, in Gothenburg, where residents can propose solutions through petitions, but they are not implemented in the form of a participatory budget, nor do they have any impact on final decisions made by the local government.

The political factor is also related to the problem of insecurity in the streets, which manifests itself, inter alia, in the form of shootings. This is not conducive to an atmosphere based on trust and knowledge sharing.

This problem was also raised in Gothenburg. Therefore, the challenge is to effectively allocate the city's resources so as to increase this security.

III.3   What determines the impact of smart organizations on local development in the light of the analysis of strategic documents of selected smart cities

Smart organizations are a source of many data and indicators of a diagnostic nature allowing for drawing development scenarios. Therefore, they have great potential to support strategic management. However, their actual use depends on the way of perceiving development opportunities and threats according to priorities dependent on cultural, economic, and natural factors. Therefore, the analysis of strategic documents looked for ways of perceiving the development strategy through the lens of the main development conditions divided, in accordance with the PESTEL methodology, into political, economic, social, technological, environmental, and legal conditions. This was the starting point for identifying the determinants associated with smart organizations.

Based on the review of strategic documents of 25 selected European cities, it can be concluded that a comprehensive and complete analysis of the conditions for the development of a smart city or resilience city is rare, despite the fact that in the twenty-first century we are observing a significant acceleration of scientific and technological progress, and recent years have also resulted in high political, economic, and epidemiological instability in many regions and areas of the world (Birmingham City Council, 2021; City of Amsterdam, 2011; City of Copenhagen, 2021; City of Dublin, 2018; City of Hamburg 2020; City of Helsinki, 2021; City of Kiel, 2019, 2022; City of Lille, 2021; City of Manchester 2021; City of Rotterdam, 2021; City of Stockholm, 2020; Endbericht Freiburg, 2017; Glasgow City Council, 2017; Municipality of Amsterdam, 2019; Senate Department for Urban Development and the Environment, 2015; Smart Climate City Strategy Vienna, 2022).

Therefore, it is surprising that out of 25 cities included in the global smart city ranking, only one city had the PEST analysis included in the smart city development strategy. The vast majority of strategic documents constitute a list of strategic goals broken down into the main spheres of socio-economic life, the development of which are more detailed strategic management tasks.

It is rare to indicate in them the main contemporary threats that appeared in 2019 and in the following years in the form of epidemiological globalization, the energy crisis and, finally, high political uncertainty in connection with the war in Ukraine. However, they are not stressed as factors that may affect the risk of failure to implement a given strategy. Contemporary threats such as the Covid-19 pandemic and the increasingly noticeable energy crisis were mentioned only incidentally, not in strategic documents, but rather in current plans. This was mainly due to the fact that a large proportion of the strategic documents were prepared in the period before the Covid-19 pandemic.

Strategic documents usually lack updated strategic assumptions and do not take into account mechanisms enabling the selection and implementation of scenarios according to the development of the situation. The lack of a scenario approach means that in most cases strategic documents are mainly a list of goals and tasks without indicating risk management methods in individual spheres (political, economic, social, environmental, or legal).

The growth of the resource potential of smart organizations (intellectual capital, ICT) and the development of management structures based on data and knowledge flows is possible when cities have their own strengths or development opportunities resulting from external stimuli. Moreover, it is important what kind of demand is developing with regard to management information.

In turn, the weakening of smart organizations is associated with the weaknesses of cities and external threats, as well as a decline in demand for information and knowledge.

The analysis of strategic documents of the cities in question indicates the determinants of the development of smart cities. They are analyzed by authors from the angle of their impact on the development of smart organizations as a catalyst for local development. The author's conclusions and comments resulting from the analysis carried out in this way are divided into groups according to the PESTEL model.

III.3.1 Political conditions

With regard to the political determinants of smart city development, the EU energy policy can be perceived as an opportunity, especially in terms of the full transition to renewable energy sources (Vienna). Distributed energy sources must be included in the general energy system not only on a regional and area scale but also on a national and even international scale, e.g., in border areas. This will increase the demand for information systems dedicated to renewable energy sources.

The political views of the decision-makers on the development of their cities are very important. Visionary leadership combined with agency allows the city to enter the path of development toward a smart city or consistently follow it (Leeds). If this is accompanied by uniform political leadership, as pointed out in Gothenburg, then these decisions have a driving force and may, for example, result in long-term efforts to evolve toward a smart city, even if at the beginning the goals are clearly promotional. This theme of promotion, for example, appeared as a crucial factor of the interest in the creation of information systems in Gdynia, the first city in Poland to obtain the ISO 37122 certificate for smart city; similar was the case with Kielce – one of the first centers that obtained the ISO 37120 certificate.

Experience in the implementation of the sustainable development policy is also important, which translates into an increase in demand for information systems and solutions based on ICT (Zaragoza). The concern to ensure an increasingly rising quality of life by reducing noise, improving the quality of the air, better management of water resources, and sustainable mobility contributes to increasing the awareness of residents about the need to combine efforts in these areas.

Changes in affiliation to political groups have been indicated as a development barrier, for example, in Glasgow. They indicate that the outlook for the economy is uncertain, and one should take into account a decline in internal investment in the city. This will require the support of the Scottish and British Governments.

Similarly, a political and an economic constraint is the city's growing financing gap in terms of commitments, as also pointed out by Glasgow. The gap (rising costs) arises from unexpected events, which creates challenges and financial pressures. These were set out in the Council's financial framework for 2017–2023.

Leeds also highlighted the difficulties arising from local politics in the face of the diverging interests of different types of stakeholders. Tech players want to obtain business benefits, while stakeholders – recipients of technologies and smart products – want to maximize utility benefits.

III.3.2 Economic/financial conditions

Business smart organizations are typical of high technology sectors. They are also a carrier of smart products which, thanks to additional digital functions, not only revolutionize the IT industry but also bring benefits to many other sectors. The strengths of digital technologies in the form of increased labor productivity, reduced operational failure and usually much higher profitability indirectly impact many other sectors, being a source of innovation in traditional sectors of production, construction, retail as well as product and service design (Manchester, Leeds Vienna). This creates a growing demand for ICT-based solutions, while cities are becoming specialized in the HT sector, attracting technology startups, which increases the development potential of smart organizations. There is also a growing demand for smart services in local government units as recipients of digital services, e.g., through public utility companies or enterprises performing their own tasks on behalf of local government units. Modern forms of work organization (e.g., agile techniques) are also introduced as part of work organization in city offices.

Therefore, it is a factor that positively influences the stimulation of the development of smart organizations in local government units.

Better-managed cities, based on smart solutions, respond better to the needs of their stakeholders and are a source of development impulses in their surroundings.

However, the influence of smart creative industries may be limited due to the high risk in running the high-tech business (Kiel), which may change the approach to implementing digital solutions in the city hall.

III.3.3 Social conditions

The development of smart organizations is limited by mental barriers in the adoption of new IT solutions by the staff and employees (Leeds). The reluctance of the staff and employees to use digital technologies creates barriers to competitiveness on an international scale, e.g. UK vs Germany, which reduces the potential for the development of smart organizations and inhibits decisions regarding the implementation of innovative digital solutions in city offices.

The strategies often raise the problem of growing differences in access to digital technologies, the problem of digital exclusion, especially among people of post-working age. Digital exclusion has a particularly discriminatory impact on communities, as well as people with disabilities and people aged 65 and over (Manchester). This inhibits the interest in smart solutions.

Another barrier to the implementation of smart solutions is the lack of 100% confidence in IT throughout the entire process of the use of certain technologies (e.g., cameras in public space, IT errors – in data encoding), which was noticed in Brussels.

This barrier is exacerbated by the lack of basic digital skills and the knowledge how to safely use the Internet, as recognized in Leeds.

III.3.4 Technological conditions

Among the main technological barriers affecting the development of smart organizations, both in the city hall and in the city it manages, the risk of know-how leakage, translating into the loss of competitive advantages of the city/region, should be noticed.

There is a risk that due to leakage of know-how from companies and professionals, local value chains or local companies (Kiel) will be damaged. This is also related to the problem of ensuring cybersecurity, which was pointed out in Vienna.

There is also a risk of misuse of IC technology, as noted in Brussels. Fears of unfair or civil rights-breaking solutions pose a great threat to the development of smart solutions in the public sector.

III.3.5 Ecological/natural/spatial conditions

Urban development strategies in the case of centers with a similar origin, structure, and economic base are aimed at overcoming barriers resulting from the growing conflict in spatial development. Competition for land for the implementation of individual functions of the city space is directly indicated.

The lack of land reserves and competition of various stakeholder groups for real estate, as well as the increasing costs of revitalization of industrial areas or depreciated housing structures in the central parts of the city require a strategy for activities in the field of shaping spatial order (Düsseldorf). Such needs appear rarely, but more often in smart city development strategies built on the basis of port cities. The natural limitation in the form of a coastline is therefore a factor supporting not only the care for the best use of urban space, but also the rationalization of the use of infrastructure in order to avoid local overloads. This is achieved by numerous ICT-based solutions as a result of city plans implemented on the basis of strategies.

Other development problems are included in low-population cities where undeveloped lands are perceived as unsafe and unattractive. This applies to sparsely populated countries, developing in conditions of discontinuous space (e.g., Scandinavian cities). Strategies are more geared toward the development of shared public spaces than the revitalization of post-industrial areas or slums.

The need for spatial order arises during the transition from dispersed development to compact – the densification of the city – empty spaces between buildings that create gaps and interfere with urban life. There are also large car parks that can be used more often and more efficiently or low-quality green zones that are not used. The role of the street as a public place was ignored in favor of road accessibility and safety (Gothenburg). This raises the need to monitor these areas, optimize their use based on monitoring, and create equal spatial development scenarios for such areas.

Among the factors driving the demand for digital services is the need to conserve resources. As explained in the Vienna strategy, the city's digital infrastructure must operate at maximum efficiency in a resource-saving, renewable-oriented manner. This creates a demand for digital services provided by the city hall.

The need to develop smart city monitoring systems is also created by climatic threats (warming, floods). An intensively used and densely built-up city with heavy traffic is struggling with the consequences of global warming. Longer periods of heat and heavy rains are becoming more common (Düsseldorf, Helsinki, Zaragoza), which requires early warning systems as well as the development of IoT solutions.

III.3.6 *Legal/organizational conditions*

In this group, bureaucratic barriers deserve attention, which can be summed up: the law has not kept pace with technological progress, as highlighted in Kiel.

III.4 Mechanisms of IO influence on local development and key recommendations

The mechanism that enhances the impact of smart organizations is related to leadership and the role of leadership competences of local development leaders. According to Badran, the managerial abilities of managers in local development are more useful than employees' abilities (Badran, 22007). Shared vision, mental model, systems thinking, team learning, and personal mastery can be used to enhance local development.

Not only the local leader but also strategic public service leaders and their willingness to learn and do so quickly are key to the sustainable development of public services. Being a learning organization requires a competent workforce and very careful succession systems to protect the organization's knowledge base. As a learning organization, the public service must proactively create an environment and mechanisms that enable it to think and act systematically to achieve the goals of sustainable growth and to deliver services effectively and efficiently. Therefore, strategic leaders in the public service need to carefully plan the implementation of a learning organization, bearing in mind that it is a long-term process that requires the unconditional commitment of all stakeholders (Schutte & Barkhuizen, 2014, p. 165).

Local and regional managers recognize that a more successful future depends on the development of human and social capital, and issues such as the learning city are considered by city managers and policymakers (Bednarczyk et al., 2019). A learning city brings together all providers of educational services to meet the needs and aspirations of its citizens. By pooling local resources, learning cities can find local solutions to local challenges (Saraei & Hajforoush, 2018, p. 1695).

Local governments, especially local government officials, should respond to social and economic changes in their communities. Organizations created by local leaders can be agile and become "adaptive organizations". They can take a systemic approach to organizational systems and structures to make the necessary changes to the organization in order to respond to changes in the community. Of key importance for the organization's ability to adapt to changes is the need for a positive organizational culture created by local leaders (Jensen, 2014, p. 293).

Hence, the intellectual capital created by the local development management team is of great importance. The influence of leadership is visible not only through the implementation of tasks assigned to the city's president/mayor but also through the method of selecting associates and creating principles for the organization of local administration.

The leadership style and decision-making competences influenced, for example, the commencement of works on the development strategy based on the smart city concept in Kielce and the certification of the city based on the ISO 37120 standard, as well as in Gdynia in the city certification process in accordance with the ISO 37122 standard. In both cases, the city authorities initiated and were directly involved in the process of creating a city development strategy based on the smart city concept. Interviews conducted among representatives of selected cities show that the smart city concept is not the same in individual cases, which means that not every local leader understands the concept the same. However, the common element that appears in the understanding of the essence of a smart city is the pursuit of a high quality of life in the city by basing its functioning on IT systems, ICT, databases, and the automation of management processes. Most often it concerns communication and management of parking spaces, municipal waste management, security, and public order infrastructure.

In turn, the intellectual capital inherent in project teams triggered the mechanism of diffusion of innovation within a given organization. Basing some of the tasks related to data acquisition and automation of management processes in the city's infrastructure also led to the dissemination of comprehensive thinking about the city's development strategy and its management based on the smart city concept, for example in Wrocław.

The influence of the personality of city presidents or their closest associates (e.g., vice presidents) also has an impact on the readiness to absorb innovations from outside the native local environment. Thanks to the flow of information between partner cities, participants of events dedicated to local government units or members of smart city organizations or other local government units territorial, there was a flow of information concerning not only the smart city concept itself but also specific methods of introducing smart solutions.

Thanks to the exchange of information between people who had a direct or indirect influence on decisions regarding the management of individual cities, it was possible to disseminate good practices regarding smart organizations as a factor stimulating local development. Information flow channels in the form of websites for certified smart cities, especially on the basis of international standards ISO 37120, ISO 37122, and ISO 37123, are useful for this type of impact. Moreover, study visits organized especially by partner cities contribute to the exchange of experiences. During the exchange of experiences, it is possible to develop solutions tailored to the specificity of a given city. An important function of the information channel is also played by large cyclical events for various groups of stakeholders. For example, the Economic Forum in Karpacz in Poland (previously in Krynica) is an opportunity to exchange experiences between businesses, politicians, local government units, and scientists from Poland and other countries of Central and Eastern Europe. As part of panel discussions, not only experience is exchanged, but also informal relationships that favor the exchange of information and the flow of non-modified knowledge are established.

Official internet portal of city of Amsterdam – amsterdam.nl, Official internet portal of city of Berlin – berlin.de, Official internet portal of city of Bilbao – bilbao.eus, Official internet portal of city of Bordeaux – bordeaux.fr, Official internet portal of city of Brussels – brucity.be, Official internet portal of city of Copenhagen – international.kk.dk, Official internet portal of city of Glasgow –- glasgow.gov.uk, Official internet portal of city of Gothenburg – goteborg.se, Official internet portal of city of Hamburg – hamburg.de, Official internet portal of city of Helsinki – hel.fi. Official internet portal of city of London – london.gov. uk, Official internet portal of city of Madrid – madrid.es, Official internet portal of city of Rotterdam – rotterdam.nl, Official internet portal of city of Stockholm – international.stockholm.se, Official internet portal of city of Vienna – wien.at.

Partner cities are usually similar in terms of existing development paths based on a similar economic base (e.g., port cities, cities with mining and metallurgical traditions, cities with strong long-term commercial functions and the like), therefore, it is particularly valuable to be inspired by good practices developed by a city with a higher level of socio-economic and technological development with similar development conditions.

Problems already resolved by a more developed city may provide inspiration or a ready-made model of conduct for a city with a lower level of economic development and thus at a different stage of smart city development. For example, a highly developed city may already be creating a smart city 4.0, while a city with a lower level of economic development is capable of development in line with the smart city 2.0 concept.

The similarity regarding historical conditions described in the path dependence concept is therefore a source of inspiration regarding management methods, tools, and specific plans allowing to overcome new emerging barriers to development, or as a source of ready-made solutions in the case of long-term barriers (e.g., the form of IT exclusion of the population, aging of the population, degradation of housing infrastructure in traditional city districts, growing disproportions in the standard of living of the population, and increasing environmental threats).

The analysis of both strategic documents and the audit of websites and interviews with representatives of selected cities also show a conclusion regarding the significant role of territorial marketing in the implementation of the smart city concept, and thus the possibility of smart organizations influencing local development. It is most visible in the certification process of cities based on ISO 37120:2019 or ISO 37122:2019.

The certification process comes down to adapting databases to the possibility of monitoring city development in accordance with the overarching values contained in the description of a given standard. In the case of ISO 37120, the main value is the quality of life of the inhabitants. In the case of the ISO 37122 standard, emphasis is placed on the use of modern IT tools in city management. According to this standard, the factors supporting the development of cities are the methods of joint leadership and improving the use of data and modern technologies in order to provide better services and ensure a high quality of life for local stakeholders (ISO 37122:2019, 2019).

In turn, in the ISO 37123:2019 standard, the most important thing is to ensure the city's resilience to shocks caused by various types of threats of a natural, economic, or technological nature. The definition provided in this document highlights the smart city's ability to accelerate its achievements in the field of social, economic, and ecological sustainability. The ability to respond to such global challenges as climate change, population growth, and political and economic instability is also underlined. Therefore, it includes the key determinants of smart city development, which result from global phenomena taking place in the twenty-first century.

Cities that apply for the certificate are required to collect data in a way that allows monitoring of individual spheres of the city's functioning.

For this purpose, they have directional indicators specified in the standard in the form of either a ready-made proposal or pointing to a certain group of possible partial indicators. The city receives a certificate if it creates an appropriate database and makes it available, for example, in an open data system. However, in order to certify the city, it is not required to use databases created in accordance with the standard for the purposes of making management decisions by the city administration.

In this situation, the certificate itself means creating an information basis for making management decisions in a rational, factual, transparent manner and ensuring better management of risk arising in various spheres of the city's functioning, rather than in situations where such databases do not exist. In the case of Polish cities, at the current stage of development, the marketing approach, mainly promotional, to obtaining awards and certificates is visible. However, our research shows that as the open data system develops, supported not only by local government units, but also other stakeholder groups, it is possible to generate unique databases devoid of initial errors or incomparability. The more these databases are refined and free of various types of defects, the more they can actually support management processes. Nevertheless, it should be noted that territorial marketing is a mechanism that initiates activities aimed at creating smart organizations but does not guarantee the use of the potential of a smart organization to actually strengthen the decision-making process, and thus make a real impact on development effects.

It is also important to promote smart solutions. This is highlighted by Claire Thorne and Catherine Griffiths, based on research regarding London. The authors notice that there is a real educational need to disseminate knowledge about the developed smart solutions. "Marketing" efforts are also needed to inform the public about the ubiquitous IT integration and to highlight the benefits of a smarter future for London. Most citizens may still consider "smart London" irrelevant or a waste of public money as the true use has not been effectively communicated (Thorne & Griffith, 2014).

Marketing activities are a catalyst for the development of a smart city based on creating or strengthening the city's brand (Baccarne, Mechant & Schuurman, 2014). The greater the marketing needs, the smarter solutions are needed for the management of a given city or territory.

Territorial marketing is also expressed by creating a territorial product in the form of a smart city built on the basis of stimulating local entrepreneurs and start-ups with the help of innovation centers. In this way, it is possible to support the investment attractiveness of a smart city for high-tech enterprises and to strengthen the migration attractiveness. It is a phenomenon that strengthens the activities of smart local government, which develops open databases for all local stakeholders (Sánchez-Corcuera et al., 2019).

III.5   Key entities – elements – mechanisms and barriers to the development of smart organizations in local administration

III.5.1   *Key entities of smart organization in a local government unit*

When considering the key entities of smart organization in a local government unit, one should distinguish between smart organizations created within the Offices and smart organizations formed by external stakeholders such as the business sector, research and development sphere, and social organizations.

In the case of smart organizations created by local administration, the key entities include local administrative authorities (president/mayor), city board/city council or local government assembly (in the case of cities that are regional or federal capitals in federal states), and middle-level managerial staff administering individual departments or enterprises separated from the administration, which carry out own tasks of local self-government.

Due to the decision-making competences, as well the legal framework related to shaping the development strategy of the city or other local government unit, it is the people at the head of the administration who have a very large impact on initiating and developing a smart organization supporting the development of a given local government unit. City authorities make management decisions, propose development strategies for a given city, and come up with initiatives for priority solutions.

An important entity of internal smart organizations is also city boards or city councils. The nature of cooperation between the city council and the president is very often political. Hence, the relationship between the organs of the executive power and the legislative authorities is of great importance at every stage of the development of smart organizations.

These relations are also of great importance for maintaining the budgeting of individual projects that create the development potential of a smart organization. Important entities in the local administration office are also managers or heads of departments responsible for the economy and entrepreneurship, as well as departments dedicated to the implementation of IT needs. Middle management is not subject to as much political pressure as mayors of cities or city councils. Therefore, they often have well-established views and visions of how a given city should be supported through an information and knowledge management system in the office itself and in the area subject to a given administration.

In the case of smart organizations covering not only the area of a given local government unit, but also social and economic ties with different entities from outside a given territory, of great importance become also other entities, such as the business sector. In the case of German cities, corporations and other large industrial units are of particular importance, as these constitute a very important group of stakeholders for the local government, and at the same time they act as creators of solutions based on information and communication technologies financed from private funds. This is especially visible in cities with strong commercial traditions. Many solutions supporting business processes are complementary to the tools prepared by the local administration or are provided on attractive terms for public use.

Small and medium-sized companies, especially technology startups, are also of great importance. They are a source of inspiration in the field of working methods and generating prototype technological solutions that are used in various spheres of the urban management. This dependency is reinforced by the fact that residents expect the digitization of public services with a quality similar to digital products and services offered by business due to the need to use more and more effective solutions in the field of municipal economy or other areas of the city. Another important subject of smart organizations is R&D units. Academic centers are an excellent example of strong support for local smart organizations by means of educating people with high digital qualifications, providing modern technological solutions, and including prototype solutions that can be used on a mass scale.

An example of such a relationship can be found, for example, in cities such as Barcelona, Vienna, or Leeds. The academic sector as an entity creating smart organizations is more often found in cities located in countries with a highly developed economy or in cities with long-standing traditions of implementing the smart city concept.

III.5.2 Key subject elements of smart organization in a local government unit

For the development of smart organizations, resources and competences assigned to IT departments, as well as departments dealing with economic development and entrepreneurship, are of key importance. During the pandemic, administrative units performing their own tasks in the field of health protection, education, and public safety also grew in importance.

Limiting direct interpersonal contacts, introducing distance learning, and providing medical services, especially advice using IT solutions, created an unprecedented demand for e-services and accelerated the development of the public administration's offer based on modern technological solutions. Currently, they constitute an equally important component of the digitization of public office activities as the previously introduced elements of management processes digitization in the field of municipal economy, public transport, and security systems.

III.5.3 Key mechanisms for the development of smart organizations as a factor influencing local development

Based on the analysis of selected European cities, there can be distinguished four basic mechanisms for the development of smart organizations, understood as a factor supporting decision-making processes in offices, directly or indirectly influencing the development effects in a given local environment. These are mechanisms such as diffusion of innovation, territorial marketing, historical determinism defining the trajectory development of a given territory, and behavioral mechanism expressed in the leadership style of local development leaders.

Among the above-mentioned mechanisms, particular attention should be paid to conditions based on innovations not only considered in the context of diffusion, but also in the context of local and supra-local innovation systems, while historical conditions and behavioral factors are of less importance.

Diffusion of innovation, as well as links within local/regional innovation systems, is manifested in the form of mutual inspiration from good practices in the field of information technology application. As a result of direct contacts between city authorities, managerial staff from local administration, and enterprises performing public tasks, the diffusion of innovation shows a multi-point and dispersed character. This is related to the search for the best models in the use of information technologies in various spheres of city functioning.

At the same time, no particular importance of the links between the twin towns was noticed. More characteristic channels of innovation flow are conferences dedicated to the development of smart city and websites supporting the smart city network, for example, https://www.smartcitiesnetwork.net/.

Moreover, often sought-after innovations are inspired by specific solutions observed during study visits. An example of such a mechanism may be the decision of Wrocław authorities to implement electric tickets, a solution inspired by London's experiences. Vienna, for example, in the search for new solutions looked for good practices in Dutch cities. Some cities are also looking for inspiration on other continents, especially by analyzing modern solutions in Asian and American cities.

III.5.4 Key catalysts for the development of smart organizations

Smart organizations appear as a tool supporting local administration at various stages of city development. The catalyst for this process is obtaining funding from public funds for the development of digital solutions positively influencing the quality of life of residents. This is especially characteristic of cities that have obtained funding from EU funds.

Another mechanism influencing the acceleration of the development of smart organizations in offices is the emergence of new IT opportunities offered by specialized enterprises that adjust their digital product to the specificity of a given city. The possibility of solving growing management problems along with the uncontrolled and unplanned development of the city using modern IT tools is a significant incentive, especially for cities that are at the first stage of creating a smart city, i.e., smart city 1.0.

This type of mechanism of stimulating the development of smart organizations can be strengthened by the development of technological entrepreneurship incubators, an example of which can be Barcelona, where local startups and technology companies have supported solving local development problems. Another catalyst for the development of smart organizations may be the needs of residents articulated in an organized manner through growing social participation, which is characteristic of smart city 3.0, where the carrier of IT solutions are the needs reported, for example, as part of civic projects. Research also shows that the use of smart solutions can be catalyzed by regulations and standards related to the need to protect civil rights. Such regulations, for example, relate to the protection of personal data or the recognition of electronic signatures.

III.5.5 Barriers to the development of smart organizations

Taking into account the website audit, its interviews and the collected survey material, the most important barriers in the development of smart organizations are social barriers, especially the lack of digital skills, as well as unwillingness to introduce changes in the existing administrative procedures or activities, both on the part of the administration and citizens.

Moreover, it is worth noting that the implementation of smart solutions requires financial resources, the budgeting of which, due to public procurement, is in contradiction with the high volatility and short life cycle of digital products and services.

Hence, great difficulties in creating smart organizations are characteristic of regions located in countries with a moderately developed economy or those struggling with a large budget deficit.

The difficult situation is exacerbated by the fact that the larger the city, the higher its development thresholds are. This is related to the depletion of building land reserves. In such situations, restructuring and revitalization of urban space require much greater resources than in the case of small settlement units. Hence, IT projects related to the flow of information and knowledge, despite their key importance, are not the subject of the most important points of the election programs and implemented local or regional development strategies.

III.5.6 Good practices for the development of smart organizations supporting local development

Smart cities 4.0 noticed this need when preparing a digitization strategy, including the preparation of specific programs and tasks, along with the planned budgets of individual projects. Therefore, it is a good practice that we can recommend based on the conducted research. Another good practice may be to undergo ISO 37122 or ISO 37123 certification.

Preparation based on the guidelines contained in both of the abovementioned standards allows for the adaptation of the collected information system to the actual development needs not only in the context of the development of smart organizations but also in preparing cities for various types of previously unknown shocks. Particularly noteworthy is the ISO 37123 standard, where the individual proposed parameters are tied to the goals of sustainable development. Thanks to this, it is not only possible to prepare a smart city for various unexpected types of development shocks, but also to control the goals of sustainable development, taking into account the social, economic, natural, and technological context.

The digital twin allows:

- identifying the needs of residents while presenting the possible variants of the city's development,
- visualizing the contemporary look of the city and its current functioning. On this basis, it is possible to control, plan and model various functions in the city based on what is happening now in real time,
- developing and visualizing development scenarios for new planned areas, and
- managing risk through the possibility of generating various types of scenarios for the development of problematic situations with the given assumptions of the model.

References

Baccarne, B., Mechant, P., & Schuurman, D. (2014). Empowered Cities? An Analysis of the Structure and Generated Value of the Smart City Ghent. In Dameri, R., & Rosenthal-Sabroux, C. (Eds.), *Smart City. How to Create Public and Economic Value with High Technology in Urban Space* (pp. 157–182). Genova: Springer.

Badran, M. A. (2007). Creating Learning Organizations for Local Development. *International Journal of Business Research,* 7(4), pp. 1–8.

Bednarczyk, Z., Kołos, N., Nosarzewski, K., Jagaciak, M., & Macander, Ł. (2019). *Kompetencje, jakich nie było. Kompetencje przyszłości na mazowieckim rynku pracy w perspektywie do 2040 roku.* Warszawa: Wojewódzki Urząd Pracy w Warszawie.

Birmingham City Council (2021). *Sustainability Appraisal Scoping. Report for the Birmingham Plan Review. Draft.* https://www.birmingham.gov.uk (accessed on 12.10.2022).

City of Amsterdam (2011). *Structuurvisie Amsterdam 2040 Economisch sterk en duurzaam. Amsterdam.* https://assets.amsterdam.nl/publish/pages/867639/ structuurvisie_amsterdam_2040_2011.pdf (accessed on 12.10.2022).

City of Copenhagen (2021). *The City of Copenhagen's Business and Growth Policy 2015–2020 – a Business Friendly Copenhagen.* https://international.kk.dk/sites/ default/files/202109/Business_and_%20Growth_%20Policy.pdf (accessed on 11.10.2022).

City of Dublin (2018). *Dublin City Development Plan 2016C2022 Progress Report.* https://www.dublincity.ie/sites/default/files/2021-05/report-no.-3132018-of- the-assistant-chief-executive-r.-shakespeare-dublin-city-development-plan. pdf (accessed on 11.09.2022).

City of Hamburg (2020). *Die Digitale Stadt gemeinsam gestalten. Koalitionsvertrag, Hamburg 2020.* https://www.hamburg.de/senatsthemen/koalitionsvertrag/ digitale-stadt-hamburg (accessed on 10.09.2022).

City of Helsinki (2021) *A Place of Growth. Helsinki City Strategy 2021–2025.* https:// www.hel.fi/static/kanslia/Julkaisut/2021/helsinki-city-strategy-2021-2025. pdf (accessed on 10.09.2022).

City of Kiel (2019). *Digitale Strategie der Landeshauptstadt Kiel.* https://www.kiel. de/de/kiel_zukunft/digitalisierung/_dokumente_digitale_strategie/digitale_ strategie_der_landeshauptstadt_kiel.pdf (accessed on 11.09.2022).

City of Kiel (2022). *Kommunale Innovationsstrategie für die Landeshauptstadt Kiel.* https://ratsinfo.kiel.de/bi/vo020.asp?VOLFDNR=26307 (accessed on 11.10. 2022).

City of Lille (2021). *Plan Lillois pour le climat 2021–2026.* https://www.lille.fr/content/ download/228672/2902930/file/PLAN+LILLOIS+POUR+LE+CLIMAT+- +NUMERIQUE.PDF.

City of Manchester (2021). *Manchester Digital Strategy: Creating an Inclusive, Sustainable and Resilient Smart City. Revised Copy for Continuing Consultation. January 29th 2021.* https://www.manchester.gov.uk/downloads/download/7344/ manchesters_digital_strategy (accessed on 12.10.2022).

City of Rotterdam (2021). *Voortgangsrapportage Aanpak Nul Emissie Mobiliteit.* https://www.rotterdam.nl/wonen-leven/nul-emissie-mobiliteit/ voortgangsrapportage-NEM-2020-2021.pdf (accessed on 12.10.2022).

City of Stockholm (2020). *Climate Action Plan 2020–2023 for a Fossil-Free and Climate-Positive Stockholm by 2040. Adopted by the City Council 25 May 2020.* https://international.stockholm.se/globalassets/rapporter/climate-action-plan-2020-2023_ta.pdf (accessed on 10.09.2022).

Endbericht Freiburg (2017). *Klimaschutzziel und – Strategie. München 2050.* https://stadt.muenchen.de/dam/jcr:8fab7200-cc0b-4e9b-8a9a-319d459e1a57/fachgutachten_2050.pdf (accessed on 11.10.2022).

Glasgow City Council (2017). *Glasgow City Council Strategic Plan 2017 to 2022.* https://glasgow.gov.uk/CHttpHandler.ashx?id=40052&p=0 (accessed on 11.09.2022).

ISO 37122:2019; Sustainable Cities and Communities — Indicators for Smart Cities, https://www.iso.org/obp/ui/#iso:std:iso:37122:ed-1:v1:en.

ISO 37123:2019. Sustainable Cities and Communities — Indicators for Resilient Cities, https://www.iso.org/obp/ui/#iso:std:iso:37123:ed-1:v1:en (accessed on 11.10.2022).

Jensen, J. (2014). City Libraries Townsville as a Learning Organisation within a Local Government Framework. *The Australian Library Journal*, 63(4), pp. 292–300.

Municipality of Amsterdam (2019). *City in Balance 2018–2022. Towards a New Equilibrium between Quality of Life and Hospitality.* https://assets.amsterdam.nl/publish/pages/868689/programme_city_in_balance_2018-2022_1.pdf (accessed on 10.09.2022).

Sánchez-Corcuera R., Nuñez-Marcos A., Sesma-Solance J., & others. (2019). Smart Cities Survey: Technologies, Application Domains and Challenges for the Cities of the Future. *International Journal of Distributed Sensor Networks*, 15(6). https://doi.org/10.1177/1550147719853984.

Saraei, M. H., & Hajforoush, S. (2018). Assessment and Prioritizing "Indicators Social and Legal of Learning City" in the Areas of Yazd City. *Revista de Direito da Cidade*, 10(3), pp. 1692–1712.

Schutte, N., & Barkhuizen, N. (2014). Creating Public Service Excellence Applying Learning Organisation Methods: The Role of Strategic Leadership. *Mediterranean Journal of Social Sciences*, 5(4), pp. 159–165.

Senate Department for Urban Development and the Environment (2015). *Berlin Strategy. Urban Development Concept Berlin 2030.* Berlin. https://www.stadtentwicklung.berlin.de/planen/stadtentwicklungskonzept/download/strategie/BerlinStrategie_Broschuere_en.pdf (accessed on 10.09.2022).

Smart Climate City Strategy Vienna. Our Way to Becoming a Model Climate City. Vienna's Strategy for Sustainable Development. 2022. https://smart-city.wien.gv.at/wp-content/uploads/sites/3/2022/05/scwr_klima_2022_web-EN.pdf (accessed on 12.10.2022).

The official website of the city Amsterdam – amsterdam.nl.

The official website of the city Berlin – berlin.de.

The official website of the city Bilbao – bilbao.es.

The official website of the city Bordeaux – bordeaux.fr.

The official website of the city Brussel – brucity.be.

The official website of the city Copenhagen – international.kk.dk.

The official website of the city Glasgow – glasgow.gov.uk.

The official website of the city Gothenburg – goteborg.se.

The official website of the city Hamburg – hamburg.de.

The official website of the city Helsinki – hel.fi.

The official website of the city London – london.gov.uk.

The official website of the city Madrid – madrid.es.

The official website of the city Rotterdam – rotterdam.nl.

The official website of the city Stockholm – international.stockholm.se.

The official website of the city Vienne – wien.at cdx.

Thorne Claire, Griffiths C. (2014). Smart, Smarter, Smartest: Redefining Our Cities. In Dameri, R., & Rosenthal-Sabroux, C. (Eds.), *Smart City. How to Create Public and Economic Value with High Technology in Urban Space* (pp. 89–100). Genova: Springer.

Summary and conclusions

In November 2021, the focus of researchers dealing with regional and local development was on the uncertainty in the regional and local development brought on by the global character of the Covid-19 pandemic. The main thrust of theoretical and practical search was aligned with the need to identify administrative and technological solutions which enable rapid decision-making by local government units amid lockdowns and mass infections. The year 2022 proved to be even more difficult due to other very serious developmental hazards of varying nature coming to the surface. Hence, research in European cities was a very difficult process which often required shifting the area of the search to manifestations of how smart organizations work. On the other hand, it was necessary to keep track of new technological solutions emerging in response to new hazards to the development of the population of individual regions and areas in the world.

This had an impact on the course of the research and the unique nature of the empirical material obtained. In spite of numerous difficulties, we managed to collect material that made it possible to address the posed research questions and to show the impact of a smart organization on local development. The research questions and answers to them are described below.

1 How are smart organizations defined, operationalized, and classified, in particular smart organizations in the public sector?
   In scientific terms, ten definitions of intelligent organizations and ten definitions of smart organizations were identified, including five specifically related to smart organizations in the public sector. Smart organizations consciously and skilfully identify and articulate organizational goals going beyond current organizational existence and survival, and they focus on meeting the identified and emerging new needs of their stakeholders, as well as on responding to the feedback received from them. The culture of smart organizations is very much modeled on agile ways of working and cooperation, as well as entrepreneurial behaviors. Smart organizations exploit already developed organizational knowledge and explore new knowledge that does not

DOI: 10.4324/9781003265870-14

exist at the organizational level. They identify and meet the needs of relevant stakeholders, using organizational and inter-organizational learning methods.

By dynamically adapting, networking, and using local, regional, and international cooperation networks, smart organizations "spill over" in terms of the rigidly defined boundaries of the constructs that organizations are. When functioning, smart organizations draw from virtual organizations, at the same time maintaining their physical form with the indispensable "hardware" infrastructure and human capital. The characteristics of smart organizations are complemented by skillful application of technology and creating "developmental leverage" using that technology, including, primarily, with respect to collecting, processing, and obtaining valuable decision insights from data and information.

In relation to autonomous organizations and local government units, smart organizations are subject to taxonomic classification and can go beyond such classifications, i.e., occur at the locoregional, microregional, submesoregional, mesoregional and macroregional (national), and even international levels (for intensively cooperating local government units located in various countries). Smart organizations lend themselves to being classified according to an organizational life cycle, so it is possible to identify organizations as they emerge and become active, grow and develop, and mature and decline.

2 How do smart organizations fit into the scientific discourse and how can they be used for further improvement and advancement of public sector organizations?

Smart organizations are a relatively new tendency that has been noted and studied in a systematic manner over the past 30 years. The immediate predecessors of smart organizations were intelligent organizations, ambidextrous organizations (exploring new knowledge and exploiting existing knowledge), and learning organizations. Smart organizations complete the picture of the evolution in leading paradigms of how organizations function that emerged in science and management (as a young scientific discipline of just over 100 years). They can be anchored more broadly in the context of improving management by objectives, strategic management, the market school, and the resource school. What immediately catalyzed and contributed to the emergence of smart organizations was the processes of skilful and purposeful processing of knowledge and information driven by the desire to increase competitiveness and selectivity (being attractive) in the eyes of organization's stakeholders. Smart organizations evolve and draw in a discernible manner upon other forms that derive from management and quality sciences, such as virtual organizations, agile organizations, resilient organizations, and finally, self-managing/holacratic organizations.

3 How are smart organizations measured in scientific and academic terms, as well as in industry and business practice?

This work presents 32 identified ways of measuring organizations that can be used to determine the maturity of smart organizations. The characteristic features of scientific methods include their focus on the intensity of acquiring and processing knowledge, and identifying, improving, and changing organizational competencies. Methodologies drawn from business practice highlight to a greater extent the aspects related to technology, connectivity, the flow of data and information between the organization and its external environment, and digitization. A particular type of method dedicated to so-called smart cities takes note of both infrastructural, and human and technological issues in measuring an organization's smartness. Whatever the environment of origin of the identified measurement methods, it is important to point out an important methodological gap typical for them, which is that they do not take into account of ways in which organizations prepare and make decisions. The book's authors venture to address this issue by conducting their own research and proposing measurement solutions of their own.

4 What factors and mechanisms enable the proliferation of smart organizations in local government?

The key factors and mechanisms identified in the research and which support the emergence and development of smart organizations in local government units are knowledge-based economy and intra- and inter-organizational learning, the concept of Industry 4.0 following a process approach and automation of some of the work performed, digitalization of the ways in which the public sector functions supported by regulations and funding, digitalization enabling a number of interactions, and the handling of issues between the local government administration and the residents, entrepreneurs, and investors. Last but not least, as an example of an external shock and a transformational and developmental impulse, the COVID-19 pandemic is counted by the co-authors of the work among the mechanisms that can further stimulate the emergence of smart organizations in local government units. The opportunities for further development and strengthening of smart organizations in the EU regard EU funds for 2021–2027, including those available under the *National Reconstruction Plans and Cohesion Funds*, a significant portion of which is dedicated to the digitization of work and cooperation.

5 How does the EU institutional environment affect the development and functioning of smart organizations in local government units?

Without a smart environment and relevant saturation with new digital technologies, smart organizations in local government units will not be effective. Smart organizations develop, for instance, due to interactive processes of learning and implementing innovations which are determined by institutional structure. Institutions provide information and reduce decision uncertainty, manage conflicts, and cooperation, offer incentives to implement the ideas of sustainable development, and allocate resources to foster the development of smart technologies. Institutions shape communication processes and adjust relations among people and groups of people in organizations, among organizations and beyond. Not only do they affect the process in which smart organizations emerge, but they also decide on the number of resources earmarked for development in the context of creating innovations and technologies used in smart local government units.

6 What types of potential of EU innovation systems over the NUTS-2 spatial scale create the institutional environment of smart organizations, how do they vary, and what are their typologies territorially?

The typology of European regions has shown that smart organizations function in various institutional and innovation environments. Because of regional disproportions and due to a lack of cohesion, the initial seed capital for the organizations varies. This applies particularly to human and innovation capital. Regions characterized by high developmental parameters are already taking on the role of innovation leaders and they achieve measurable effects in implementing new smart development concepts. For regions where there is a deficit in potential, institutional solutions should be put in place which provide a cooperation framework for knowledge and information flow. However, the foregoing should not follow the principle of growth drivers with respect to which diffusion and spillover of the developmental effect were expected. Missions set forth in the EU strategy involve everyone in the goal-attaining process, which becomes a priority challenge for both leading as well as peripheral regions. Moreover, their participation in the process is directly proportional to their resources and endogenous types of potential.

7 What endogenous conditions should be met within territorial systems for smart organizations to contribute to sustainable development?

New energy solutions and technologies aimed at sustainable development involve investment risks which local government leaders responsible for sustainable development programs refer to in their decisions. Investment projects related to the implementation of zero-emission transportation, urban bicycles, electric buses, modern energy systems, transportation and communication systems, and utility applications are costly and require good management of local government budgets and finance. In addition, residents may not approve of, and lack skills, thus precluding the implementation of innovative solutions. Changes in daily habits and rules and the development of skills and competencies are necessary. Consequently, they will generate a need for a system of promotion and training and the introduction of relevant laws and regulations. Thus sustainable development should not only be technological but also social innovation based, which will boost the competitive advantage of local government units in the global economy in the long run.

8 What is the role of territorial innovation systems in the diffusion of knowledge, information, and innovation?

Territorial information systems play a major role in how a smart organization functions, as its volatile environment generates a constant need to adapt to changes and to produce new, often innovative, solutions. Such systems are primarily social systems that pertain to systematic interactions among various groups of institutions in the public and private sectors alike. In order to increase local capacities for knowledge flows and innovations aimed at sustainable development, channels supported by modern IT technologies are being established as part of innovation systems among smart organizations. Local government units that want to participate in the processes of creation, absorption, and diffusion of new technologies and solutions must be active participants in such systems. This is a prerequisite for the effectiveness of their smart management and crisis handling.

9 What is the essence of local sustainable development today?

The essence of local sustainable development is to attain environmental, economic, and social goals which determine the welfare of the present and future generations inhabiting a local territory. It should also incorporate a digital dimension that is dependent on ICT infrastructure, knowledge flows, and technological innovations absorbed and developed by all the local stakeholders.

10 How can you identify the impact of smart organizations in local government with respect to local development in the era of digitalization?

To identify the influence of smart organizations in local government versus sustainable local development in the era of digitalization, our idea is to holistically employ the DPSIR method (Drivers, Pressures, State, Impact and Response) developed by the Organization of Economic Cooperation and Development (OECD, 2003). This will be a means of providing a structure and organization for environmental factors to create a comprehensive framework for decision-makers. It is recommended for evaluating smart and sustainable development, as it involves an evaluation of the effects of decisions made by decision-makers.

Indicators recommended in smart city certification based on the ISO 37122 standard can be of help, too. The certification process based on this standard allows databases to be adjusted to monitor the achievement of the city's development goals in line with a resolution of the United Nations General Assembly which determines 17 development goals. In this way, it is possible to identify the impact of smart solutions applied in smart cities, especially in terms of the needs of the local community and its habitat, as well as the effects of management decisions made by the local government authority in a given administrative unit.

11 What theories can be considered sources of knowledge on the impact of smart organizations on local sustainable development in the digital era?

The impact of smart organizations on local sustainable development in the era of digitization can be explained by innovation diffusion theory. Based on competitive advantages being due to a better use of information and knowledge, smart organizations promote the rationalization of management decisions made by the authorities of individual local government units, which yields social economic and natural effects.

Based on the theory of diffusion of innovations, we can show that the sources of innovative solutions and the paths (channels) of their dissemination are of major importance. Sources of innovation can also include local government units which develop original IT solutions and enterprises providing universal IT solutions. By recognizing the type of information flows within the local environment, as well as those involving participants other than local participants in decision-making processes, it is possible to account for how new digital solutions emerge and extend, thus fostering sustainable local development in various regions of Europe.

Our research shows that this diffusion is a tendency spreading from the West to the East of Europe, i.e., from the economically more developed regions forming the center of the European space (the *blue banana*) toward the peripheral areas. This strongly corresponds to the level of economic development of individual European regions.

Another theory comes into play here that explains well the impact of smart organizations on the local development – a path dependence concept. This theory holds that the past barriers that determined the survival of previous economic specializations create similar barriers preventing the absorption of innovative solutions, especially those based on ICT.

Hence, regions with a past mining and metallurgic profile experience similar difficulties in implementing innovative solutions despite advanced restructuring processes. What is more, sources of innovation created by the industrial sector are also observed as exerting an increased influence on the creation of smart solutions in the region. This, for example, does not hold for regions that have formed an economic base using the coastal function (maritime shipping, industry based on trans-shipment structure).

The concept of regional innovation systems is also useful in accounting for the impact of smart organizations on local development. This explains why in regions with highly interconnected business sectors, administrative sectors and organizations, contacts are more frequent, and thus information and innovative solutions based on ICT are exchanged more intensely.

12 How can a case study be used to enhance the current body of knowledge with elements regarding the impact of smart organizations on local sustainable development?

In analyzing the impact of smart organizations on local sustainable development, it is worth employing the case study method to supplement statistical analyses. Case studies enable deeper analysis based on elements that are absent from regional and local databases.

In addition, by analyzing the case studies, it is possible to identify the most topical tendencies and ongoing processes, especially amid unexpected and rapid changes in the local government units themselves and in their environment. The case studies can also provide inspiration for areas or regions that have similar solutions in their strategies, yet no practical experience.

Thus, with the case study method, it is important to make the right choice of local units to be analyzed. First of all, a choice of units that are representative of the type of region given the economic base, previous developmental trajectory, previous demographic character, geographical location and the like is especially important in research on the application of smart organizations as a tool to support sustainable local development.

As a subject of case studies, the units selected should have the experience that can be promoted and/or enhanced in other local circumstances as it is essential for the solutions identified to apply elsewhere, that is, to be universal.

There is one more, purely practical, condition. Namely, it is necessary to consider the actual accessibility of people who have the knowledge and experience to identify the key content. Even the most experienced local government units are not always willing to share their knowledge, which significantly limits the odds of acquiring knowledge useful to other local communities.

13 Are smart organizations a factor encouraging sustainable development of local government units amid severe and unpredictable random tendencies, the so-called *black swan*?

Smart organizations are a factor encouraging the sustainable development of local government units amid severe and unpredictable random tendencies, the so-called *black swan*. This is because, using smart solutions, information flows faster, and the number of signals coming from residents and infrastructure systems allows for effective and reasonable decision-making.

As shown by studies carried out in Poland on smart local shields, the main initiator of unusual actions is representatives of the city hall/municipal/communal office. The more advanced the hall/

office's information system, the greater the chance of decisions that make it possible to cope with unexpected catastrophic events. It is also possible to reduce the cost of administrative activities caused by unpredicted occurrences, and therefore not included in the local government budget.

In the pandemic era, smart organizations are also the foundation for new e-service solutions to reduce the frequency of personal contacts between citizens and local administration. This solution would not have been feasible but for an earlier or accelerated implementation of modern ICT solutions.

In regions with more advanced civic society, where the regional or local innovation system is fully established, smart organizations formed by the administration are also supported by smart organizations created in businesses and NGOs.

This is a source of great potential, encouraging local development through smart local organizations created by all groups of local as well as supra-local stakeholders, the latter being active, however, in a given territory.

14 What growth-oriented measures are undertaken by local government units having smart organizations which are more advanced?

Growth-oriented solutions that emerged in cities in which there is a higher number of advanced smart organizations are those deriving directly from the latest technological solutions based on artificial intelligence and the Internet of Things. In turn, no interest was recorded for solutions improving data management, such as blockchain.

On the other hand, the introduction of a tool in the form of a digital twin is recommendable. A digital twin is a three-dimensional miniature of an actual city that can be used to identify the present and future needs of the residents, generate various scenarios of spatial development of the city, and apply scenario-based methods of risk management in city development.

On the other hand, it is quite common to create electronic applications that allow direct involvement of the public in the process of urban space management and that improve access to the facilities the city offers. These facilities include for instance, tourism, mobility and public transportation, the labor market, or the real estate market.

Due to the answers to the questions above, it is possible to formulate answers to more universal questions about the impact of smart organizations on local development.

1   How does the model of smart organizations support local government in pursuing the policy of local and regional development in a way that is sustainable and resilient to internal disruption?

Based on the author's own model of smart organizations shown in this study, it is possible to identify both the potential for growth of smart organizations and the mechanisms that enable rationalization and higher effectiveness of decisions made in the local government unit and, indirectly, developmental effects broken down into natural social economic and natural effects. Each of the model's elements can be monitored by variables selected on the basis of a smart city certificate (ISO 37 122) or resilient city certificate (ISO 37 123). This idea can be implemented through the development of open data systems, as well as the digital twin as a tool to create more elaborate models describing both smart organizations and complex structures created by cities or other local entities.

2   What are the major characteristics of smart organizations that impact local government's effectiveness in attracting and retaining inhabitants, entrepreneurs, and investors?

In light of the research, the major characteristics of smart organizations include scalability, i.e., the ability to modularly scale up the deployed high-tech solutions and to bring compatible subsets of data together so that individual databases can network locally, regionally, and even internationally.

The second important characteristic is the ability to sustain and improve the implemented solutions. This is vital given both the short life cycle of high-tech products and rapid obsolescence of digital competencies of both employees and users of information systems.

It is also worth noting the applicability of IT solutions aligned with the present and anticipated needs of various stakeholders. Various groups of local stakeholders co-creating applications for mobile phones and computers means opportunities for synergy of efforts by administration, business, and the public. It also reduces the cost of digitization of public sector management.

What determines the production of an effective smart organization is openness to innovation on the part of local leaders, as well as a willingness to participate in the diffusion of digital innovations on the part of other stakeholders in the process. The process of innovation diffusion requires both openness to sharing innovations and readiness to implement them.

In our view, the theoretical gap was partly filled thanks to the attempts to answer the above questions. The argument supporting this is the development of a model perspective of the impact of smart organizations on the mechanism of management decision-making in local government units, and then on developmental effects viewed in four categories: natural, social, economic, and technological. In addition, 20 definitions of smart organizations were reviewed in detail, the definition of a smart organization in the public sector was coined, and 32 methods for measuring such organizations were reviewed allowing for the methods' backgrounds (including academics and the business community).

The empirical gap in research on smart organizations in the public sector was filled by an electronic audit technique applied to the official website of the top 25 European cities in the Smart Cities Index 2021, and by surveying their representatives based on the direct interview technique. The research findings identified a number of specific good practices followed by smart organizations in the public sector. They can be a source of inspiration and developmental stimulus for other local government units aspiring to transform into smart organizations.

In the context of the methodological gap, the co-authors came up with an explanatory model for the formation, functioning, and impact on the environment of smart organizations in the public sector. The model can provide a direction for further detailed research and verification both by academics and in managerial practice at the local government level.

Based on the conclusions presented, the following hypothesis can be deemed true: The greater the access to human capital resources and to infrastructural resources, the greater the potential for local government to develop into a smart organization (a hypothesis inspired by the research of Filos and Banahan, 2001 and Filos, 2006).

The research shows a link between the regions having the resources and the location of smart organizations. As many as 26 highly rated smart cities are located in the regions with the highest potential. The formation of smart cities is encouraged by a multidimensional institutional environment and the mechanism of interaction between not only technological and infrastructural types of capital but also social aspects that are of tremendous importance. They prepare the residents to welcome new technologies and to desire to explore and use the technologies in everyday life. The conclusion is that other regions willing to participate in the processes of implementing smart solutions will therefore have to overcome not only infrastructural and technological but also social barriers. Changes in the mindset of the population will in many cases pose a major challenge for local authorities responsible for implementing smart strategies. Being among the highest-rated cities in the ranking discussed, Zurich emphasizes in its strategy that "smart" means combining people, organizations, and infrastructure. Effective city management is determined by dialogue and communication between the city administration and its residents. In this way, joint city management is enabled, as well as the creation of grassroot initiatives in the form of civic budgets. In addition, participation and direct democracy become strengthened. This is what seems to be the main challenge in the coming years of digital transformation.

The remaining hypotheses were not verified, as it was impossible to collect empirical material from cities with the highest potential for developing smart organizations. In spite of repeated attempts to obtain consent to conduct a survey or an interview, we were faced with either no or a negative response. Thus further research is necessary, albeit with less disruption to city functioning. A reluctance to participate in the research may also be down to the (cities considered) smart cities visibly lacking information systems to generate reports on activities carried out for the local environment. Such is the conclusion of research conducted in Polish cities in 2021. At that time, for the purposes of smart loyalty shield study, cities only collected information on social and economic activities during the pandemic, instead of using automatically generated reports.

Further research paths that the co-authors believe are worth pursuing include identifying detailed mechanisms for attaining organizational sustainability in functioning typical of smart organizations, as well as mechanisms for responding to and achieving sustainable resilience to development shocks occurring in the developmental environment of local government units.

References

Filos, E., & Banahan, E. (2001). Towards the smart organization: An emerging organizational paradigm and the contribution of the European RTD programs. *Journal of Intelligent Manufacturing*, 12, pp. 101–119.

Filos, E. (2006). Smart organisations in the digital age. In Mazgar I. (ed.) *Integration of ICT in Smart Organisations* (pp. 1–38). Hershey, PA: Idea Group Publishing.

Garvin D. (1993). Building the learning organization. *Harvard Business Review*, 1(4), pp. 78–91.

OECD (2003). Environmental indicators – development, measurement and use. Report. Organisation of Economic Co-operation and Development, 37 pp. https://www.oecd.org/environment/indicators-modelling-outlooks/24993546.pdf

Appendix

Appendix 1 PESTEL analysis of the development conditions of smart cities based on strategic documents of selected European cities

Political factors

No.	Factor	Type of impact (positive/ negative)	Description	Example
	Striving for a full transition to renewable energy in line with the established principles of the EU energy policy	Positive	Renewable energy sources will provide 75% of the energy needs for digitization and digital services by 2030 and will cover 100% of these needs by 2050. This also includes power supply for data centers, workstations, etc.	Vienna
	Local policy toward a conflict of interest (technological players – local stakeholders)	?		Leeds
	Visionary leadership of city leaders	Positive		Indirectly Leeds
	Uniform political leadership	Positive		Gothenburg
	Financial feasibility of political decisions	Positive		Indirectly Leeds

(Continued)

Continued

No.	Factor	Type of impact (positive/ negative)	Description	Example
	The city's financial commitments to the budget gap	Negative	The gap (rising costs) arises as a result of unexpected events – financial challenges and pressures. These were set out in the council's Financial Framework 2017 to 2023. It confirmed that it is a reasonable assumption that the level of spending gap experienced by the council over the last five years is likely to continue to at least the scale experienced, £220 million. The Council Strategic Plan has to reflect the Financial Framework and recently issued Financial Forecast when setting out any commitments.	Glasgow
	Experience in the implementation of sustainable development policies, political/ administrative authorities with social participation	Positive	An example of such activities may be the city's activities to reduce noise levels, improve air quality, water management, sustainable mobility, etc. It is also important to use the experience of city officials in increasing citizens' awareness of the above-mentioned aspects of sustainable development.	Zaragoza
	Consequences of leaving the EU	Negative	The economic outlook is uncertain, and we need to plan for the long term. The risk of a decline in internal investments in the city. This will require the support of the Scottish and British Governments.	Glasgow

Source: Own elaboration.

The economic factors

No.	Factor	Type of impact (positive/negative)	Description	Example
	ICT as a source of key and interdisciplinary technologies for other sectors and areas of life	Positive	Attractive location for IT and start-ups.	Vienna
	Excellent digital infrastructure	Positive	Constantly developed digital infrastructure with its implementation integrated into the organizational structure of the city.	Vienna
	Competing for investments and talent with other regions	Negative	Creating value elsewhere (e.g., through collaboration).	Leeds, Kiel
	Automation of "typically" female sectors, e.g., office and administrative work, has negative effects on jobs for women	Negative		
	100% lack of trust in IT during the entire process of use of certain technologies	Negative	Distrust is related to placement of, for example, cameras in public space, IT errors – when encoding data.	Brussels
	Mental barriers to the absorption of new IT solutions by the staff and employees	Negative	The reluctance of the staff to use digital technologies causes barriers to competitiveness on an international scale, e.g., UK vs Germany.	Leeds
	Hybridization of industrial and other types of development and creation of attractive spaces for the new economy	?		Madrid
	New forms of hybrid and remote work	?	Limiting the demand for office space.	Helsinki
	The development of the use of digital solutions in various types of activities, including traditional ones	Positive		Leeds

(Continued)

No.	Factor	Type of impact (positive/negative)	Description	Example
	High risk in running a technologically advanced business	Negative		Kiel
	Digital technologies destabilize markets and displace entrenched companies	Negative	Digital technologies are disruptive to the entire world. Retail, tourism, transport, and media are shaking up in the same way as new "technology" sectors. Both companies representing traditional sectors and technology enterprises rooted in the local market, which have a hard time assimilating innovative solutions, may be replaced by business innovators, thus leading to a crisis on the local market. This is a trend that is likely to continue and impact other sectors as digital technologies advance and smart business solutions are deployed.	Glasgow
	The extent and manner of using ICT in production and services as a leading factor of competitiveness	Negative	The extent to which enterprises use digital technologies becomes a critical factor in their ability to survive and/or grow. It concerns mainly activities in the field of: 1 promotion and creation of the company's image, 2 Internet security, 3 compliance with data protection rules, 4 communication with employees, partners, and customers.	Glasgow
	Competitive potential of IT innovations for many other sectors	Positive	The digital aspect of business is a critical success factor for the broad business community. IT-based solutions also have an impact on many other sectors, being at the forefront of innovation for traditional manufacturing, construction, and retail. This is particularly true for the design stage of products and services.	Manchester

Source: Own elaboration.

Social factors

No.	Factor	Type of impact (positive/negative)	Description	Example
	Growing inequalities in the world	Negative		Helsinki
	Growing social injustice caused by inequalities in basic digital skills	Negative	The entire United Kingdom.	Glasgow
	Digital alienation	Negative	Digital exclusion has a particularly discriminatory impact on communities as well as on people with disabilities and those aged 65+.	Manchester
	Aging of the population, growing senior population; indispensable reform of social and health services	Negative		Helsinki, Zaragoza
	Growing social (cultural) diversification	?	It triggers the need to create a safe and attractive space for everyone.	Helsinki
	Accessibility and digital equality	Positive		Vienna, Manchester Brussels
	Excluding certain social groups from access to ICT	Negative		
	Impact of ICT on health (e.g., radiation impact)	Negative		
	Lack of basic digital skills and safe internet use	Negative		Leeds
	Fall in demand for some jobs and increase in demand for others	Negative	Workplaces that consist of routine tasks are at greater risk of falling, while those professions that require interpersonal and cognitive skills have good opportunities for growth.	Leeds

Source: Own elaboration.

Technological factors

No.	Factor	Type of impact (positive/negative)	Description	Example
	IT security	Positive		Vienna
	Strengthening the fast-growing ICT sector while ensuring social justice	Positive	Technological factor, but related to social accessibility to ICT.	Vienna
	Risk of misuse of IC technology	Negative		Brussels
	The risk of leakage of know-how translating into the loss of competitive advantages of the city/region	Negative	There is a risk that local value chains will be breached due to leakage of know-how from companies and professionals. In addition, local businesses may lose their ability to compete outside their home territory.	Kiel

Source: Own elaboration.

Ecological and spatial factors

No.	Factor	Type of impact (positive/negative)	Description	Example
	Conserving resources		The digital infrastructure of the city must work with maximum efficiency, in a way that saves resources and focuses on renewable sources.	Vienna
	Competitive functions of urban space	Negative	Revitalization or restructuring of industrial areas requires pro-ecological solutions.	Madrid, Düsseldorf
	The lack of land reserves in the face of growing population causes competing functions in spatial development	Negative		Düsseldorf
	Imbalance in the management of natural resources in urban space	Negative	Need to improve the territorial balance and structure of areas and neighborhoods with less dependence on central districts and greater resilience and durability of the city as a whole, as well as its inhabitants.	Madrid
	Climate threats (global warming, floods)	Negative	An intensively used and densely built-up city with heavy traffic struggles with the consequences of global warming. Longer periods of heat and heavy rains increase (Düsseldorf).	Helsinki, Zaragoza Düsseldorf
	Landslides	Negative		Zaragoza
	Noise	Negative		Gothenburg
	Large contrasts in the city's spatial structure – growing disproportions	Negative	Decapitalization of traditional housing resources, high-density built-up areas in traditional districts, the problem of vertical and horizontal accessibility.	Zaragoza
	The need for spatial order in the transition from dispersed development to compact – city *densification*	?	Empty spaces between buildings that create gaps and interfere with city life, large parking lots that can be used more effectively, or low-quality green zones that are not used; the role of the street as a public place has been ignored in favor of road accessibility and safety.	Gothenburg

Source: Own elaboration.

Legal (legislative) factors

No.	Factor	Type of impact (positive/negative)	Description	Example
	Legal obligations resulting from the EU energy policy	Positive		Vienna
	bureaucratic barriers (the law does not keep up with technological progress)	Negative		Kiel

Source: Own elaboration based on the official websites of the surveyed cities.

Appendix 2 List of smart city development conditions as a substantive basis for monitoring opportunities and threats to smart city development

Development conditions are either a stimulant or an inhibitor. Sometimes their impact is ambiguous, depending on the specificity of a given city. Their measurability also varies. Therefore, the table below presents the development conditions for smart cities broken down by type (PESTEL). Factors identified as positive should be included in database system models as stimulants, and those identified as negative as inhibitors.

Political factors

Chances/stimulants

- political integration, which gives the possibility of co-financing key investments in information and communication technologies,
- the possibility of creating international teams working in partnership to solve modern-age problems, and
- development of international financial instruments by means of common EU policy in the field of smart city development.

Threats/Inhibitors

- wars and political conflicts,
- terrorism,
- divergent political interests of members of decision-making bodies in local government units,
- conflicting interests of various stakeholder groups, especially companies versus residents, local government units,
- political conflicts regarding minorities, and
- lack of political will on the part of the mayor or city council.

Technological conditions

Chances/stimulants

- large implementation of high ICT-based technologies to traditional types of activity,
- the ability to quickly update databases,
- possibility of including new resources into open databases,
- the ability to connect databases and the computing power of the world computer network, and
- development of technological entrepreneurship, which is the basis of new business models adapted to contemporary social, economic, and technological challenges to a greater extent than is the case with traditional business models.

Threats/Inhibitors

- emancipation of artificial intelligence,
- technical requirements grow too quickly relative to users' readiness to use them,
- unfair use of knowledge, such as white hat hackers and black hat hackers,
- unforeseen side effects of the technologies used, for example, artificial intelligence may recommend decisions that are based on the wrong premises,
- malfunctioning notification systems, i.e., also the result of a wrongly made or wrongly suggested decision,
- rapid obsolescence of technology, which creates difficulties for public procurement,
- applications becoming obsolete too quickly relative to the changing needs, hence the need to modernize them, maintain service, and introduce appropriate changes,
- the use of technology for political purposes, which is associated, for example, with controlling political opponents,
- high dependence on constant electricity supply, as the lack of electricity causes great perturbations in the use of modern solutions of modern technologies, and
- physical efficiency of the server rooms and their security.

Economic conditions

Chances/stimulants

- expansion of sales markets thanks to virtualization of operations,
- access to labor resources is increased today by the missing resources,

- possible acquisition of talented people thanks to the use of remote and hybrid work,
- running a business based on high technologies, which, compared to traditional industries, is characterized by greater profitability,
- new technological solutions become cheaper with time, thanks to which competitive advantages arise,
- the possibility of creating crowdfunding, which helps to reduce local capital deficits, and
- reducing the waste of all resources in enterprises and local government units.

Threats/Inhibitors

- unpredictability of financial expenses due to the difficult to estimate expenses related to the maintenance of the smart city infrastructure,
- unprofitability of developing smart organizations in peculiar or sparsely populated places,
- lack of adequately qualified human capital causing bottlenecks in the workings of a smart organization and its beneficiaries,
- the increase in the capital intensity of investments with the growing costs of urban development causes a capital barrier,
- investment in ICT is not profitable with too few users, this applies to unpopulated or sparsely populated areas, and
- lack of spatial order resulting in higher revitalization costs of decapitalized housing and industrial infrastructure.

Social conditions

Chances/stimulants

- the emergence of generation Z, which is characterized by a much greater level of acquiring technological skills compared to the older generations,
- growing awareness among the society of ecological threats,
- the use of information and communication technologies makes it possible to virtualize markets, and
- smart solutions make it possible to limit the personal contacts of the population under threatened conditions, e.g. epidemics, natural disasters, warfare, and terrorist attacks.

Threats/Inhibitors

- the problem of lack of trust in modern digital solutions of users,
- resistance to adopting innovative digital solutions resulting from satisfaction with existing solutions,

- digital exclusion increasing with the aging of the population,
- social conflicts intensifying in line with the growing social diversity, especially in cities, which causes mass immigration, which results in reluctance to share knowledge and resources of a smart organization,
- treating digital competences as an advantage on the labor market, which hinders the dissemination of digital skills among the population, and
- virtual solutions weaken local interpersonal ties, thus local social networks lose their importance, which also results in less consolidation of the city's society around common goals.

The spatial and natural conditions are related to the spatial structures created by the city in a specific natural habitat.

Chances/stimulants

- the possibility of reducing the consumption of raw materials, improving the efficiency of recycling and, at the same time, reducing supply chains thanks to the use of modern digital solutions dedicated to the circular economy and
- it is easier to monitor the environment with ICT than with traditional methods, therefore the use of notification systems is a direct source of more effective environmental protection.

Threats/Inhibitors

- unpredictability of natural phenomena, which makes it difficult to create appropriate solutions in the field of ICT,
- the lack of investment areas makes it necessary to expand the boundaries, which means that if smart solutions are not developed, then architectural, legal, and social obstacles can appear,
- conflicts of interest in the use of the limited urban space of the city create barriers in shaping the spatial order of the city, as well as inconsistency in IT solutions created in the open data system models, and
- the insular nature of the smart city space adjacent to traditional districts with high development barriers causes perturbations in the implementation of coherent city management mechanisms using smart solutions.

Legal and administrative conditions

Chances/stimulants

- optimizing decision-making processes in local government units,

- improving the rationality of decisions made thanks to the larger available sets of possibilities for collecting information about the real needs of individual stakeholders,
- creating new administrative solutions based on electronic document circulation, for example electronic signature,
- the possibility of using completely new solutions that will ensure data security, and at the same time will make them more accessible to users, for example blockchains, and
- the possibility of combining efforts on experimental solutions in cooperating cities of the same country operating under the same legal framework.

Threats/Inhibitors

- lack of flexibility in the sphere of public finances with the simultaneous politicization of decisions, which has a limiting effect on the development of smart cities,
- blending of cities with different needs and specializations,
- no scenario approach to the development of existing threats, for example, there are no scenarios prepared for the event of a terrorist attack,
- no clear allocation of competences in the field of smart organizations to the structure of offices – only in some cities there are dedicated units dealing with development based on the smart city concept,
- low availability of knowledge workers in the public sphere, and
- lack of institutions competent to make decisions for the real needs of residents.

Source: Own elaboration.

Appendix 3 Electronic audit questionnaire on European smart cities websites

1 Does smart city strategy exist and is visible in the website?
2 Does smart city plenipotentiary/team exist and is visible in the website?
3 What types of strategies are published (smart city, circular economy, etc.)
4 What smart city/smart organization projects examples are visible in the website?
5 What concrete examples of technology solutions for local managers, and/or citizens are exposed in the website (e.g. mobile applications)
6 In what format city enables open feedback from citizens/is open for being contacted by citizens in a friendly manner (e.g. suggestion box, etc.)
7 In what format city clearly demonstrates its purpose (e.g. via brand-promise or mission statement)?
8 In what format city enables and/or promotes learning initiatives for citizens?
9 What types of cooperation and partnerships are exposed in the website (with business, with education sector, with other cities, etc.)
10 What types of competitive advantages and benefits are promoted by the city from general view/welcome page of the website?
11 What types of threats are included in the smart city strategy/urban development strategy according to the PESTEL model?
12 What types of opportunities are included in the smart city strategy/urban development strategy according to the PESTEL model?
13 What risk management solutions related to the deployment of smart organizations are included in the smart city strategy/urban development strategy?
14 What solutions exist to take advantage of the opportunities associated with the deployment of smart organizations as envisioned in the smart city/urban development strategy?
15 Other sources of information (i.e. papers)
16 Important links
17 Other important information

Appendix 4 Individual interview questionnaire

Introduction

- Thank you for participating in an interview on the impact of smart organizations on smart and sustainable development. Before we begin, let me briefly present the context and format.
- This interview will last around 60 minutes and will be recorded and transcribed for research purposes. Results of the interviews will be published in 2023 in "Smart Organizations in the Public Sector: Sustainable Local Development in the European Union" in Citizenship and Sustainability in Organizations series by Routledge.
- My name is Michał Mądry and I will be the interviewer on behalf of Warsaw School of Economics and researchers Hanna Godlewska-Majkowska and Tomasz Pilewicz.
- We are conducting several interviews with chosen municipalities across Europe. Our goal is to research best practices and contribute to knowledge and know-how development on smart organizations and sustainable development.

Questions

1 Please introduce yourself and briefly present your role in [Municipality]?
2 What specific solutions have you been using in your city to identify and analyze data and information for local socio-economic development support?
3 For how long have you been utilizing these solutions?
4 What are the advantages and benefits of such solutions?
5 What are the key barriers and risks associated with such approach?
6 What solutions are in place to take advantage of the opportunities associated with the deployment of smart organizations in your city?
7 According to the PESTEL model, what types of threats are currently the most important for your city?
8 According to the PESTEL model, what types of opportunities are currently the most important for your city?
9 What are some of the best practices you are leveraging in municipal decision-making processes oriented on local development?

10 What would you recommend to other municipalities of similar size and development level?

11 What are some bad experiences in relation to the usage of smart cities solutions which you would not recommend to other municipalities?

12 How are you dealing with the most pressing problems of your city indicated in the Smart City Index 2021 report – affordable housing, unemployment, road congestion, and health services?

13 What are the specific smart solutions that contributed or will contribute to solving these problems?

14 What is the assessment of performance results of smart solutions oriented on solving the problems in short, medium, and long term?

15 What methods and measurement indicators are used to monitor efficiency of smart solutions oriented on improvement of the situation related to the problems?

16 What risk management solutions related to the deployment of smart organizations are already deployed or soon to be deployed in your city?

17 What mistakes and failures related to efforts oriented on solving the problems would you advise to avoid?

18 How do you provide an easy access to local government decisions? What are the impacts of this approach for the decision-making process?

19 How do residents contribute to the decision-making process?

20 How do residents provide feedback to local government projects?

21 Do you enable online voting?

22 Do you provide an online platform where residents can propose ideas for improved city life?

23 What are other key local development stakeholders that support the implementation of smart city concept in your municipality?

24 Are there any other additional information sources relevant to indicating impact of smart city-oriented solutions you are using in the city oriented on sustainable development?

25 Please provide your closing thoughts on best practices and most important areas of smart city-oriented solutions?

Closing

Thank you very much for your participation, if you wish to enquire about research progress and monograph publication, please reach out to me via e-mail.

Source: Own work.

Index

Note: **Bold** page numbers refer to tables; *italic* page numbers refer to figures and page numbers followed by "n" denote endnotes.

technological conditions, and smart
local government organizations 178
technological intelligence 82
technological knowledge 95
technology transfer 95
Territorial Agenda of the European
Union 87
territorial capital 88
territorial cohesion 88
territorial governance 87
territorial innovation systems 196
tertiary education 101
Theory X 21
Theory Y 22
Thorne, C. 183
threats 1, 56, 61, 85, 104, 117, 128, 131,
133, 152, 156, 166, 170, 174– 176,
178, 179, 182, 183, 211–215
Toruń 158
total quality management (TQM) 22
Toyota 22
TQM *see* total quality management
(TQM)
transaction cost economics 64
Trzcieliński, S. 39

U4SSC *see* United for Smart
Sustainable Cities, The (U4SSC)
UK *see* United Kingdom (UK)
uncertainty: reduction 127–129; smart
organizations in times of 117–119
United for Smart Sustainable Cities,
The (U4SSC) **46**
United Kingdom (UK): human capital
110; "London Curriculum" initiative
161–162; public sector, smart
organization in 100; relational capital
110; social conditions in 178

United Nations General Assembly
142, 196

VAIC *see* Value Added Intellectual
Capital (VAIC)
Value Added Intellectual Capital
(VAIC) **39**
Veža, I. **45**
Verona: local government organizations,
smart organizations in 174
Vico, G.: *Scienza Nuova* 74
Vienna: ecological/natural/spatial
conditions in 179; technological
conditions in 178; "Urban Mobility
Plan Vienna" 165
Villet, H. **63**

Wachowiak, P. **15**
Warsaw: local government
organizations, smart organizations in
173, 174; Warsaw 19115 system 170;
Warsaw City Hall 170
waste management 164
Wereda, W. **18**, 31
Wilkin, J. 71
Wodecka-Hyjek, A. **63**
Wrocław: local government
organizations, smart organizations in
170, 171, 174

Yamanari, J. S. **17**
Yolles, M. 24

Zaragoza: ecological/natural/
spatial conditions in 179; political
conditions in 177
ZEBRA Technologies **45**
Ziębicki, B. **15**